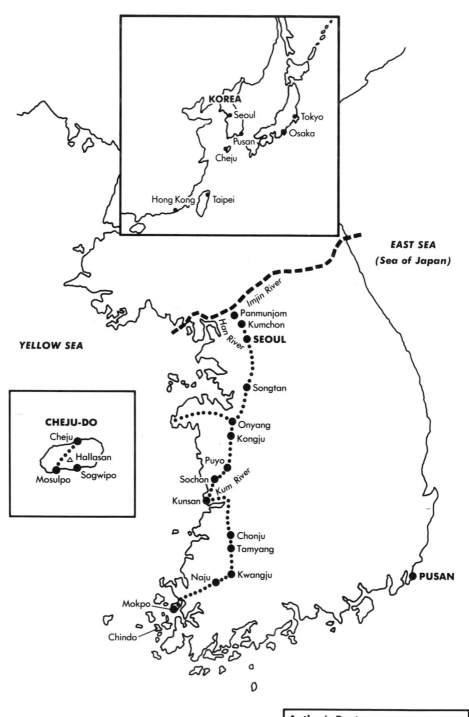

KOREA

Seoul

Tokyo

Pusan
Osaka

Cheju

Hong Kong
Taipei

EAST SEA
(Sea of Japan)

Imjin River

Panmunjom

Kumchon

SEOUL

Han River

YELLOW SEA

Songtan

Onyang

Kongju

CHEJU-DO

Cheju

△ Hallasan

Mosulpo
Sogwipo

Puyo

Sochon

Kum River

Kunsan

Chonju

Tamyang

Naju
Kwangju

PUSAN

Mokpo

Chindo

Author's Route	••••••••••••••
Military Demarcation Line	– – – – –

KOREA

KOREA

A Walk through

SIMON WINCHESTER

Illustrations by Ko Seouk-young

PRENTICE HALL PRESS

New York London Toronto Sydney Tokyo

the Land of Miracles

For P. W.

Insert photographs courtesy of the Korean National Tourism Corporation, except photographs by Robert Holmes and Michael O'Brien/Archive Pictures as noted

Photograph research by Amla Sanghui
Map by Michael Freeland

Published by Prentice Hall Press
A Division of Simon & Schuster, Inc.
Gulf+Western Building
One Gulf+Western Plaza
New York, NY   10023

PRENTICE HALL PRESS is a registered trademark of Simon & Schuster, Inc.

LIBRARY OF CONGRESS CATALOGING IN PUBLICATION DATA

Winchester, Simon.
  Korea : a walk through the land of miracles / Simon Winchester.
    p.   cm.
  Bibliography: p.
  Includes index.
  ISBN 0-13-516626-8
  1. Korea (South)—Description and travel. 2. Winchester, Simon
Journeys—Korea (South) I. Title.
DS902.4.W56 1988
915.19′ 0443—dc19   87-27133
                                                                          CIP

Manufactured in the United States of America

10 9 8 7 6 5 4 3 2 1   88 .10 – 363

First Edition

ACKNOWLEDGMENTS

❖   ❖   ❖

THE INSPIRATION FOR THIS BOOK CAME FROM MISS
Park Choon-sil, the interpreter who showed me around Seoul on my first visit
in the late summer of 1985. Miss Park said many times that she was eager that
her country, so little known abroad and of such uncertain reputation, should
be better and more sympathetically understood out in the English-speaking
world. My present hope is that this very modest account, born of her initial
suggestion, should go some way toward realizing her wishes.

Philip Wetton, then the commercial counselor at the British Embassy in
Seoul, and a man well disposed toward and hugely knowledgeable about Korea,
was equally keen that a kindly book about this country should be published
in the West, and he was generous to a fault with advice, contacts, and constructive criticism. Both Philip Wetton and George Robinson, who also lived
and worked in Seoul, read the typescript and made innumerable helpful sug-
gestions. I owe a very considerable debt to both of them, though they are in
no way responsible if any errors or misjudgments escaped their scrutiny: That
responsibility, of course, is my own.

Both Cathay Pacific Airways and the Seoul Hilton Hotel were kind enough
to provide support for the venture; and in ways other than the purely practical,
David Bell of Cathay Pacific's parent company, The Swire Group, and Christian Schuecking, Siegbert Beller, and Mrs. S. H. Ahn of the Hilton were
immensely helpful.

During my weeks on the road I met scores of people who were invariably curious to know why I was walking and, when I told them, were in a variety of ways helpful or supportive or both—a glass of water here, the offer of a lift there, a shared lunch in a field in one province, a few glasses of *soju* in a roadside drinking stall in another. To all of this vast anonymous band, my sincerest thanks.

But others I do know by name, and so to all of them, my gratitude for helping with what turned out to be a most pleasurable mission: Ian Buruma, Chang Kyung-soon, Sangon Chu, the Columban Fathers, Roger Crabb, Paul Ensor, James Fenton, Billy Fullerton, Brigadier Tim Hackworth, Max Hastings, Adrian Hill, Christopher Hitchens, Peter Hyun, Kim Dae Jung, Ko Seouk-young, Lt. Joe LaMarca, Lee Seong Cheol, Hwi J. Lee, the Reverend Pat Lohan, Gavin Mackay, Boyd McCleary, Ferris Miller, Michael O'Brien, Oh Kyoung-sook, Birgit Schwarz, Shin Hyun Gook, Edwin Shum, Lucretia Stewart, Bob Sweeney, Yvonne Townley, Max Whitby, and Paul Whitelaw.

I wish in addition to thank both Philip Pochoda, my editor in New York, and Lois Wallace, my agent there, for their support and for their sustained belief that Korea, so little known in the West, should in fact be written about.

My family, of whom I saw too little during my Korean spring and summer, were as delightfully helpful as ever: My gratitude to them all is incalculable.

PREFACE

❖   ❖   ❖

IN THE FOREWORD TO HIS BRILLIANT AND DEFINITIVE book *The Korean War*, the British military historian Max Hastings muses on the reasons for the curious popular neglect that has been visited on this most savage of modern conflicts. Almost all of the other struggles of the past century—from the Boer War to Vietnam, from Ypres to Gallipoli, from Northern Ireland to West Beirut—have found their place in legends, novels, films, and sad and popular songs. But with the single exception of television's "M*A*S*H*" series, which Korean veterans deride as presenting too comfortable an image of a very uncomfortable war, the Korean War seems to have passed without being consciously memorialized at all. It is somehow as though the world wanted to forget, to blot out those terrible three years of fighting. Westerners in particular, Hastings notes, were "soured by the taste of costly stalemate, robbed of any hint of glory." They just didn't want to know.

And as with the Korean War, so with Korea. I am sure I breach no confidences of the publishing world if I mention that this book, when it was little more than a half-formed idea mentioned over coffee tables, met a wall of skepticism and fusillades of stiff resistance. "Are you quite *sure?*" colleagues would inquire, kindly. "Isn't Korea just a trifle, well, how to say, *unpopular?* Not at all sure anyone would ever actually want to go there. Frightfully cold, for a start. The Korean people are so wretchedly *unfriendly.* Terribly violent place. Nothing to eat but cabbage."

And that, too, was more or less the way I felt, when I readied myself to travel on my very first expedition to Seoul. Under normal circumstances a journey from a fog-bound, drizzle-dampened London to some city—any city— out in that vast geographical and cultural mystery zone known as The Orient would prompt strangulated wails of envy from those doomed to be left behind. But my journey to Korea produced no such anguished outpourings. Colleagues greeted the news with an uninterested equanimity. No one else, it later transpired, had wanted to go. Friends merely offered me their sympathy, and their thermal underwear (even though it was September). There was the near-universal conviction that I had drawn the short straw.

Near, but not wholly universal. One friend in the office, a shy and retiring young woman who generally kept her own counsel, telephoned me shortly before my plane took off. "You are so lucky," she whispered, her voice almost breaking. "It is perhaps the most lovely country in the world. It is an unforgettable place. I just wish I could be going, too." She had lived there for six months, I later learned. None of the skeptics had ever set foot in Korea. All that they had said to me was born of the same kind of barely rational prejudice that caused the Korean War to pass nearly unremembered—an inexplicable association of the word *Korea* with a multitudinous assortment of synonyms for *grim*.

"Don't listen to them," breathed the young woman. "It's a remarkable place. Utterly unforgettable."

So I flew away, stayed in the Republic for a busy fortnight, and then returned, and my impressions, as I hope the following chapters will illustrate, coincided more or less exactly with hers. Korea *is* a truly remarkable place, a country that deserves to be better known and understood, yet known in a way that keeps to the very minimum the dour trinity of headings under which the place is normally filed. I decided that if I was going to write a book, I would not write one that viewed Korea in the context of war, economics, or politics. In the heady aftermath of that first visit, and with all the enthusiasm of a naif, I planned a book that would present a series of ruminations about the Korean people, who are quite unsullied by the evils of money making, are uninterested in the mechanics of power seeking, and had long forgotten the miseries of battle. I would, I vowed, go straight for the *kokoro*, the often-ignored, rarely understood *heart* of modern Korea, and let the rest of the peninsula's story go hang.

That might have been a reasonable approach in any year other than 1987. But as it happened, the weeks and months during which I researched and later wrote this account coincided with the most volatile, most fascinating, and perhaps—time will have to tell—most historically profound period in Korea's modern history. So while I might at some other time—ten years past, say, or ten years hence—have been able to tell a story unadorned by the stern realities of politics, it would be manifest folly to ignore today the political context in which this brief journey was set, if for no other reason than that this context seems very likely to change the face of Korea for a long while to come.

The political wool, then, started to unravel halfway through my journey, during the time I was in the old Paekche capital of Puyo trying to fathom the intricacies of ginseng manufacture. Quite suddenly, and almost unexpectedly, I had to break off my studies to watch television: President Chun Doo-Hwan, a rather less-than-popular military man who had seized power seven years before and ruled with an exceptionally heavy hand ever since, was broadcasting an announcement to the effect that no, he was not, after all, prepared to amend the country's constitution to allow for the direct popular election of a president. The people might have argued for such a change, he conceded, but he would not grant it. The Republic would have to bear with him while he and the bosses of his political party chose a successor (for Chun would step down in 1988) and allowed him to be elected in the time-honored manner that had, sad to say, precious little to do with democracy.

The moment the television was snapped off—we were in a small café in the center of Puyo—there was a roar of disapproval from the assembled customers. There would be trouble, everyone said. The people had displayed an overwhelming craving for real democracy, and they would not be cheated of it. Not without a fight.

The people of Puyo—a long way from Seoul, and thus a long way from political sophistication—were more prescient than any outsiders might have supposed them to be.

There were skirmishes almost immediately: minor tribulations for a regime, minor stories in the newspapers, a rash of trivial protests. But a month later the fight began in earnest when President Chun went on television once again to announce that his successor was to be, as expected, a colleague from army days, one General Roh Tae Woo. Roh, whose name, confusingly, was pronounced "noh," had a reputation that was considerably besmirched by the army's role in the infamous affair at Kwangju (which is recounted in detail in chapter four). This reputation, taken together with the manner in which his candidacy had been forced upon the people, prompted an outcry, which fast developed into riots.

And what riots! In almost every Korean city, from Seoul in the north to Pusan in the south, hundreds of thousands of young people poured from their universities and colleges and schools and apprentice shops; in a brilliantly orchestrated crescendo of early summer violence, they displayed both to the generals and to a grimly fascinated outside world (for this was all good television) that a political limit had been reached. They rioted. Then—crucially— the middle classes, similarly angered by the high-handed ways of the Chun regime, spurred on by the excitement of all the action, joined in. Stones, fire bombs, chunks of iron and glass, tear-gas grenades (stolen from the police)—anything that could be hurled at the impassive walls of samurai-kitted riot policemen was hurled. For a while the policemen—courageous men, all were later to admit—stood their ground. Then their commanders unleashed them, and charges were ordered, and people were hurt, and crowds of innocents were tear-gassed, and a couple of young men died.

Warnings of martial law were issued. Urgent talks began in Seoul. The American government weighed in with warnings about the similarities (superficial, but nonetheless beguiling) between Seoul and Manila, between Chun and Marcos, between popular disorder in Korea and people power in the Philippines. At first the warnings went unheeded. The proud and stubborn men in the Blue House—the advisers in Chun's inner circle—were adamant: They would solve their problems in their own, inimitable way, without advice from the outside or concessions to anyone inside. So more tear gas was hurled, more heads were broken, and there was public speculation in Korea and overseas about whether the Olympic Games might actually have to be held elsewhere. A few cities equipped with the necessary stadiums and swimming pools peered, vulturelike, above the parapets, and sent telegrams to Switzerland, hoping to be considered for a chance to feed off the corpse.

In the end it probably was this horrifying thought—that Seoul might be denied the chance to stage the Olympiad—that prompted General Roh to climb down. Of course some loss of face, so important to this country, was inevitable. But the degree of loss at having to make a political concession was nothing, the regime calculated, compared to the potential loss to be suffered if the games were taken away. And so Roh capitulated. He invited the television cameras into an apparently unremarkable midsummer meeting of the ruling political party and made a historic announcement. Not martial law, not a fresh round of arrests, not fresh military resolve, but there would be a free referendum staged to ask the Korean people for their views on the desirability of political change. Should their verdict demand such change, then an election for a new president, a free and fair election such as Korea has not known for a generation, would be held.

Korea, the United States, the world—all were delighted. A referendum was duly held in late autumn, and as anticipated it proved that by an immense majority the Korean people keenly wanted to be *allowed* to choose their own leader. "Our country has come of age," someone said, and there was a sage nodding of heads throughout Korea and indeed throughout the East, a general taking of pleasure in the notion that a country that had worked miracles with its economy was about to match its monetary and industrial maturity with sophistication and maturity at the ballot box. An election was planned for December—General Roh Tae Woo standing for the continuation of government policies; the populist hero Mr. Kim Dae Jung standing for an altogether more liberal regime (with overtures to be made toward North Korea); the pleasantly smooth Mr. Kim Young Sam (once an ally of Kim Dae Jung, but now keen to win power for himself) standing for another, only subtly different shade of liberalism; and a former prime minister Mr. Kim Jong Pil trying to divert establishment votes from the general.

Koreans entered into the spirit of the campaigning with great gusto, and all the candidates pitched in, too, quite undaunted by the newness of the experience. Even General Roh, who was hit by many eggs and rendered bleary-eyed by wafts of tear gas when he ventured into the south (where he is not popular, to say the very least), seemed to take such matters in his stride, supposing that they went with the new territory that his country was bent upon exploring. The army looked down its nose with corporate disdain, and—if the journalism of the day was to be believed—the officers' messes were thick with anxious conversations about whether or not a *coup* should be staged, since there was more unrest than seemed healthy, at least to the soldiery.

The election went off reasonably peaceably, and General Roh—or Mr. Roh, as the world was now pleased to call him—won, handsomely. The triumvirate of opposing Kims ("We Three Kims of Orient Are" was said to be the favored carol of the Korean Christmas season) cried foul, but in the end they had to concede that their loss was their own silly fault. Had they presented a unified opposition, instead of bickering among themselves like schoolchildren, they would now be running Korea. As it is, they must now wait at least five more years before they are allowed to try again.

It would be most unwise to forecast the stability of the new regime or to hazard much of a guess at the mood of the country over which this regime now presides. There were riots immediately following Mr. Roh's victory, but these seemed confined—at least at first—to the universities and the more radically minded quarters of the country. The middle classes kept the peace. And those Koreans who professed some hope that the political turmoil in their country might eventually abate suggested that by doing so—by staying clear of the street disturbances, by keeping silent—these middle classes guaranteed that the new regime, the new, properly elected government, might preside over a more constructive and less bitterly divided period, at least in the short term.

But in the long term? Who can tell? Can the Morning Calm, an unlikely name with which old Korea was once blessed, settle again on this small, half-forgotten, mysterious, and faraway peninsula? Or is there more domestic anguish, perhaps a yet wider struggle, still to come?

The brief account that follows does not offer any answers to such questions, important as they are to some. I have taken a much easier road by attempting simply to present a few of the more timeless elements of a land whose lingering loveliness far outweighs, for me at least, the wayward behavior of some of her people. Such behavior makes for good television, of course, and for headlines of much gravity, but it seems to me to have little enough to do with the realities of an ancient, and deservedly very proud, country, of which all too little is known and for which all too little sympathy is offered. Over the years ahead—perhaps even starting with the Olympic Games—this situation, one hopes, may reverse itself, and the world may come to accept Korea for what she is, and for what she has been for a long, long time.

AUTHOR'S NOTE

❖ ❖ ❖

THROUGHOUT THIS BOOK I HAVE GENERALLY USED the McCune-Reischauer system of transliterating words originally written in Korea's *hangul* script. In addition, and to help make the acceptance of many unfamiliar Korean words a little easier for the innocent reader, I have left out all but the most essential hyphens and all of the apostrophes and other diacritics with which romanized Korean is liberally littered. I hope purists and linguists will forgive this deliberate lapse, which was perpetrated with the very best of intentions.

In a while, with good luck and a fair wind, the people of South Korea will enjoy a high degree of human rights. But for now it is a sad reality that they do not. So to protect a small number of people who were good enough to talk to me during my journey, but whose remarks might well cause offense to some of the more sensitive members of the republic's hierarchy, I have changed some names and muddled some identities. The events they described, however, remain unaltered.

CHAPTER

ONE

"The Kingdom known to us by the Name of Corea, and by the Natives call'd Tiozencouk, and sometimes Caoli, reaches from 34 to 44 Degrees of North Latitude, being about 150 Leagues in length from North to South, and about 75 in breadth from East to West. Therefore the Coresians represent it in the shape of a long square, like a playing Card. Nevertheless it has several Points of Land which run far out into the Sea.

"It is divided into 8 provinces, containing 360 Cities and Towns, without reckoning the Forts and Castles, which are all on the Mountains.

"This Kingdom is very dangerous, and difficult for Strangers. . . ."

—FROM *THE DESCRIPTION OF THE KINGDOM OF COREA*, WRITTEN IN 1668 BY HENDRICK HAMEL—THE FIRST WESTERN ACCOUNT OF THE ''HERMIT KINGDOM''

❖　❖　❖

THIS STORY STARTS A VERY LONG WAY FROM KOREA— indeed, very nearly halfway across the world from Hendrick Hamel's "dangerous and difficult Kingdom"—on a gloomy, rainswept, industrial street in the ancient English city of Newcastle upon Tyne.

Newcastle, as it is usually abbreviated, was where I had my first job on a newspaper in the middle sixties: It was a grimy and then rather depressed old place tucked away up in the far northeast, a place of deep coal mines and half-closed factories that were worked by men (the luckier ones, that is—many had been out of work for years) who still wore overalls and cloth caps, drank the strongest beer brewed in Britain, and had a tradition of making the sturdier items of advanced society—things made of iron and brass and heavy alloys, things like battle tanks and cantilever bridges, artillery pieces and cranes, telescope mirrors, power-station turbines and railway locomotives.

But it had a softer side, too. As robust and no-nonsense a place as it might have been, the Newcastle I came to know was a city surrounded by and shaped by a wild and starkly beautiful countryside, and a place whose whole life and economy and folk history were dominated by two mighty waterways that were born high up in the nearby hills, the River Tees and the River Tyne.

The Tyne! Such—or so it seems at this distance—such a grand old river and such grand old memories! The Tyne remains for me, and probably for anyone who has ever fallen under the subtle spell of what they call the Geordie country, one of the great streams of the world. It is neither a very long nor in truth

3

a very great river, yet somehow in its brief passage from source to sea it manages to capture all the alluring mixtures and contrasts that make England what she is—grace and power, rustic charm and ironbound sinew, breeze-ruffled heather and hot industrial oil, lonely moorlands and bustling factory gates. These contrasts exist in many river passages, perhaps, but in the case of the Tyne seem to represent so accurately all that for which the country once stood and all that had been for so long part of the leitmotiv of Empire.

The Tyne rises high in the broom-covered hills near the border between England and Scotland. It chuckles merrily through narrow gorges and across small waterfalls. It matures and lazes through meadows and prosperous suburban villages. It washes grandly between the great old cathedral cities of Newcastle and Gateshead, cities of gray sandstone and marble monuments, vaulted railway stations and imposing city halls; and finally it passes by the low-lying, swampy slakes of Jarrow and Wallsend—the latter named for the eastern end of the mighty wall Hadrian had built to protect Rome's English dominion—on its way to the cold and gray heavings of the North Sea. And in those last ten miles of its brief course, by which time it has widened and deepened and slowed to a kind of majesty, the River Tyne became over the centuries the home for an industry that perhaps more than any other has made the northeast of England famous throughout the world: On the lower reaches of the River Tyne *they build ships.*

Vessels of war and passenger liners, gritty little tramp steamers and sleek container ships, ugly grain haulers and bulk carriers, motor vessels of every imaginable type that now ply between faraway ports, Baltimore and Capetown, Pago Pago and Papeete, Shanghai and Port Moresby, Colombo and Mombasa and (with a cruel irony that will shortly be apparent) the Korean ports like Inchon and Pusan, and a thousand places besides. Anything that was made of iron, and that floated, and that was made in England seemed to have some inevitable association with the River Tyne. So many of these ships in their uncountable armadas have, on some 'tween-deck bulkhead, an oval brass plate with the engraved name of the shipyard and a final phrase of simple geography that still stands out proudly like a mariners' seal of approval—made, the plaques say, in Newcastle upon Tyne.

When I arrived there as a reporter in 1967, they had just started work on the last family of truly great ships ever to be built on the river. The first, the flagship, was called the *Esso Northumbria,* and she weighed in at something like a quarter of a million tons—a supertanker, everyone called her. The people of Wallsend, where she was built, were glad indeed after many months of short orders and short time—for the Tyne was suffering from a near-terminal case of slump—to have won the order to build her. I was fascinated by her construction. (I had been brought up in Dorset, and the biggest boat I had ever seen was a six-man whaler built of teak.) Each weekend I, along with scores of other local people, would drive down to Wallsend to watch her progress. I would

4

walk down to the tiny lanes of terraced houses where the shipyard workers lived, and I would watch her mighty hull rise behind them.

Week after week a wall of steel, fireworked by rivet throwers and welders, resonant with hammering and flecked with red lead and rustproof paint, would rise higher and higher, blocking out the view, the light, and the wind. Walls-end housewives who were normally muffled to the eyes would walk to the shops in summer dresses. The icy gales that so often roared across the river had been stopped in their tracks by the *Northumbria's* ever-growing hull, which, within its cobweb of cranes and scaffolding, climbed higher and higher into the sky.

And then one day in early May 1969, Princess Anne came by, a young girl in a big yellow hat and a warm yellow coat, and ended it all. She cracked a bottle of champagne over the bows of the mighty new ship. With a roar of drag chains and a muted roar of pride from her Geordie builders, the *Esso Northumbria* was let go. She gathered speed down the slipway, slid effortlessly into the dark waters of the Tyne, performed the traditional curtsy of buoyancy to the thousands waiting on the riverbanks, and proceeded downriver to be fitted out and to undergo her sea trials. Then, probably (for I lost track and now cannot find her in *Lloyd's Register of Shipping*), she took off for the distant destinations for the petroleum trade, like Kharg Island and Kuwait, Philadelphia and Kagoshima, and all the oil ports of the world. Newcastle upon Tyne would never see her again. (She was broken up in Taiwan thirteen years later.)

The housewives in Wallsend complained that night that their protective wall had suddenly vanished and that cold gales blew grittily up their terraced streets once again.

What the women of Wallsend may then also have vaguely suspected, and what the months and years ahead would confirm, was that Newcastle upon Tyne, and indeed the River Tyne itself, would never see so great a vessel again. It was not simply that the *Esso Northumbria* and her sisters were the last of the massive supertankers to be built there; they were also the last really big ships to be built in the English northeast. The *Northumbria's* launching and the empty slipway she left behind were powerful in their symbolism. They represented in a mournful way the formal close to a lengthy and glorious industrial era—the end of a historical chapter for the Tyne, for Britain, for Europe, and, one might say, for the once-ascendant countries grouped around the Atlantic Ocean. As each tanker vanished downriver and out to the ocean, so it became the turn of the nations grouped around the Pacific to take up the duties of the Old World and begin to accept the benefits and the responsibilities of being the world's new industrial powerhouses, for the remainder of the century and beyond.

Sixteen years after the *Northumbria* had gone I traveled on assignment for a newspaper out to that Pacific Ocean, and I spent a couple of weeks in the Republic of South Korea. On the Wednesday of my second week I flew down to a small seaside town in the deep south of the country, an unlovely place with the unlovely name of Ulsan. And in Ulsan I came to realize in an instant just why the River Tyne, so very far away and to these people so very unknown, was in the throes of dying.

For here, on a huge plain below a heather-covered bluff jutting into the Sea of Japan, was the headquarters of the shipbuilding division of a new Korean "miracle" company called Hyundai. I was shown around, as I remember, by a young man named Lee Seong Cheol (though some of his cards gave his name in the more Westernized syle: Mr. S. C. Lee). He was an assistant in the company's protocol division. What he showed me would make any Tynesiders—any Europeans, indeed, and many Americans too—shiver in their shoes.

Any one of the yards on the Tyne, in the river's heyday, could possibly manufacture four or five ships at once—in wartime, perhaps, or during a period of grave emergency or extraordinary prosperity. The Hyundai Heavy Industries Company's shipyard at Ulsan, however, could make *forty-six* ships at once. And it could do so without any of the romantic Victorian nonsense of tallow and drag chains and bottles of champagne and princesses in flowery hats. Out here it was all much more businesslike—the yard had seven immense dry docks, and when a hull was finished the dock was simply flooded and the monster was floated away. In one of their docks—the biggest—they could build a million-ton tanker; two more of them could hold a 700,000-tonner apiece, two more still could each build 250,000-tonners like the *Esso Northumbria*, and one dock each could accommodate a 400,000-ton and a 350,000-ton monster— or any combination of smaller vessels that the buyers appeared to need. Three million six hundred and fifty thousand tons of shipping could thus be manufactured at any one time in the Hyundai yards.

And superquickly, too. From the moment the immense plates of steel were cut in the foundry shops until the moment the dry-dock sluices were opened and the sea waters were allowed to float a new behemoth away, it took the Korean workers only nine months. With a further nine months spent in the fitting-out yard, this meant that any new Hyundai vessel took just a year and a half to make. A ship order placed at Hyundai took half the time it would in a European yard—and at a price a good 10 percent lower than the nearest-priced competition (which happened to be, rubbing in the prosperity of the New Pacific, just across the sea in Japan).

Eighteen thousand men worked at the Ulsan yard. They worked six days a week. They started at 6:30 A.M. with thirty minutes of compulsory jogging. They then reported for work at the yard at 7:30 A.M., and labored uncomplaining until they were allowed home at 5:30 P.M. They had an hour off for lunch— invariably they would be handed a plastic box filled with the mess of Korean pickled cabbage known as *kimchi* (which now has so much status as the country's national dish that a museum has been dedicated to it in Seoul). They were permitted two ten-minute breaks, one at ten, the other at three. A worker of average diligence, competence, and seniority was paid about $500 a month. (Although, two years later in this story, this sum came to be regarded as so derisory that Korea suffered a period of major industrial unrest, with rashes of strikes and riots, back in 1985, when I made my first visit, the workers seemed docile and content and behaved peaceably enough.)

They enjoyed, in any case, many fringe benefits. The men lived in Hyundai dormitories and ate at Hyundai canteens. They wore Hyundai clothes—even Hyundai underclothes and Hyundai plastic shoes—and were given, at appropriate times in the year, appropriate Hyundai gifts. They had a Hyundai motto: Diligence. Cooperation. Self-reliance. (The word *hyundai* simply means "modern.") They read Hyundai newspapers. They watched Hyundai films. Every possible need, from the moment of a young man's application until the moment of a foreman's retirement, was taken care of by Hyundai. And further, to ensure that an employee, a member of the Hyundai family, spent as little time as possible in the uncomfortable and unknown world beyond Hyundai's protective wings, he was allowed only three days' holiday each year—and many of them seemed reluctant, so Mr. Lee informed us with gravity, to take even those.

I daresay most European shipbuilders could have learned a great deal from a visit to Hyundai—about styles of management, about efficiency, about the means of inculcating keenness in a work force. But the Europeans I met didn't seem to want to know. They just seemed overwhelmed and rather miserable. During my expedition through the yard I had an instructive conversation with one shipowner from the Old World, a Swede, as lugubrious a man as a caricaturist might wish. He had come to Hyundai to inspect his company's new ship, a 160,000-ton bulk carrier called the *Nord See*—a vessel that might once have been built on the Tyne but was now being finished in Hyundai's Dry Dock Number Two.

I stayed with him for a good hour as he shinned up the *Nord See's* companionways and clambered down her bulkhead ladders, peered at her tracery of pipework, measured the officers' swimming pool ("Nice time they'll have in this, eh?" he grinned, rather bitterly I thought), idly polished the brass journal at the end of her waiting propeller shaft, and knocked at the solid oak of the wardroom door.

Then he came out into the hot late-summer sunshine, and we clambered down the steps onto the dockside, and he looked admiringly up at the great wall of rust-red steel with the fireflies of welding torches glittering here and there along its immense length. He turned to me and said, with a note of very real sadness in his voice: "You know, I think that Europe is quite finished."

I prompted him to explain. He warmed to his miserable theme as only a Scandinavian could: "There was a time, you know, when we were past masters at building things like this. Ships so grand, so beautiful. . . . But now, looking at this. . . . Oh, sure, from my owner's point of view I'm pleased. We've saved some money, we've got a ship delivered on time, everything's fine in the balance books. But seeing how they do it, these Koreans—I just can't see how we back in Europe can continue to make ships, how we can continue to have any real industry at all. I suppose what I mean to say is, I don't see how Europe can survive in the face of competition from miracle workers like the people here. For that's what this is—it's a sheer, bloody miracle."

And that, I suppose, is when my fascination with Korea began.

❖   ❖   ❖

I knew, as my Swedish companion had, that Korea had quite literally risen from the ashes of recent ruin. Just thirty-two years before this particular autumn day, a war that had lasted for three years, claimed a 1.5 million casualties, and raged quite pointlessly up and down the playing-card-shape Korean Peninsula, had been concluded: A cease-fire had been announced, a truce that divided a nation in two and separated it by barbed wire and minefields and ever-vigilant guards was put into effect. And South Korea, utterly devastated and demoralized, an emasculated shambles of a country, started shakily to get up onto its two feet again.

And get up it most certainly did. With an effort that, more than any other postwar recovery effort in the world's history, appears now to have been superhuman, truly miraculous, Korea stood, then took a first step, then began to walk with confidence, then to trot, and finally to run until—as now—it has started seriously to challenge the world's industrial leaders, with a seemingly unbeatable combination of energy and efficiency, national pride and Confucian determination.

There was no shipyard at Ulsan thirty years ago. There was not even a company called Hyundai. But now the Hyundai plant at Ulsan is one of the best and most productive in the world; and the men who had the idea to make it thus, and whose pride and vision have kept Korea's shipyards and Korea's car plants and, indeed, the Republic of Korea as a whole forging ahead and pulling away from all others, were, it seemed to me, true miracle workers.

I was not, I must confess, either terribly interested in studying nor competent to explore the mechanics of Korea's industry, nor the unfathomable mysteries of Korea's economics. The price of steel plate and the costs of fuel oil, the insurance rates for the Strait of Hormuz and the cumbersome tables of freight rates for the North Atlantic Conference remain among the arcana that I could never hope to master. But I was, I soon discovered, fascinated by the Koreans themselves, by the Korean people. How, I wondered, had they managed it? What was it that had allowed them, or had perhaps impelled them, to become so hugely successful when all the Cassandras would have marked them down for Third World ignominy, for poverty, for oblivion. In short, what sort of people were they? So I made up my mind there and then, while talking to that dour Swede on that Ulsan jetty, to go back one day and try to find out. And indeed, in the early spring two years later, and armed with enough time to make a stab at understanding, I flew out to Hong Kong and boarded a nonstop jet bound for the Korean capital, Seoul.

❖   ❖   ❖

It was a late afternoon in the middle of March when I arrived, during a bout of what the immigration officer at Kimpo Airport called "flower-jealousy weather." It had been warm the day before, he said, but in the night the wind had unexpectedly backed round to the northwest, blowing miserably cold continental air across the Yellow Sea from Harbin and the plains of Manchuria, and bringing flurries of snow down upon the Korean capital. The Great North Mountain Fortress was dusted with ice, and all over the city people were wrapped up in overcoats that they would have been foolish to suppose had now done their bit for yet another Korean winter.

Worst of all, the early cherry blossom was being whipped from the trees and whirled up into busy little blizzards, the branches left bare and forlorn looking. Back in the West we would shrug our shoulders and huddle into our cashmeres. Out here, though, everything had to be answered by the application of a most complicated formula, and I was promptly given a lecture about it while everyone else was forced to wait. The situation, I gathered from the immigration officer's seminar, was all to do with internecine envy and rivalry. The Chinese cold winds that keenly afflicted the Korean Peninsula had been dispatched because China was irritated—in fact, distinctly jealous, hence his charming phrase, *kkot saem chu wi*—that so many blooms had appeared so early in Korea and that Korea was being transformed for yet another springtime into something far more beautiful than, in Chinese eyes, it deserved to be. Did I see? Could I not understand how mad the Chinese weather gods had become?

But then—perhaps because his boss had just appeared—the immigration officer abruptly changed his demeanor, stopped discussing the weather and the crops, and asked how long I planned to be in Korea. Two months, I said brightly, whereupon he drew a long intake of breath, whistling implosively as he did so. It was a gesture I recognized well: Most of the people of northeast Asia, when faced with a problem or with a question that is not amenable to an instant answer, do much the same. It is a way of buying time, of giving the questioner the impression of deep thought and consideration, and of avoiding the face-losing notion that the answer is unknown or has been forgotten or is about to be an unwanted denial or in some other way negative. So Mr. Chung, for such was the name of the young officer who stood between me and the Korean streets, sucked and whistled and gazed impassively at my open passport.

"Where will you go?" he asked, and he whistled again when I replied that I was heading for Cheju Island, a great chunk of windy basalt best known to Koreans as a holiday and honeymoon resort down off the south coast. "Forty days in Cheju?" he hissed, incredulous, and I became aware of a vague feeling

9

of alarm creeping down my spine, as though a cup of cold syrup had been tipped down my collar. The others waiting in the queue behind me—well-dressed and identical-looking German businessmen and American bankers and a less well-dressed Indian from Madras whom I had chatted to on the plane, and who was trying to sell the Koreans one of India's less romantic commodities, like shellac or gutta percha or urea—began to shuffle impatiently. I grinned at them, trying to look confident, as though I was temporarily in the hands of a buffoon, a mere hobbledehoy of a clerk.

"What is your business? Why are you here?" Mr. Chung went on. I replied cautiously that I was going to Cheju on holiday, and that I was planning to use the island as a starting point from which I would walk the entire length of his country. *"What?"* He hadn't understood. "Walking," I said, and made two of my fingers stroll briefly across his field of vision.

"Working?" he asked, clearly having misheard and having dismissed the finger explanation as a sign of near lunacy. "No, not working, *walking.*" And at this he suddenly cheered up, as though a switch had been pressed. "Ah! *Not working.* Fine. That's good." And he inscribed my passport neatly with the words *Not Working*, stamped me and entered me into a computer file, and waved me on. I was back in Korea again, even though I had feared—despite my confident grin at the shellac peddler and the man from Citibank—that I might well not be allowed in at all.

It had something to do with a story about a fence.

❖ ❖ ❖

Some months before I had been down on the country's southeast coast, motoring idly northward after a rather less-than-successful visit to National Historic Site Number 158, the underwater burial place of a long-dead monarch, the late King Mun-mu. There had been an angry little typhoon named Wayne scurrying about in the Sea of Japan, and the narrow stretch of water between where I had stood and the rocky and half-submerged tomb of the old Shilla king was roiled and foamy, with great combers from the east pounding against the cliffs. The boatman, a grizzled and normally stout-hearted navigator, decided that for safety's sake he would rather not set out that day. I pressed thick wads of folded *won* into his hand, but to no avail: He knew his Sea of Japan, and he was not planning to do battle with it for a mere visit to an old grave. So, grumpily, I set off northward in my rented Daewoo, vowing to return to Mun-mu when Wayne had spent himself raining and storming on some distant Manchurian moors.

Now, it so happens that along the entire east coast of Korea there is a fence—a tattered and rusty old barbed wire fence that was built in the fifties with the avowed purpose of keeping out would-be assassins and spies who might row down from North Korea and try to land. The mere existence of and supposed need for the fence are extraordinary enough. But then so is the fence. It has small platforms woven into the wire at random, and on each platform stands a Coca-Cola bottle or a pile of pebbles with a device painted in white on them, so finely balanced as to tumble down if ever the fence is disturbed. There are gates, which can be unlocked to permit people to go fishing or swimming (or to allow the inquisitive to try to commune with King Mun-mu), but they close at dusk, and there are large red notices warning that the beaches are curfewed at night, and anyone found walking on or swimming from them may well be thought an inbound spy and be shot. The beaches are lit by arc lights, and the sand is raked, the better to show up footprints emerging from the sea. So, if a spoor of Vibram imprints shows up in the sand, and if fallen Coke bottles and tumbled pebbles can be seen near the fence, it is immediately apparent which route the terror monger has taken, and the police will be hot on his trail.

Though said by the coast guards to be reasonably effective, such methods were not effective enough, as I was soon to discover. Twenty miles north of Mun-mu, as I rounded a bend in the road, I came across a party of Army Pioneers who were putting up another fence. And this, in contrast to its rather forlorn sibling, was a real granddaddy of a fence—eight feet of tough chain-link steel, topped with two-foot coils of razor wire, with sandbagged watchtowers every half mile or so from which armed guards peered suspiciously. It would be tricky indeed for any swimmer or oarsman to get into Korea via this monster.

The new fence went on for dozens of miles, winding along clifftop and beachfront, to be silhouetted at dawn in scores of fishing villages, to be passed through only with permission and the unhasping of padlocks. I stopped and took a couple of pictures, and soon learned from a bored and friendly Pioneer leaning on his shovel that the entire coastline was to be protectively wrapped in barbed wire and chain link—thousands of miles of brand-new fencing were being erected, the better to preserve South Korea from all enemies, foreign and domestic. It seemed reasonable to let the outside world know of this small peculiarity, and so, when I reached a typewriter and a cable office I dispatched a brief story. It was duly published, a day or two later, in London and Washington: KOREA, the headlines read, FENCING HERSELF IN.

A week later, according to a foreign-editor friend in London, the Korean Embassy telephoned. A senior official was on his way to the newspaper to voice an official protest, the message went. Kindly be on hand to receive him. And sure enough a diplomat did eventually present himself and read in tones somewhat less than friendly a message from Seoul complaining that by publishing details of the fence a grave national security lapse had been committed, and the consequences could be dire. Was the account factually wrong? asked the editor. Oh no, by no means, coughed the diplomat. All the facts were quite correct. It was simply that the fence did not, officially, exist. Writing about it and, worse yet, photographing it were grave offenses. The consequences, the diplomat repeated, could be severe. It was likely that I would not be welcomed back to Korea, for instance, should ever I choose to return.

❖   ❖   ❖

In the event, memories being short or bureaucracies being less than efficient, no sanction was ever applied, and I squeaked in through Kimpo's gateway with no more than a few moments of uncertainty that were prompted by Mr. Chung's labored suspicions. I collected my bags—Korean customs officers invariably ask passengers to open every one, and today was no exception—and walked out into the chill. The first sight stopped me in my tracks. In front of the automatic doorway stood a quartet of soldiers in full battle dress, with helmets, gas masks, and rifles at the ready. They stood at four points of a square, facing outward, their bodies perfectly still, their eyes ranging like radar. There had been a bomb at the airport just a few weeks before, someone explained. No need to be alarmed.

But there were troops and blue-uniformed police everywhere, it seemed. Mobile yellow-and-black tiger-striped steel barriers were pushed back by every road crossing, ready to close roads, gates, bridges, tunnel entrances—whatever looked like an escape route for a putative attacker. All cars coming into the airport were being searched, hoods and trunks opened, mirrors held beneath the chassis, armed guards standing by, a caltrop spread before the front wheels and only tugged free when the searcher had signaled the all clear. I had been to Kimpo many times before, but never had it seemed such a nervous, jumpy place than on this day of flower jealousy, the day I had chosen to embark on my adventure. It all seemed rather ominous.

❖   ❖   ❖

Looking back, Korea had perhaps always seemed a rather ominous place. The image I, like so many people, first held of Korea—and it was a very faint image, indeed, one that flickered and dimmed the more closely I examined it, like a faraway star—was a mosaic of melancholy.

The image was composed of and underlain first of all by a terrible sense of cold and then colored in and fleshed out by mind-pictures of an unremitting and bladelike Siberian wind. I imagined impenetrable and unclimbable ranges of ugly mountains; endless plains of frozen mud; wrecked tanks smoking blackly against a leaden sky; mile-long lines of shambling refugees; mean, pinched little towns; bomb craters; shabbiness and raggedness; despair and injury; and cruelty and death.

These images, of course, had woven their way into my childhood mind through the old Pathé news films of the Korean War, news films seen if not watched before the cartoons and the second feature and the main attraction in the one-and-nines at the local Gaumont: "General MacArthur storms ashore at Inchon!" "The Glorious Gloucesters and Their Heroic Stand!" "The Human Wave of Chinese—'Our Guns Were Red Hot!' said GI colonel!" I have a distant memory of René Cutforth broadcasting on BBC radio about crossing the Han River, southbound (for at the time the Communists had taken Seoul again and were pushing the United Nations forces backward), and I remember his words about the flickering fires in the oil drums left on the ice, and the young soldier from Tennessee nearly freezing to death, and all the participants in this strangely awful drama wondering just what they were doing and where they were going and, indeed, exactly where they were.

And then the shutter snaps shut and the image, such as it was, halts its meager progress. After 1953, the year I vaguely recalled as the date of the cease-fire between the two unhappily and perhaps permanently divided Koreas, there is no real image at all. A few names of people and places and events swim in and out of memory—Syngman Rhee, President Park, Koreagate, Kim Il Sung, the KAL 007 disaster, Pyongyang, the Rangoon bombing, the green baize tabletop at the town of Panmunjom. But otherwise nothing. Just a distant memory of merciless and pointless fighting, a hazy knowledge of stunning economic miracles having been wrought in the subsequent years, and, pervading everything, a vague and haunting impression of a Korean face as somehow being a face that represents all that is mysterious, impassive, and vaguely frightening about the East.

Ian Fleming's Oddjob, in the Bond books, was a Korean—because to the most perceptive of Western popular writers, and, later for Hollywood casting directors, the Korean and the Korean face epitomized Asian menace, a face and a persona perfectly designed to induce a sense of fear. And then again, hadn't I read that the Japanese always used Koreans to guard the very worst of their concentration camps, because Koreans would undertake tasks that even the Japanese might be too squeamish to perform? It might not have been true (though in fact it was), but it was an idea that added to the overall impression—that of an inclement and menacing place, far away and unknown, a country at eternal war with itself or with others, peopled by strange and unforgiving Orientals, a secret and forbidding country that was probably best kept a secret, filed away and forgotten.

And then, that autumn day in 1985, I traveled there, and stayed for two weeks—the two weeks during which I journeyed down to Ulsan and to that mighty shipyard that first sparked my curiosity. But it was more than mere ships—much more—that changed my perception of Korea.

❖   ❖   ❖

I had not really wanted to go. It was a last-minute decision, prompted by a characteristic piece of newspaper-office idiocy. One Monday morning an editor came up with the not-unreasonable scheme (from my point of view) that I should fly immediately to Western Australia for a fortnight and from there to Manila, to write essays on Perth (before the America's Cup) and the Philippines (before the fall of President Marcos). But then, later that afternoon, another, more senior editor discovered that the newspaper's medical correspondent had flown off to a remote town in northern Japan to interview the "world's oldest man," and had taken no less than £7,000 in cash with him, breaking all records and, to the chagrin of the accountants (for on most newspapers these days, accountants hold more sway than editors), all departmental budgets as well.

Down came the predictable ukase: no more foreign trips to be made until the medical correspondent was found, his explanation given, and the cash returned. In vain did I protest that flights had been booked, appointments made in Perth and Fremantle, luggage packed, sobbing families comforted. I railed and I argued. In the end I was told to go to the airport, check in, and call the editor before the chocks were pulled away. I did just that, only to be told that someone else had been asked to write about Perth, and that while I was expected in Manila three weeks hence, would I kindly now go to Seoul instead and write an essay on the country that, someone had just remembered, was planning to stage the Olympic Games in 1988. A hurried change of planes—no longer Qantas to Perth but British Airways to Amsterdam and KLM to Seoul; an equally hurried change of books (the *Survival Guide to Australia* being dumped in favor of the *Insight Guide to Korea*)—and I was on my way.

It was a wretchedly long flight. I had idly mentioned to a friend in the office that we were probably flying via my old stamping ground of New Delhi, and it was only when I saw that the sun was off the port beam that I realized, cursing my stupidity, that we were in fact headed across the Pole, via Alaska. So I called the friend, collect, from Anchorage Airport, prompting a splendidly surreal argument that revolved around his much-repeated protest to the operator that, "No, I won't accept the call from him in the United States. He's in India." It took a little time before the penny dropped, and by then it was time for the flight to leave again, bound across the Pacific, down to Seoul.

During all those long hours I tried, so far as I recall, to clear my mind of most of the prejudice against Korea, the views instilled in the Gaumonts and the classrooms of old. To an extent I must have succeeded, difficult as it may have been. In any event the conversion, for that is what I underwent during the two weeks that followed, was positively Pauline in its scale and extent. I became, without a doubt, and with extraordinary suddenness, enchanted by what I found.

All the old images suddenly melted and slipped clear away. I became captivated by Korea and the Koreans, and have remained so ever since. I hope that these pages that follow will convey some of the reasons why—reasons that remain, and may remain long after this book is written, a mystery to me. The reader will not want a litany of excuses, of course: But I sometimes find my affection for poor old Korea—this "unhappy country" that so many earlier writers, half a century and more ago, discovered it to be, this "difficult and dangerous Kingdom" that Hendrick Hamel found three centuries before—sometimes I find it hard to explain, even to myself. Hence the journey, and the need to try to understand both Korea and my own reactions to Korea. The journey that I planned, then, and the words that result from it, will serve me every bit as much as I trust they may serve the reader. For, like all travels, this is as much a journey of self-discovery as the simple discovery of another country and another people. I needed to make the trip—to find out not simply what, and who, and when, but *why*.

❖   ❖   ❖

For several months I contemplated the best way to journey around the country. I had already driven and flown and taken the railway and the bus over many hundreds or even thousands of miles. Each was pleasant enough a mode of transport, yet each placed strict limits on the kind of Koreans one was able to meet. In a car, of course, you had either your companion or the very occasional hitchhikers—invariably students or drunks or American servicemen eager to get back before their two-day passes expired. The planes, on the other hand, tended to fill with blue-suited businessmen from Hyundai or Gold Star or Daewoo, men who would either read impenetrable documents about the finer points of oil tanker hull assembly or else, and more frequently, test their English on you in sometimes the most excruciating ways.

I once encountered a Mr. Jimmy Kim (as his card declared) on a flight to Ulsan: He approached me in the airport lounge and, with neither introductions or queries, announced his apparently rather urgent inquiry. Was the word *slipper*, he asked, generally used in the singular or the plural form? I thought for a moment and then replied that people normally asked for the dog or child to fetch slippers in pairs, at which news Mr. Kim suddenly looked crestfallen. I asked him why. He was, he explained sadly, the publisher of a series of English conversation books, and he had just sent his latest masterpiece to press containing a sentence that read: "Mrs. Park, would you please fetch me my slipper?" I suggested that one might well explain away the odd construction by saying that Mr. Park had only one leg or that the dog had savaged the other shoe, whereupon Mr. Kim brightened a little. He then asked for reassurance that another of his sentences was correct. Garlic and sugar, he wondered, they were usually used in the plural, were they not, as in "There are quite a lot of garlics in that soup, Mrs. Lee"?

In the end I decided to walk.

I was not accustomed to walking, nor was I very fit. But it was a means of journeying born of a noble tradition: Belloc and Byron and Laurie Lee and Patrick Leigh Fermor had all walked, and none of them, so far as I could learn from their accounts, had previously been renowned for athleticism nor belonged to any rambling club. Providing I had enough warm clothing, stout boots, and enough money to buy dinner and a bed at an inn each night, the journey could be nothing less than pleasurable. I would see the Korean people at ground level; I could linger where I wanted, go where I wished, stop and start at moments convenient only to myself. I mentioned the idea to friends at home, and they scoffed amiably; I mentioned it to Koreans, who took the Confucian view that to journey long distances alone was highly disagreeable and an almost unhealthy practice. But the more I considered it, the more the idea appealed. The only matters remaining, after buying boots, a rucksack, and an ample supply of adhesive bandage and Kendal Mint Cake, were to choose a route and select a date on which to begin. History provided me with a perfect design.

❖　　❖　　❖

Korean history is a mysterious subject and like many Eastern histories is as much a mixture of legend and hyperbole as of documented fact. If it is uncertain when the West first became officially aware of Korea's existence, it is by no means clear when and how Koreans first came to know of the existence of the strange-smelling, pale-skinned ghosts—the *yangnom*—who lived in the vast world beyond the sunset. China, Japan, and Mongolia formed the essential boundaries of Korean geographical knowledge until as late as the sixteenth century; and after two successive and brutal invasions and sieges by the Manchus, the Koreans withdrew into themselves so decisively and effectively that they referred to their land as the Hermit Kingdom, a country deliberately shunning contact with the outside Oriental world and having virtually no conception of another world in the Occident.

But Roman coins have been found in Korean burial urns, suggesting that traders must have reached Korean shores, bringing at least some form of contact with the Mediterranean civilizations. And the tentative contacts made with the West by the Chinese offered some later links between the Koreans— who sent peacetime envoys to the Peking court—and the cultures of London and Paris and Venice and Madrid. Korean writings of the early sixteenth century refer to people called the "Fo-lang-chi" overrunning the Chinese tributary state of "Man-la"—the Portuguese, undoubtedly, who annexed Malacca. A Spaniard, Gregorio de Cespedes, actually served in Korea as chaplain to Hideyoshi's troops during the Japanese campaign of 1593, but no reference can be found in any Korean source to the appearance of this strange-looking barbarian.

It was some time toward the end of the reign of King Sonjo, around 1606, that a Korean diplomat returned to Seoul from Peking with a map of Europe, offering the first certain, and presumably dismaying, knowledge that there was an advanced and civilized world beyond the great tracts of China. Then again, in 1631 an envoy named Chong Tu-won returned from a mission to the Celestial Kingdom with a collection of Western objects—a musket, a telescope, an alarm clock, a map of the then-known world, and books on astronomy. Thirteen years later still, when the Korean prince Sohyon was taken hostage by the invading Manchus and brought back to China, he met and was befriended by the Jesuit astronomer and mathematician, Adam Schall von Bell, and on his release in 1644 he brought back a number of books on Western science and a posse of Christian servants. (However, Sohyon died mysteriously, possibly of poisoning, just two months after his return to Seoul. It has long been thought that his enthusiasm for Schall's teachings, his pride in the books and presents he had been given, and his friendship with his Christian butlers proved offensive to the strict Confucian orthodoxy of his royal colleagues. In any case, such influence as he might have brought with him evaporated like perfume on a stove, and once his servants had been deported back to Peking, it was as though Sohyon, and Schall, had never been.)

But inexorably, events began to move more rapidly. A Dutch sailor named Jan Weltevree was shipwrecked on the Korean coast in 1627 and became a subject of immediate official fascination. In line with the policies of Japan and Korea, he was told he would have to remain exiled on the peninsula and could never return home. Weltevree, a master foundryman, was inducted into the Korean Military Training Command, and spent his career teaching military gunsmiths how to cast cannon, European-style. In such ways—imprisonment and exiledom, diplomacy and wreck—did knowledge seep slowly into this most perversely isolated of states on the Pacific shores.

But then, in 1653, came an event that was to bring Korea firmly to the notice of the Western world, though in truth it must be said it did little to increase Korean enthusiasm for or interest in the West.

The story of the wreck of the Dutch merchant ship the *Sparrowhawk* on the southwestern shores of Cheju Island, and the subsequent adventures of the surviving crew, was something I came across while browsing in a bookshop in the center of Seoul one wet and dismal November evening. It took me but a few moments to realize that the journey of these Dutch sailors, for reasons both symbolic and practical, would provide the perfect template for my own odyssey through Korea nearly three-and-a-half centuries later.

❖　❖　❖

The *Sparrowhawk*, or more precisely, the *Sperwer*, was a three-masted barque in the service of the Netherlands East India Company. Her crew had come out from Texel in Holland in January 1653 and had arrived at the Dutch naval station in Batavia—today's Djakarta—and then sailed on to Taiwan. There they transferred to the tiny *Sparrowhawk*, with orders to proceed to the treaty port of Nagasaki, in Japan, where the Dutch had trading rights.

According to the now-famous account of the journey written by the ship's secretary, Hendrick Hamel (with whose words I have begun this and all other chapters and ended the last one), the vessel set course to the northeast on

July 30. The bill of lading, issued in Formosa, shows the vessel to have carried the kind of exotic cargo that would have delighted Masefield: 20,000 catties (the measurement is still commonly used in China; a catty is equivalent to about 1.3 lbs.) of *putchuk* (better known as costus-root, a gingerlike aromatic root much favored by the Japanese); the same amount of camphor (listed, oddly, as Borneo camphor—odd since most of the world's camphor came in those days from a species of cinammon tree grown in Taiwan, whence the *Sparrowhawk* sailed); 20,000 catties of alum; 92,000 catties of powdered sugar; 300 wild goat skins; 3,000 eland skins; and nearly 20,000 Taiwanese deerskins.

Captain Egberts, of Amsterdam, was at the helm as the boat set sail. And Hamel wrote: "The day held fair till towards the Evening, when, as we were getting out of the Channel of Formosa, there arose a Storm, which increas'd all night."

It was a bad start to a journey that ended in catastrophe. The East India Company might well have expected it. July and August are, after all, the worst months for typhoons in the northwestern Pacific (remember the old mariners' adage: "June, too soon; July, stand by; August, *if you must*; September, remember; October, all over"), and modern mariners might have construed it as foolhardiness on a grand scale to send a heavily laden sailing vessel across the East China Sea in August. Nevertheless, the company directors confidently expected their charge to make fast on Deshima Island, off Nagasaki, by the end of September at the latest. But she never did arrive, nor did she ever return to Taiwan. The *Sparrowhawk* and her crew of sixty-four men simply vanished. The company waited for more than a year, hoping against hope for some sign; but then, in October 1654, a brief announcement in the East India Company bulletin recorded the loss of the vessel. The cargo and crew, with expressions more of inevitability than sorrow, were written off.

Twelve years later, however, in September 1666, a message was received at the Dutch agent's office in Nagasaki saying that "eight Europeans, dressed in a wondrous way and with a boat of strange fashion" had fetched up on the Goto Islands in southwestern Japan and were being transported to the Japanese authorities at Nagasaki, where the Dutch—the only local Europeans—might see them and try to discern who or what they might be. The meeting must have been an extraordinary event, for the eight men were indeed Dutchmen, some of the surviving party from the *Sparrowhawk*. Their clothes, their little fishing boat, their newly adopted language, and their eating habits all came from the country in which they had sojourned for thirteen years after their shipwreck and that was only vaguely known to any Europeans—Korea.

Their tale ranks among the most romantic of the innumerable sagas of wreck and faraway adventure, and it has been meticulously recorded by Hendrick Hamel in a book that was published in both Amsterdam and Rotterdam in 1668—a book that presented the first European account of "the Kingdom of Corea."

The *Sparrowhawk* smashed onto the rocks at night, early in the morning of August 16, 1653:

> . . . when the second Glass of the second watch being just running out, he that look'd out a Head cry'd Land, Land; adding, we were not a Musket-shot from it; the Darkness of the Night and the Rain having obstructed our discovering it sooner. We endeavoured to Anchor, but in vain, because we found no bottom, and the roughness of the Sea and the force of the Wind obstructed. Thus the anchors having no hold, three successive Waves sprang such a leak in the Vessel, that those who were in the Hold were drown'd before they could get out. Some of those that were on the deck leap'd Overboard, and the rest were carried away by the Sea. Fifteen of us got ashore at the same place, for the most part naked and much hurt, and thought at first none had escap'd but ourselves; but climbing the Rocks we heard the Voices of some Men complaining, yet could see nothing, nor help anybody, because of the darkness of the night.

The survivors had no idea where they might be; and when the first curious locals appeared on the clifftop to inspect these cold and frightened newcomers, the natives' dress suggested they had landed in China. "These men were clad after the Chinese fashion, exception only their hats, which were made of horse-hair." But then, two days later, the matter was clarified. The navigator was able to snatch a hurried sight of the sun and the horizon with his sextant. He pronounced the ship to have stranded not in China at all but at 33°32′ north latitude, 126°20′ east longitude, on an island the Dutch had sighted sufficiently often to have included it on their charts, with the name of Quelpaert, after a type of Dutch sailing vessel that, from a distance, it resembled. Quelpaert, "which the natives call *Sehesure*," was known to lie "12 or 13 leagues south of the coast of Corea."

Hendrick Hamel's account of the next thirteen years, written in a hurry while he was waiting in Nagasaki to be taken back to Batavia, is brief but vivid. He tells of the crew members' interrogation by the local magistrates on Cheju Island and of the quite astonishing arrival in their midst of another Dutchman—the same Jan Weltevree who had been wrecked some thirty-five years before, had been impressed into the Korean Army, and had fought against the Manchus. Weltevree's arrival was a piece of marvelous good fortune: He had been sent by the court in Seoul to act as interpreter:

> It was very surprising, and even wonderful, that a man of fifty-eight years of age, as he was then, would so forget his Mother-tongue, that we had much to do at first to understand him. But it must be observ'd he recovr'd it again in a month. The Governour [of Cheju] having

caus'd all our Depositions to be taken in Form, sent them to Court, and bid us be of good cheer, for we should have an Answer in short time. In the mean while he daily bestow'd new favours on us, insomuch that he gave leave to Weltevree and the Officers that came with him to see us at all times, and acquaint him with our Wants.

The decision of the court was issued within weeks: The entire party was to be brought by ship across the Strait of Cheju to the mainland and then by horse and foot was to be transported north to Seoul. Only then, when the king and his court officials had seen and interrogated the party themselves, would orders for their disposition be made.

It is not necessary at this stage to relate in detail the entire story of this hapless band of stranded seamen—no doubt some mention of them will be made in subsequent chapters. Briefly, they, like Jan Weltevree, were pressed into the service of the army, as musketeers in the Seoul palace guard. They immediately tried to escape by attempting to win over to their cause the ambassador of the Chinese court, but they failed, were punished (feeling for the first time a punishment they had seen meted out to criminals on Cheju, the uniquely painful foot beating known as bastinado, which was performed with particularly efficient unpleasantness by the Koreans), and then exiled to the very southwest of the country. It was from there that eight of them managed, after ten years of waiting, to steal a small fishing boat and set out eastward for Japan.

I read all this on that dark and wet autumn night; Korean bookshops stay open late, mercifully, and the bookseller seemed not to mind my browsing. But I had in any case decided within moments of opening the book on the route of my walk. I would follow the path that Hamel, Denijszen, Ibocken, Pieterszen, Janszen, and the rest (which included a mysterious Scotsman named Alexander Basket), the first European party to be escorted through the Hermit Kingdom, had taken.

They had left Cheju in June 1654 and had landed at the southern port city of Haenam. From there, horses having been supplied, they trotted comfortably northward—keeping to an almost die-straight path through the cities that are now called Yongam, Naju, Changsong, Taein, Chonju, Yonsan, Kongju—and finally having crossed "a river as wide as the Maese is at Dordrecht," reached the city their hearing suggested was *Sior* and that we now know as Seoul. The journey had taken them ten days. One of their number, a gunner "who had never enjoy'd his health since our shipwreck," died along the way; but otherwise the party arrived without incident before His Highness the King Hyojong, seventeenth monarch of the Yi Dynasty.

The journey I would make, then, would start at the very point on Cheju Island where the *Sparrowhawk* had stranded. I would cross the island to its capital, Cheju City, where the Dutchmen met Weltevree and were told of the court's decision to bring them north to Seoul; I would sail across to the mainland and, with compass and stick, set off due north along the track that my fellow Europeans had taken all those years before. I would go to Seoul, of course, but I would then, for the sake of completeness, walk smartly for those last few miles up to the point where South Korea ends and its other half, the implacably hostile neighbor-state of North Korea, begins. More precisely, I would try to finish my journey at the celebrated village where the country finishes—the war-wrecked hamlet of Panmunjom, through which the frontier (or the Military Demarcation Line, to be exact, for this is not a legal frontier, merely a temporary division caused by a war frozen in cease-fire) runs—and from beyond which North Korea glowers menacingly at its neighbor and the outside world.

❖   ❖   ❖

I had an early and devastatingly naive notion that it might be a comparatively simple task (for such an innocent as a British passport holder) to walk on through the frontier and make the journey run from Cheju Island to Pyongyang, the North Korean capital, or even to the Yalu River, on the Chinese border. I had visited the North Korean Embassy in Peking once and was told that there should be no problem at all about gaining access to North Korea— no problem, particularly, no matter how many times I had visited the South. But when I mentioned this possibility to friends in South Korea, inward whistling and pursing of lips began at a furious pace. No, they said in unison. You go to North Korea, and you will not—respectful regrets, mumble mumble, dreadful shame, mumble mumble—be permitted to enter the South. So there seemed no point: A walk through Korea that turned out to be only a walk through North Korea sounded monumentally lacking in point. Besides, Mr. Hamel hadn't been there, which realization finally set a cap on the matter.

There was little enough organization to be done, other than to secure the necessary time off. The journey would be about 320 miles, and at 20 miles a day I should need only 16 days if nothing of interest happened and nothing caught my fancy: I was certain to require more, so I arranged to be away from my base in Hong Kong for two months, which, it turned out, was almost exactly the time I needed.

I bought myself a stout Lowe rucksack and one of those canvas-and-Velcro purses in which you can keep all your valuables suspended from your neck. I dug my New Balance boots (last used a year before to clamber along the Crib Goch ridge in North Wales, and thus well worn in) out of a cupboard. I bought bars of Cadbury's Fruit-and-Nut chocolate and sachets of instant coffee and the inevitable slabs of Kendal Mint Cake (brown, not white). I found a long blackthorn stick with a ramshorn crook that had been made by a shepherd in the Cotswolds, somewhere near Chipping Norton. I discovered, after a long hunt, my old Silva compasses, which are the best found outside ships' bridges, are made in Finland, and must therefore be a mainstay of the Finnish export business. I bought woolen socks and gloves, cotton shirts and underwear, and a khaki-colored neck stocking known as a "headover," which I had been given one particularly frigid day in the Falkland Islands by an army sergeant who feared I might freeze to death. I begged back my Swiss army knife (two types of screwdriver, a spike for undistressing begraveled horses, several wicked blades, an ivory toothpick, tweezers, *and* a magnifying glass, the better for lighting fires with) from the son who had borrowed it. I bought a Sony Walkman Professional and clipped a weatherproof microphone to my shirt so that I could recite reassuring things to myself at lonely moments and then transcribe them at night into one of my waterproof-jacketed Alwych notebooks. I took a Sony ICF4900 lightweight shortwave radio receiver so I could hear the BBC (except I rarely could; the Spanish Service of Radio Peking used an identical frequency). And I took plenty of spare batteries; pencils; a first aid kit; sunglasses; and a Leica M6 camera with a 35mm Summicron lens, a yellow filter, and plenty of Agfa black-and-white 100 ASA film.

Thus equipped—the weight of the rucksack, like the length of the Chinese measure known as the *li*, would vary according to whether the journey was uphill, downhill, or on the flat—I squeezed myself into a pair of Rohan walking breeks and a Viyella shirt, thrust on my head a battered old Akubra drover hat I had bought in Queensland that was said to be good for drinking out of or for fanning a dying fire and, braving the puzzled looks from the Brooks Brother'd bankers in the Hong Kong departure lounge, boarded Cathay Pacific Flight CX410 from Kai Tak to Kimpo.

The Cathay people, unfailingly kind to the inquisitive, let me sit on the flight deck for the approach. Kimpo Airport is regarded with distaste by most professional pilots, said the captain, a rather dyspeptic Londoner. Not only was there a very nasty mountain that reared up in the final moments of the approach but the South Korean security services placed extraordinarily strict controls on the precision of that approach. A slight northward drift off the glide slope and, said the captain, "You're dead meat." The problem was that the North Korean aerial frontier was only three minutes' jet time away from the Kimpo glide slope, so any friendly airliner that strayed north from the slope could appear, to an unsophisticated Seoul approach radar operator, to be a North Korean intruder. And since the glide slope passed only a few miles from the Blue House—the Korean presidential palace—it *could* be that the intruder was on his way to blow up the Blue House. "So we are warned—more than at any other airport in the world—to stay exactly on the slope we're told. Any plane that makes a mistake is in deep trouble. They nearly blew the tail off a Northwest Airlines jumbo a few years ago. They mean business, those Korean boys."

But Cathay did its job this time with sedulous efficiency, and we screeched to a halt at Kimpo on time, and I began my struggle through the immigration counters. It took an hour or so, but by eveningtime I was in a hotel, asking the advice of friends, mugging up on my understanding of Korea's *hangul* script (which was pretty poor and so remained), and making the last plans for the trip.

A day later I was armed with maps. I had imagined there would be some difficulty, given the security situation—after all, it is well nigh impossible to buy decent maps of countries like India and Pakistan, and one has to make do with American aerial navigation maps bought at Stanford's in Covent Garden, where most of the world's journeying seems properly to begin. I had asked the defense attaché at the British Embassy in Seoul, and the American Defense Mapping Agency in Washington, if I could acquire some good English-language maps of Korea, but both, with weary you-should-know-better-than-to-ask sighs, had refused. In the end I discovered you could go into an ordinary Seoul shop and buy as decent a 1:250,000 or even 1:50,000 map as you could wish, but for the script being in either Chinese characters (which I did not understand) or *hangul* (which I was trying to). I thus bought coverage of the entire country in the smaller-scale 1:250,000 for about $6; and I was not particularly alarmed to notice, in red letters on the reverse, a strict enjoinment to the effect that were I to take the map abroad without permission of the director general of the National Institute of Geography, I could be sent to prison for two years or fined 2 million *won*. After use, the warning ended, the map should be destroyed by fire.

Now I was really ready. So I returned to Kimpo's domestic air terminal, bought myself a single ticket for Cheju Island, and waited as flight after flight took off, filled to the brim with honeymoon couples bound for the warm wildernesses of the south. I wondered if I would ever get on a plane—the airline seemed puzzled about how to handle someone traveling alone. But, as I was to discover a dozen times a day from that moment on, there was always someone happy to oblige an Englishman. "*Meeguk saram?*" they would inquire, asking if I was an American. "*Anio,*" I would say brightly, "*Yong guk saram.*" No, I'm English. And anxious faces would break into broad smiles, and someone would always come up with a mysterious phrase that instantly put me on my best behavior. I have no idea to this day which schoolbook taught it to them, but someone would invariably say, in tones of some gravity, "English—an *English gentleman,*" and whatever problem I had mentioned would instantly disappear.

So on this occasion, the first, the formula worked a treat.

"*Mian hamnida*—excuse me, but when may I get on a plane to Cheju-do?"

"*Meeguk saram?*"

"*Anio, yong guk saram.*"

"Ah, an *English gentleman.* Please, have this seat. Next flight. Ten minutes. *Anyonghee kashipshiyo!*"

And thus bidden Godspeed, and having presented identifications galore (travelers inside Korea are required to show passports or papers at every verse end, so troubled are the authorities that infiltrating Northerners might wander freely about), I boarded the plane for the south. They had put me right at the very back of the aircraft, and I had an interesting chat with a man who confessed to being a Korean version of a sky marshal and had a very large and wicked gun hidden under his jacket, which he was nonetheless quite happy to show me, demonstrating how he would try to stop a hijacker, should one be so foolish as to try.

The flight took fifty minutes—a journey by air that took Mr. Hamel ten days by horse and would take me, on shank's pony, rather more than a month. I stepped off the plane into a fierce westerly Cheju Island gale that nearly swept the Akubra from my head. So the journey begins, I thought to myself; and, like Hamel when he heard of the orders to remove his party to Seoul, "I knew not whether to Rejoyce, or be Troubled." I found my way to a hotel and slept my last night in luxury before beginning the long march northward, up to the border.

C H A P T E R

TWO

"On the 18th, we spent all the Morning in enlarging our Tent; and about noon there came down about 2000 Men, Horse and Foot, who drew up in order of Battel before our Hut. . . . They were as far from understanding us as if they had never known Japan; for they call that country Jeenare, or Jirpon. The Commander, perceiving he could make nothing of all we said, caus'd a cup of Arac to be fill'd to every one of us, and sent us back to our Tent.

"After Dinner they came with Ropes in their hands, which very much surpriz'd us, imagining they intended to strangle us; but our Fear vanish'd when we saw them run altogether towards the Wreck, to draw ashore what might be of use to them. At night they gave us more Rice to eat; and our Master having made an Observation, found we were in the Island of Quelpaert, which is in 33 degrees 32 minutes of Latitude."

—HENDRICK HAMEL,
1668

❖   ❖   ❖

THE MONUMENT TO HENDRICK HAMEL—MY STARTING
point—stood squat, ugly, looking out of place and very Bauhaus, on a windy
hillside of short and springy grass a hundred feet above the sea. It was built of
concrete blocks and had the legend "Hamel kinyombi" engraved in *hangul*
at the top. A plaque recording the efforts of various philanthropies—such as
the Borneo Sumatra Trading Company Ltd. and one Carel H. Pappenheim—
that were responsible for its construction was weathering nicely in the rain on
one side; and on the other, a plaque recorded the wreck of the *Sparrowhawk*
and the consequent writing of "the first description of Korea ever published
in the West." This, then, undistinguished a structure though it might be, was
as much a memorial to a book as to a shipwreck—a pleasant symmetry, I
thought, as I hitched my pack onto my shoulders, turned my back on the sea,
dug my stick firmly into the turf, switched on my tape recorder, and took the
first step to the north.

I was at a village called Mosulpo, a pretty affair of blue- and orange-roofed
cottages that huddled out of the wind in the shadow of a huge basalt cliff at
the southwest tip of Cheju-do. (The island's name, given by mainlanders, is
memorably prosaic: *che* means "across" or "over there," *ju* means "district,"
and *do* means, in this instance, "island"—hence Cheju-do is "the island district over there.") The locals either fished or farmed, and one might have
supposed, being so far away from the realities of the Korean politics (and that
is one reason why so many peninsular Koreans come to Cheju on holiday,

27

removing themselves from the tensions prompted by the proximity of the North and the DMZ), that there would be no sign of the more distressingly martial side of life. But even down here the military were all around. High up on the cliff—my notebook records it, as though I were a birdwatcher, as my very first sighting—were two men quite obviously from the U.S. Army. They were wearing full combat gear—packs, rifles, gas masks, rain capes, heavy boots, helmets—and when I spotted them they were gaily abseiling down the sheer basalt face. The first to get back to solid earth—a large man with more muscles than seemed decent—came over to me.

"You 'murican?" he inquired, in an accent indubitably from south of the Mason-Dixon line. I confessed that I was not. He spoke in a machine-gun staccato. "Limey, huh? How're ya doin'? Goddamn shit hole of a place this is, Korea. You like it?—shit, you must be crazy. Come over 'n' see us at the camp. We'll set you right. I can tell you a thing or two about this place. Nothin' else to do in this place 'cept get seriously drunk. No pussy. No pussy for miles. Nothin'. Come over 'n' see us." And with that he left to retrieve his friend, who was shouting anxiously and appeared to be stuck on his rock.

I hauled up a steady rise along the flanks of the cliff, and was soon, puffing like a pug engine, in open country. It was just like the West of Ireland, like Connemara or Donegal. There were dry stone walls between the little fields, and there was cotton grass, and the green shoots of new barley, and a dusting of bright yellow from the spring meadows of rape. Curlews were singing, and early swallows swooped low over the little rivers. A steady, soughing wind riffled the moorland grasses, and over to my right a ragged line of foam showed where the land tilted down, via a narrow paludal plain, to its drowning in the sea. The weather was very Irish, too; there was a thin gray mist, through which a milky sun shone fitfully, and occasionally great gusts of cool and pleasant dampness whirled down from the sky. It was refreshing, exhilarating weather— perfect, had I been a professional walker, for a marathon.

But on this first day I was not planning more than the gentlest of hikes. "Wearing in my boots," was how I excused myself. A friend in Hong Kong had given me the name of a young Cantonese man, Lawrence, who ran a hotel at Sogwipo—a honeymoon hotel, the friend had said with a knowing leer. So I kept to a more easterly track than Hamel's men had done, and by nightfall I had reached the outskirts of the village and had found the hotel. It looked like an immense inverted jelly mold—it had been designed by a firm of Hawaiian architects—standing on the clifftop overlooking the southern sea. Lawrence was waiting for me. "You really did walk here?" he asked, incredulous. He was a plumpish young man with a disagreeable pallor of gray on yellow, and he made it abundantly clear that he found it unpleasant even to have to walk across a room. "You know the Chinese. Just lie in bed and make money, that's us."

His business was, indeed, honeymoons. I had seen dozens of young couples speeding by in taxis already that day (and the plane from Seoul had been three-quarters filled with them, nervous youngsters holding hands and clearly having little idea what to say to each other). The island is to Korean couples what the Adirondacks are to New Yorkers and the Channel Islands to Britons—with one significant exception. As it is well-nigh impossible for a Korean to obtain a passport (the well-worn excuse offered by the government being the need to conserve foreign exchange, the actual reason being far more complex and steeped in a political paranoia that I will discuss later), it is almost unthinkable for any Korean to travel abroad. (A businessman may, but he is obliged to hand his passport back to the government when he resigns or retires—the privilege of overseas ventures belonging more properly to his company than to him as an individual. Confucian respect for elders, however, allows passports to be kept by people over fifty, and soon, the government promises, by those over forty-five.) So most Korean couples, be they wealthy or working class, have almost no hope of spending their postmarital holiday anywhere abroad—no basking in the Balinese sun for them, unlike their Japanese or Hong Kong counterparts. The only serious transocean adventure open to them is thus a journey to Cheju, the island "over there." And so over there, by the tens of thousands, they flock. The Adirondacks and the Channel Islands may generally prove to be a convenient magnet for the less well-off in the West: Cheju is for everyone, with the entire spectrum of a generation there beginning its first, halting experiments in living and sleeping together.

Seven out of ten of the couples that Lawrence sees in his hotel—he reckons he sees some 36,000 a year (and to gauge the scale of this cottage industry one must note that his is but one of ten first-class honeymoon hotels on Cheju, and there are any number of meaner inns for the Korean *Lumpenproletariat*)—are brought together by professional matchmakers. Lawrence was not altogether approving. "I suppose it's my hotelier's greed, really. You see these wretched matchmakers sitting in the hotel coffee shops up in Seoul, with the groom's family on one side, the bride's on the other, and no one eating a thing. Oh yes, the matchmaker herself does; she's not nervous at all. She'll have chocolate cakes—they're usually pretty fat, these old Korean women. But everyone else is scared stiff, and if they order one cup of coffee each for the afternoon, we're lucky. The young boy and girl probably only have a glass of water. They don't know what to say or do. They just sit there, looking at the table, fidgeting, looking at the backs of their hands. I've known café managers wanting to tear their hair out on a Saturday afternoon—every table full, seven people to a table, and no one eating anything! The manager's lucky if he can pay one waitress's wages for the day. Wretched women. Bane of my life."

Usually the youngsters meet three times: once in a Seoul (or Pusan or Taegu or Inchon or wherever) coffee shop, for that initial encounter under their parents' gaze; once at a formal dinner in one of the prospective in-laws' homes; and once, if they're particularly bold, on their own at a cinema or in a park or, if she's lucky to have found a young man rich enough, in the prospective groom's new car. (By this stage, if the arrangement has "taken," the match-maker gets her money, invariably from the parents of the bride: 5 million *won* in many cases—$5,200—and often a great deal more. In weddings arranged among the *yangban*, those who like to think of themselves as the relics of the Korean nobility, or in weddings where the prospective husband is a lawyer or a doctor or an accountant and is thus an excellent catch, the bride's parents are commonly supposed to offer him "three keys" as an inducement: a key to a new car, a key to a new apartment, and a key to the new office in which to practice his calling. Finding a suitable husband for your daughter is thus a tall order for even the most fortunate of today's Koreans.)

The reason is a mathematical consequence of war and of the peculiar mar-rying habits of the Korean people. There is a custom of sorts that decrees that a girl should marry a man about four years older than herself, once he has done his compulsory stint with one of the arms of the Korean military. Girls born in the mid-1950s were the first to discover that there was a problem: When it was their turn to marry, in the late 1970s (they were then in their early twenties), they looked around for men who were then in their mid- to late twenties—born, in other words, in 1952 or 1953. But thanks to the travails of the Korean War, almost no children were conceived or born in those years, and the girls in the class of '56, as it were, found they had to look for younger men. Like locusts, they descended on men born in 1954 and 1955, meaning that the girls poised for matrimonial bliss in the years below them suffered from what might vulgarly be termed a knock-on effect. There have, in con-sequence of the war, been many thousands of girls anxiously pursuing a very much reduced pool of men of the desirable age, meaning that, in order to win a traditionally suitable spouse, girls—or, rather, their parents—have to resort to extortion, bribery, and emotional grand larceny on a mighty scale. Hence the matchmakers, and hence the sobering fact that no Korean matchmaker who nailed up her shingle since the Panmunjom cease-fire was signed has ever gone to bed hungry.

The union thus arranged, it has to be sanctified and then consummated. The service in a wedding hall (everything rented by the hour—the wedding dress, the music cassettes, the videotape, the formal Korean *hangbok* the pair wear for a photograph that is taken against an acrylic painting of a traditional background) is, except for the more devout families, perfunctory and rather mechanical, and it culminates in the pair flying off, with unimaginative in-evitability, to Cheju. Once island-bound, they place themselves in the hands of one of a small army of professional icebreakers, like the ever-beaming, ever-genial, and very small Mr. Chu, who has worked in Lawrence's hotel since it opened, and who, when we met, claimed to have been vicariously responsible "for the deflowering of more virgins than any man in Asia."

"It is a challenge just to get these people to talk to each other. They come down here quite tired, very tense, very shy. But I have worked out a formula, and it seems to produce results.

"In the spring season we may get two hundred couples down in a night. They'll be here for two nights, perhaps three if their husbands have very kindly employers. Usually, though, the husband has just finished his military service, and he's now in his first job and he doesn't want to spoil his work record. So he's keen to get back to his desk. It means we don't have much time.

"So I get them all down to the disco—they'll have had notes under the door telling them when to come down. We give them trays full of trinkets—loving ducks [the Asian equivalent of turtle doves], bath salts, heart-shaped cakes, and small bottles of *insam* extract, as a bit of a joke for the boys [*insam* is better known as ginseng, and the extract, a sweetish red liquid, is said to be heap good magic for a troublesome libido].

"We play the only games they can all be certain of knowing—the games they played at school. It's all very nostalgic for them; the men are all about twenty-six or so, the women twenty-two, and they won't have played the games for ten years or more. But then I introduce slightly erotic forfeits—I get a girl to confess which film star she likes and why, or I get her to massage the boy's neck, or I get the boy to drink ten sips of *soju*, so he gets a little drunk, and then I get him to sing *Arirang* or some song they all know, so they get a bit teary. By midnight they're all in quite a sentimental mood, and the bolder couples slip away up to their rooms.

"But there are always the problem cases. There are the girls who fall asleep at the bar because they've had such a long day, what with getting up at five to put on all that makeup. And there are the boys who are quite terrified of what they've got to do next, and they just want to stay together in the bar and get drunk. But slowly we push them all out, and by one o'clock we lock up downstairs, and take a look around to make sure no one's lingering by the indoor waterfalls [of which the hotel has many, as well as lots of pools stuffed with sluggish, barely mobile, and very fat old carp].

"Then, once we know they're all in their rooms, we all go back to the office for a drink. We have a saying for what happens next. We say we're 'waiting for the earthquake.' "

The next morning the young couples, who did not appear at all sheepish, emerged and tucked into their fish and seaweed and *kimchi* breakfasts. Hundreds of taxi drivers were on hand—each man in uniform, each advertising the fact that he carried a prodigious amount of color film and a camera, and each keen to take the new Mr. and Mrs. Park or Mr. and Mrs. Kim or Mr. and Mrs. Lee on a whirlwind tour of the island. The important thing from this moment on was to go everywhere and be seen to have been everywhere, hence the cameras and the self-promoting Cartier-Bressons *manqués* who, sad to say, had each found his career prospects so limited (as he would recount in the car) that he had been forced to take this menial job of taxi driving in order to support wife, children, and family dog. The couple wouldn't care: All they needed—and they really *needed* it—was a photographic record of the honeymoon, to fulfill the Confucian desire *to be seen to be doing the right thing* and to have proof of having done it for the elders back home.

(Strangers might find it perplexing—I certainly did—to confront a population that is overwhelmingly composed of people all seemingly belonging to the same very small number of families. Most Koreans are either called Park, Kim, or Lee, which latter is also spelled Rhee, Ee, Ea, Yi, Yih, Lih, Li, Ri, Rhi, Rii, and Ree—the Koreans having a great talent to confuse—and it can on occasion be trying if a Mr. Park wishes to marry a Miss Park, or a Miss Kim a Captain Kim, or Ms. Rhee a Mr. Li. Only if it can be proved that the pair do not belong to the same clan are they permitted to marry. A Kimhae Kim—a Kim from the Kimhae clan—may marry an Andong Kim without any major problems; but it can happen that two less well-distanced Kims may to their horror discover on consulting their *chokbo*, the family-tree book most Koreans keep in a bottom drawer, that they share the same recent antecedents and are thus *of the same clan.* They are forbidden by law to marry. They often do, but illegally, and their children will not be registered.)

Thus we talked, late into the night and over tumblers of brandy, my Hong Kong friend drinking his with peppermint cordial, a mixture of such stunning vulgarity that only the Cantonese, I thought, could conjure it up, let alone drink it and stay living. Dawn was beginning to break when I finally slumped into my bed, my head reeling with Andong Kims and Pusan Parks and Namwon Rhees. And when I woke, head still reeling, the sun was glaring down on a copper sea. I had a mountain to climb.

❖   ❖   ❖

"In this Island there is a Mountain of a vast Height," wrote Hamel, "all cover'd with woods and several small Hills which are naked, and enclose many Vales abounding in Rice. . . ."

Cheju Island, to which Hamel referred, is a vast volcano, the flanks peppered with fumaroles and lesser escape routes—now built into substantial hills themselves—from which steady streams of basalt lava once eased themselves down toward the sea. The island summit is in fact Korea's highest mountain, Halla-san, 6,397 feet, and at this time of early spring, quite covered with snow. (British charts once named the peak Mount Auckland. The Royal Navy had brief imperial ambitions for Korea's southern coast, annexed a tiny island now named Komun-do, and with rather absurd grandiloquence styled it Port Hamilton. Nowadays there are two ratings' graves there, the headstones roped off as a sanctuary, a memorial to a somewhat forlorn and unconsummated colonial idea.)

I was far from fit, but a friend who had flown down from Seoul to guide me—a tough young Korean woman named Kim Mae-young, whose firmest

friend in Seoul was, she said, one of the country's best-known rock climbers—
goaded me: To travel through Cheju without climbing Halla mountain would
be an omission verging on sacrilege. I laced my climbing boots, she tied on a
dainty pair of sneakers, and we set off on the trail.

It was a crisp early spring day, and the woods behind the small Buddhist
temple where the trail began were flecked with patches of melting snow. A
tiny stream trilled down beside the path, and in places it broadened, and on
its sandy banks small birds picked twigs to build their new nests. Tiny alpine
flowers, pale blue and primrose yellow, grew by the stream, and on the trees
there were clumps of bright scarlet or umber lichens—all very Scandinavian,
wintry, and starkly beautiful.

The path was well marked and utterly without litter; the Koreans who climb
have, I had been told, the utmost respect for their countryside. Every half mile
or so there was a map and a shelter, and beside some of these rest stops a
basalt trough of water, constantly fed by the stream, and a wooden dipper
nearby to make it easy to take a drink. The dipper had evidently been there
for years: In Korea, no one would think of stealing it.

We rounded the plump bole of a tree, and there, sitting with solemn equanimity beside the trail, was an old man. He was dressed in a dark gray coat
with a white blouse beneath and brown baggy trousers and white slippers. He
wore a tall hat, slightly tapered toward the top, with a wide, oddly transparent
brim. His face was an almost perfect oval but with a straggling gray beard and
a long mustache that reached well down the front of his tunic. His umbrella
was open and standing next to him should there be a rainstorm or should the
sun become too strong. He was smoking a cigarette in a contemplative sort of
way and looked a vision of peace and contentment, though as we approached
him he looked up, sat up straight, and beckoned to us.

He was a fortune-teller, so strategically located that it was quite impossible
to pass him without buying a reading. He asked me two questions only—the
date I was born and the time. I told him, whereupon he took an enormous
chart from a pocket in his tunic and wrote with great unhurried speed in
Chinese characters. He frowned a lot, then smiled, put away his notes, and
spoke in Korean. Mae-young interpreted. "This man says you are a writer, and
you come from England. He could tell that from your voice, I suppose. He
says that you have written six books, and that you will write fifteen more, and
you will be successful and happy. You will die when you are eighty-eight.
Please give him two thousand won. That is all."

I was astonished. Had she said anything to him? I wondered. She insisted
not. Had she winked, given him any sort of clue? She swore blind she had
not. She was as amazed as I was, for she knew that in all he said about my
past, he was exactly right. There was no vague dissembling, no catchall gen-
eralization. This man was sure—his entire attitude and demeanor radiated self-
confidence and certitude—that I was a writer, and yet I carried no notebook,

gave no hint that I might be anything other than a foreigner on his holidays. He had the number of books exactly correct. How on earth could he have known? "He knows," said Mae-young, and that was all she said on the subject. So we tramped on, with me beginning to wonder exactly what the next four-teen books would be about, and whether it would be prudent to begin planning my funeral for some time after September in the year 2032.

After an hour the trees thinned out, and the mountainside became domi-nated by huge vaulting walls of dark brown basalt, with shrubs nestling in the fissures, and occasional clumps of hardy stunted pines. It was cold up here, above three thousand feet, and a thick air-frost had settled on everything, whitening the rocks, adorning branches with fronds of ghostly crystals, making the narrow paths treacherous. At one stage we inched our way along a tiny ledge, slick with new ice, and with a thousand-foot sheer drop between us and—I could just make out his hat—the old fortune-teller in a clearing in the woods below. Logic and faith imbued me with the certainty that I would not, could not, fall: The old man had told me I had another four decades to go, so there was no need to hang on like grim death to the mountain wall and pray. I did, however, just in case he had made a slight miscalculation.

The climb became more arduous, and I began to slow down. It was, at first, quite humiliating. Not only Mae-young bounded ahead, leaving me gasping in her wake. Koreans have the capacity to be fantastically energetic and quite tireless. Old Korean grandmothers, small children, a man in his eighties with a tweed suit and a Harry Lauder walking stick—they all scrambled up the pathway like goats, and whenever I stopped, panting like a grampus, legions more would pass without the slightest trace of weariness or sweat. By using them as pacemakers it had taken me no more than an hour to reach the frost line, where the views (for I stopped a great deal to look about me) took in villages and farms in every quarter of the compass, and it became clear that this was, after all, an island, shaped like a lozenge and out of sight of any other land. But once we were up in the cold, they rushed past me, totally in their element.

We stopped at a hut at the 5,577-foot mark, broke the ice on a spring, and drank deeply of the purest and sweetest water. I had a bar of chocolate and found a tiny bottle of whiskey I had been given on the plane. It might have done on a Scottish mountain, but here it was very much spartan fare. The other climbers had more ambitious luncheon plans: The same grandmothers who had whizzed past me now untied their haversacks and produced, in short order, positively Lucullan feasts—sausages, fried fish, boiled eggs, seaweed, pickled vegetables, seasoned squid, tuna rolls, kimchi and rice, and packets of strong soup, which they heated in pots filled with melting snow. A small fire was glowing in a corner of the hut's living room, and we all sat close to it, huddling out of the cold winds that now blew incessantly. But without warning a thick bank of cloud suddenly descended over the main peak, which rose, jagged and formidable, a temptingly few hundred feet above us. A frost-covered climber clinking with expensive-looking ironmongery (which both the Koreans and the Japanese will spend small fortunes on, just so that they achieve the correct *look* up on a mountain) appeared from its slopes and made an announcement that sent up a groan from the waiting throng: We were advised not to go farther; it was going to snow, and the peak would be doubly dangerous.

So we all set off back down again, some to the north of the island, and the hotels of Cheju City, while others, like Mae-young and I, retraced our steps back down to Sogwipo. Late lunch parties had sprung up on the hillside—gatherings of ten and fifteen people getting pleasantly tight on bottles of milk-white *makkoli* and singing mournful ballads into the wind. No one climbed alone: The Koreans claim that they dislike solitude, and the contemplative Korean, even on hills where contemplation seems so suitable, is rarely found. Wordsworth is not popular: Wandering lonely as a cloud is an unfathomable Western trait. Mountains, someone explained, are for group enjoyment: "People don't come here to enjoy nature. You Westerners talk about communing with nature. Here people come to commune with each other. The nature is incidental."

❖ ❖ ❖

From back down at sea level the yellowish, waxy clouds that quite obscured the mountaintop looked full of snow; but down here it was warm, the wind had eased, and the setting sun was reddening the western sky. We found a pathway down to a beach of iron black sand, and dabbled our toes in the freezing water. I had come to look for a group of Cheju's women divers—the *haenyo*—who might, about now, be finishing their daily hunt for abalone and sea cucumbers in the shallow waters off the cliffs.

The most difficult task for anyone wandering through a foreign land with the hope of gaining some insight into it is the profound need "to come to terms with the lives and thoughts of strangers." William Franklin Sands, an American diplomat who was invited to become a counselor of the Korean royal house in 1900, when he was only twenty-five, was one of those rare individuals who tried thus to come to terms. He left a slim book, *Undiplomatic Memories*, as a record of his ventures into the wilder parts of the country he so dearly loved. He came to Cheju—though he called it Quelpaert, as Hamel's men had done—and he found it dominated by a remarkable society of women.

> Man, in this lost corner of the world, was an inferior being; the woman was everything. She was the real house-bond. She owned all the property; her children bore her family name, and she never took a permanent husband. Men were allowed to come over from the mainland once a year, but they were not encouraged to stay long,

and when they returned took with them all boys who had reached thirteen years. . . .

It was more like a matriarchy, a real Amazon community, for the women were always ready to assert their power and uphold it by force.

The women were fine swimmers and divers. Young and old would swim out through the breakers, leave a basket buoyed by gourds floating on the surface and dive fathoms down for abalone shell or a bunch of edible seaweed. They would cut it out with a short sickle (the same weapon they used on the men when annoyed), attach an empty gourd to it, drop the stone with which they had weighted the gourd and let it float to the surface to be picked up when they were ready to come up themselves. They could swim and float about for hours, dive as simply as a duck, and work or move about from place to place under the water as easily and as long as so many sea fowl. While resting on the surface they would keep up a monotonous whistling in different keys to warn chance men in the fishing boats to keep their distance.

I played the chance man. Whether they whistled or not I could not tell, but here they were, emerging from the sea like seals—a dozen or so women, most of them near middle age, all in tight-fitting black rubber suits. From a distance they looked like police frogmen or a team of specialists from the Special Boat Squadron who had been laying limpet mines on the hull of the *Scharnhorst*. They scampered out of the foam and up across the rocks with great agility, and each sat down at a little chosen site sheltered from the breeze to sort and pack her catch. Most of them had slimy bubbles of sea cucumber or bundles of weed—sea kale, perhaps—while a few of the luckier ones had managed to pluck up ear-shaped abalone, whose shells looked like oysters and that had (as I remembered from a seaside dinner some months before) the consistency of eraser rubber and the taste of Styrofoam. Abalone is reputed— along with ginseng, dog soup, snake stew, and powdered deer antler—to work wonders with a male's sexual performance: To me it has always, in Korea at least, tasted so awful as to quite put me off any experimentation.

There was a small concrete hut up on the cliff where the women stored their gear—their rubber suits, their face masks, their catching baskets. A few of them gathered by the hut to change into their market clothes—baggy trousers, drab shirts, sandals—and gossip about the day's catch. "Bad day, *onnyi*," said one woman to another who was slightly older and deserved the term of respect. "Only four kilos of *hae-sam*, and the water is so cold." She said she could only stay under for a minute at a time; in the summer she could easily make four minutes without once coming up for air and might pack ten kilos of sea cucumber into her basket before swimming back to shore. But early spring is not the best of times; the wind and currents ruin the visibility, and the storms have loosened some of the more fragile creatures from their moorings. The divers work all year, though, and they fell into helpless giggles when I asked why. "The money," they yelled. "How do you think we live if we don't work?"

They were completely without shame—not at all the prim and modest figures of the tourist posters—and they stripped naked while talking to me, changing out of their wetsuits and into their street clothes as innocently as if I didn't exist (though perhaps as a white "ghost," I didn't, in their eyes). Their bodies were muscular and pale; they had large shoulders and flattish breasts and thighs as solid as trees. I had seen advertisements in Japan touting the erotic charms of Cheju (for Japanese tourists flock in from Osaka Airport in the hope of finding affordable sex—very affordable indeed at the time of writing, thanks to the *yen/won* exchange rate), and all had portrayed the *haenyo* as part of the erotic scene. The divers, as portrayed by the Japanese travel agents, are slender youngsters in white cotton swimsuits, who swim with grace and courage, narrowly escaping death in the jaws of giant clams. The disappointment of the Japanese tourists who fetch up here, and see the Cheju foreshores fill up with what look like Russian female construction workers and part-time Olympic javelin throwers on an annual jaunt to the Black Sea, must be considerable.

At dinner that night—we were eating *chonbokchuk*, a quite tasty gruel made from rice and abalone—I got into a terrific argument with a young woman, a friend of Mae-young's, when I asked whether the *haenyo* were organized—did they have an employer, were they members of some kind of cooperative? The woman, who had also come down from Seoul, was furious. "Why do you bring your Western prejudices to Korea. Of course they are not organized. They are traditional people. They dive wherever and whenever they like. They have done so for hundreds of years."

I was flattened by the vigor of her response. I protested that I was not a victim of any prejudice but simply wanted to know. "Well, you should know better than to ask. The *haenyo* are independent and courageous people. They would not accept any organization."

Not content to let matters rest, I produced a trump card. If they were not organized, I said with what must have been an unpleasantly smug grin, then who built their concrete hut? But I had made, I later found out, a tactical error of the gravest kind. The girl faltered, blushed, looked down at her rice. Someone at the table sniggered. She had no answer. She was embarrassed. She had *lost face*. And while Confucian teaching points out how bad it is to lose face, the sin of *making someone else lose face* is inexcusable. So I, in a curiously Oriental way, had lost the argument. Her facts may have been flawed (they certainly were: the *haenyo* are rigorously organized, access to the beaches and times of diving all being laid down by bosses who, it seems, are all men), but my style of debate had been so offensive as to cost me the battle. We left the restaurant in strained silence and went to a bar and drank *soju* in a concerted effort to forget and thus save the evening. At some hazy moment in the small hours all was forgiven, glasses were clinked, and we retired firm friends again. *Soju* is a brand of firewater with splendidly restorative effects.

The next morning Mae-young had to fly home, and I saw her off on the bus to the Cheju Airport. I would miss her: She had been infectiously cheerful, ever optimistic, a good companion; she seemed then to have none of the darker, more brooding side that is said to be a characteristic of the Koreans, a side that has made more than one visitor talk of "the Irish of the Orient." As I tramped away northward from the bus stop in a thin rain I felt in a dark and brooding mood: Would she come back? I wondered. What had she felt about the weekend? Had she taken as much pleasure from the day on Hallasan as I had? There was a curious dissonance to our friendship; I was struck that I had no firm idea of what she was thinking about almost anything.

The drizzle became a steady downpour. I had deliberately left any wet-weather clothing out of my pack to save weight. Before I left England I had asked the Meteorological Research Department of the University of Reading for an analysis of spring rains in the southern half of the Korean Peninsula, and they had obliged, offering the cheering news that only two or three wet days might be expected in a month. (The department can offer weather records for almost anywhere on earth: The last time I had consulted a friend there I had been off to Ulan Bator in December, and he had given me complete snowfall records for every settlement around the Gobi Desert.) Whether or not the forecast was correct I would not now dispute: I was getting soaked.

❖   ❖   ❖

A car slowed down beside me, and the driver rolled down his window. "Would you be Simon?" asked an Irish voice, and when I said that I would he roared with delight. "I thought I recognized you. Not many people are fool enough to walk in this rain! Patrick McGlinchey. Father McGlinchey of Hallim. You remember? You wrote to me last winter? It's good to be seeing a foreign face again. You'll be coming to dinner, of course. You'll be staying the night?" And then, looking at his wristwatch, he started. "Jesus, Mary, and Joseph, I must be off! I've an appointment with the bank manager. Another blessed money crisis." He gunned his car and drove off again northward, in the direction of Cheju City, with a promise that he'd be "back at the farm" by dusk. "Make yourself at home!" he cried as the car sped away. "They all know you're coming."

What a tonic! I had indeed written to Father P. J. McGlinchey at something mysteriously called the Isidore Development Association when I read in an old guidebook that he and a small community of Irish missionaries enjoyed the somewhat eccentric pastime of making Aran sweaters on Cheju. I had no idea whether he was still alive—the guidebook was a good twenty years old— but indeed he was, for a fortnight after my inquiry I had his reply, written in a spidery hand. "It's a novel idea you have, and I wish you every success. If God does not in the meantime untie me from these shackles of space and time, I should be here when you arrive, and I look forward to meeting you. . . ."

The Columban Fathers in Navan sent Patrick McGlinchey out from Ireland to Korea in 1952. He left a country of comparative peace and came thousands of miles east to live with a war still raging around him. His task was formidable, but simple: He had to help bring Christianity into this darkest (and very Buddhist) corner of the world. Another hundred or so similarly young and energetic brothers were dispatched from Ireland—men with names so redolent of the sea and the peat bogs and the soft Irish rain, names like Sean Hogan and Kevin Fleming and Padraig O'Hara and Flynn Brennan. From Patrick Bannon to Thomas Walsh, through all the O'Briens and O'Keefes and O'Neills and O'Rourkes, the names of Ireland are now firmly woven into the very south of the Korean Peninsula. In villages and towns obscure and renowned, the Irishmen built little stone churches and tiny wooden schools, they learned Korean, they preached, they converted, they gathered about them small co- teries of the faithful, and they ministered to a people confused and wasted by war and perhaps disappointed by the languorous resignation and fatalism taught by their Buddhist masters. "They were an ambitious people," one priest said to me later by way of explanation, "and they wanted an ambitious church. We showed them that it was possible to combine faith with ambition and aspiration. It was one of the secrets of our success."

They preached and they converted and ministered—and, most important of all, they stayed. Patrick McGlinchey goes back every four years to see his brother in Donegal and to visit the grave of his father, who was a veterinary surgeon, and who taught young Patrick a fondness for the countryside, for animals, and the rhythms of crops. But essentially, he is now a part of Korea; he doubts that he will ever go back to Ireland to live but will see out his days on Cheju Island, which looks, after all, "so much like Connemara I could be home right now, really."

I reached the farm after another hour or so, and indeed the staff were ex- pecting me and had made up a bed for me in a room just off the main chapel. I eased off my boots and glumly inspected my blisters. Dusk was settling into the valleys when P. J., as everyone seemed to call him, arrived home. He had settled his argument with the bank, and was in high good humor. "Will you not take a small drink or a cup of tea first, perhaps? It looks like a whiskey by the fire is what you need."

He was a giant of a man—red face, a shock of white hair, his frame covered in the black cloth of his calling. His living room, a pleasantly untidy library, had a noisy stove in the middle, and it was within its corona of fierce heat that we sat as the darkness deepened outside. The windows faced west, and the setting sun, now glimmering weakly through the scudding clouds, glinted on the distant sea. The grasslands were dotted with sheep, and from somewhere unseen came the constant lowing of cattle ready for their evening milking. It was a moment of the purest tranquility. P. J. splashed whiskey into a cracked glass—"Sorry it's not Bushmills, damned hard to get out here"—and he told me something of the place they call Isidore Ranch.

Saint Isidore is one of Catholicism's more robust and bucolic saints. He was Spanish, a seventh-century farm worker from Seville. As the papers relating to his beatification have it, he was a man who spent more time than his colleagues thought suitable reading the Bible and praying, and he was denounced for what they charged was his laziness. The farm manager, an ungodly fellow, agreed: The sack was mentioned, unless Isidore pulled his socks up. Which of course he did. He ploughed and sowed and reaped like a maniac, so keenly that his fellow workers began to suspect that he had a seventh-century version of a Massey-Ferguson hidden in his room. One morning as he was turning over a meadow, a couple of them spied on him, and to their general astonishment spotted two angels swoop down from heaven and put their hands to the plough. Verily, they thought, this Bible-reading habit of Isidore's must have something; they promptly converted to the faith, and within a couple of years all rural Seville had gone Catholic, and Isidore was made a saint, the patron saint of the farm laborer. A concrete statue of him pushing a hand plough stands outside P. J.'s office.

"I suppose I subscribe to the philosophy of that American Indian—what was his name—Geronimo," P. J. said suddenly. "The only way to cross a river is to cross it. That's what he said. I came here in 1952, the island was unbelievably poor, the farmers were the basest of peasants. My father having been a vet—and vets in Ireland in those days did a bit of everything, they knew quite a bit about farming—I thought I could persuade these people to farm properly. But Jesus, it was difficult.

"I started with pigs. I organized 4-H clubs in all the tiny villages, and I gave pigs to the teenagers who were members. They were good pigs I had had imported—Durocs, Landraces, Yorkshires, much better than the scrawny little black things they had running about. And the deal was the same as in any 4-H club back in the States: The members could have the pigs free, except that they paid me back by giving me two piglets from the first litter born. I would give these two piglets to other members, and so it went on.

"I had hoped the teenagers' ideas would filter upward to their parents. Not a bit of it. Confucius never permitted the idea that a child could teach anything to his father. Everything went the other way. Besides, by the time the annual ceremony to honor the ancestors came round, father looked about for something nice to sacrifice, saw this nice plump pig of his son's, and bingo, the blessed thing was roasted and carved while the son grizzled in the corner. End of experiment. It was like that, Cheju in the old days.

"Same with sheep. I'd say, 'Why don't you raise sheep, you've got great country for it?' They'd say, 'No, the Japanese tried it and got nowhere, so why should we?' I persisted. 'Okay,' I said, 'why not resow the uplands with good quality grasses to give the sheep something to eat for most of the year?' 'Nope,' they said, 'the soil up on the hills is too acid, and the grass wouldn't grow.' But still—I was young in those days—I went on. 'Why not control the acidity by putting down lime?' And then came the coup de grace. 'Nope,' they said. 'That can't possibly be done on Cheju because if it had been possible *our ancestors would have done it long ago.*' Could you credit it? Damn Confucianism all over again. Dead pigs. No sheep. I tell you, it was depressing in those early days."

But the good father persisted, and in time there were sheep, and there were cattle, and the government allowed the church to buy land, and the priests set up credit unions to help the farmers finance themselves—it was a real revolution, and it helped turn Cheju from a wasteland of ignorance and penury into an island that is now well farmed, even moderately prosperous. "Every time I see a farmer driving a Daewoo car, I think, We helped him do that. The church can do a great deal more than merely preaching the good word, you know."

There were moments of luck, too. P. J. talked with great amusement of one hot and dusty day in the early fifties, when he was at his church in Hallim, the tiny coastal village to which the Columbans first directed him. He was troubled by a pressing problem: There had been no rain for months, and the local water supply had failed. He knew of an unfailing spring high up on the slopes of Halla-san, but the only way he could bring the water down to the coast was to get hold of about ten miles of plastic piping—impossible to acquire in Korea in those days other than by importing it from abroad. The Isidore Ranch had little money, so he had written to Oxfam asking for help. A pro forma reply had come back from Oxford, but nothing since. And that was six months before. It was very much on the young priest's mind.

"I remember vividly. I was standing out in the roadway when all of a sudden a U.S. Army jeep came bumping along down the hill. It was all bashed about; something had gone through the windscreen, and it had a big hole in it. It stopped by me and a white couple got out, a middle-aged man and his poor wife, covered with dust and looking terribly tired. It was the British ambassador and his wife, down from Seoul on an inspection tour! Bless me, they were a courageous couple. But so tired and fed up. I invited them into the parlor, and by chance one of the sisters had taught my young Korean cook how to make apple pie. She had had a lesson only that Saturday, and this was her first experiment. You can imagine the smell, and how the lady ambassadress or whatever you call her felt when she smelled it. She went weak at the knees, I could see it. Anyway, she and her husband sat in the parlor—just like Ireland, it was—eating this pie, and we had some fresh cream. And we had tea. They were transported, positively transported.

"And I mentioned the Oxfam business. Well, you can imagine the rest. The ambassador had been at Oxford with the boss of Oxfam; he promised he'd do something, and sure enough, when he got back to Seoul a week later he fired off a cable, and we got a telegram saying the pipe was on its way. Two months later, there was the pipe. They laid it in six months, and water has flowed in all the farms round Hallim ever since. Bless that apple pie, that's all I can say!"

The Isidore Ranch is now a mighty operation: 13 British-style self-feeding cattle bars; 56 pig sheds; 3 hay and grain storage warehouses; 8 silos; 7 reservoirs; 4 dipping tanks; 110 tractors and trucks and bulldozers; 1,700 head of milk and beef cattle; 1,900 sheep (which supply wool to the ladies who make the Aran sweaters in a co-op down at Hallim); and 4,000 pigs. The farms range over 3.6 million *pyong* (which equates to about 5,000 acres, the *pyong* being quite tiny, "like a tatami mat," as a Japanese friend once said), and Father McGlinchey mentions with evident pride that the fence enclosing the property is 130 miles long, while the paved road around the periphery of Cheju Island is 16 miles shorter.

And Isidore makes a handsome profit—scores of millions of *won* each year that go to pay for nonprofit institutions, homes for the handicapped and destitute, "for the weakest people in our society." I mention that he calls it "our society," and he takes the point. "I think of Cheju as home and the people as my brothers and sisters. I am Irish, no doubt. I still like to watch a tape of a hurling game (we had just been talking about the legendary Cup Final involving Offaly and Meath) and read the *Irish Times* when I can get it. But my real home is here. These are my people."

Sometimes he seems a little lonely. He has no one to come and cook for him or look after him, and it is abundantly clear he's not very good at looking after himself: He has some difficulty just making tea and can only just about operate the small toaster in his kitchen. So the nuns at a nearby convent have taken on the role of distant housekeepers, and they feed him lunch each day. But it is a far-from-ideal arrangement—theirs is a closed and contemplative order, and the sisters are not permitted to speak to their Father McGlinchey (even though he says mass for them many times a week), and he has to take his commons alone. I went with him once: A time was assigned, a room was prepared, and I thought I saw a nun passing quickly out of it by a side door as we approached. Inside, on a deal table, was a simple lunch, magicked from the very air, it seemed. We ate, we left, and then I heard the door of the room open quietly and as I glanced round saw two nuns dash in and collect the plates and forks. It had been like dining in an airlock, with no human contact possible. Small wonder P. J. was keen for company.

❖   ❖   ❖

And we dined down at Camp MacNab, the tiny American base back at Mosulpo, from where the climbers had come. Maybe it was the relentless rain that made it seem so depressing and spiritless a place. A dozen or so old Quonset huts, painted in green drab, dripped and leaked. A few rusting jeeps were parked outside. The sentries shone torches in our faces and let down the chain and waved us on to the mess. Inside was the enormous soldier, the Great Abseiler: He was avidly watching a film that seemed to involve a girl who grew an extra mouth somewhere in her armpit and who attacked and sucked blood from a variety of victims. Father McGlinchey and I ate hamburgers and I drank a Budweiser, and we watched, disconsolately, until someone shot the girl dead and the film ended. "Hey, Limey! My man! You came over!" said the soldier. He explained that Camp MacNab offered servicemen from farther north a chance to have a few days' exercise—special forces training went on too, but most of all "It gives the guys a few days in the fresh air, climbing the cliffs and so on. But no pussy, begging your reverend's pardon, of course. And in weather like this. . . ." He made a gesture of disgust, went and found another videotape and another beer, and settled down for more.

MacNab was more interesting than it looked that night. The Japanese had built an airstrip at Mosulpo in the thirties and had used it when they had bombed Shanghai, only a few hundred miles away across the Yellow Sea. Then the Americans had used it during the Korean War as a prison camp for captured Chinese, forcing the prisoners, at the time of the armistice, to choose whether to be repatriated to Communist China or to Taiwan. Most went to Taiwan, of course; in fact, it has long been supposed that troops in the invading Chinese armies knew they had a remarkable opportunity once they had crossed the Yalu: If they managed to avoid being killed then, assuming the war would one day be over, they would have a choice of countries to which to be repatriated. Nearly all would have chose Taiwan, hence the choice presented to them once they stormed the great river was, essentially, death or freedom. A droll situation indeed for a soldier in a Communist army.

I left P. J.'s ranch after a couple of days. He was in an exceptionally good mood the night before I went. A letter had just come from the Rockefeller Brothers Fund in New York inviting him to a thirtieth anniversary gathering of all the living winners of the Ramon Magsaysay Award—a prize he had been given ten years before for his work at Isidore. He was to go to Bangkok, all expenses paid, to help celebrate the birthday of a prize given "for those men and women in Asia who have personified the achievement of the ideals of the great Filipino president Ramón Magsaysay, and who have thus contributed significantly to the public good."

"Bangkok," he said, rolling the word around his palate like wine and grinning a puckish grin. "Sounds like fun." And he gave me a strong handshake and bade me Godspeed. "You know where I am if you need me. I'll always be here."

I didn't see him when I left next morning at eight. He read, or listened to

43

the BBC World Service, until four or five every morning, almost until the sun came up. He was in consequence rarely awake before eleven, and when I passed by his room he was snoring softly. He had been a most remarkable man, a giant in many more ways than the merely physical.

❖   ❖   ❖

It was still spitting with rain as I stretched out my stride on the high road to Cheju City. The road was die-straight for miles and very exposed, and when storms rumbled down from the slopes of Halla-san to the east, it became uncomfortably chilly. I tucked my head down against the blast and considered the odds and ends of life. It wasn't long before my reverie was interrupted.

First, two buses driving hell-for-leather in opposite directions clipped each other, neatly severing wing mirrors, radio aerials, and an assortment of other chrome-covered or glass-filled chunks of hardware that clattered like a hailstorm along half a mile of roadway. The two drivers clambered down from their charges and promptly collapsed *fou rire*, while their passengers looked on, glum and bewildered. Most of them were elderly—travelers on the so-called *hyodo kwan guang* tours, in which children pay for holidays for their parents or grandparents, in the best Confucian tradition. And then again, and suddenly and from nowhere, a horseman galloped past me; he was on a normal, full-size horse, not one of the classic Cheju horses, which are minute dwarfs said to be descended from those brought down from Mongolia by Genghis Khan in the thirteenth century. (The Mongols brought many things—Buddhism, fur hats and coats, and a language that has had a lingering influence on the peculiar dialect still spoken on the island.) I must have been no more than a blurred image as the horseman raced past, but something about the image must have registered, for a couple of furlongs later he pulled up his charge and turned around and cantered back to me for the sole purpose of asking for a cigarette. He tried to light it while his horse snorted and steamed in the rain, and he exchanged the occasional phrase, ending on the usual surprised and optimistic note about all Englishmen being gentlemen. He then turned his horse once again and thundered off until his hoofbeats were drowned out by the rush of the Halla-san winds.

And then I breasted a hill, and Cheju City lay before me—an unlovely sprawl of modern buildings, tall hotels (for honeymooners either too tired or impoverished to take the taxi down to Sogwipo), and rows of single-story houses. Most of Cheju City has been built in the last twenty years, though not, like Seoul and Inchon, because its predecessor had been destroyed in the war. Indeed, the war had left Cheju Island relatively unscarred except psychologically, and in a manner peculiar to many islands around the world.

The Communist invasion of South Korea began in June 1950. But war came to Cheju Island a great deal earlier and, indeed, in a more classically Marxist manner. In the summer of 1947, not long after the People's Committee for

North Korea had been formally convened in the Northern capital, Pyongyang, a number of Communist cells were formed on Cheju (which then had a population of a quarter of a million; today there are twice that number). The strategy, so far as one can gather now, was for the island to be subverted and used as a southern springboard from which a secondary invasion could be mounted against the republic. Had the scheme worked, the Americans—or the United Nations—would have been in direct difficulty. The so-called Pusan perimeter inside which the Allied forces took refuge would simply not have existed, and it would have taken the most enormous of battle skills to repulse an onslaught that was both terrific in scale and double-pronged in design. Had the Communist ploy succeeded in Cheju, the whole of Korea might now be united—under the malevolent leadership of Kim Il Sung.

But Cheju did not take easily to subversion and insurgency. Well-trained guerrillas, led by tacticians trained in Moscow, fanned out into the long valleys that radiate down from Halla-san and made lightning raids into the villages— villages that in those days were still protected by medieval stone walls and where a positively Sicilian code of brotherhood and *omertà* reigned. (The walls were demolished, the stones used to build the dry-stone walls that make up the little fields that give the island so Irish a character.) But the villagers fought hard and well, and the Communists made little enough headway, though some villages, like the hamlets of Sangmyong-ri and Kumak-ri close to Father McGlinchey's Isidore, were thoroughly Marxist, and remained so for some while after the war.

It took three years before Seoul realized the depth of the insurgent problem on Cheju; but by 1950, when President Syngman Rhee decided to dispatch a regiment of militia to Cheju City docks, there was already an uneasy stalemate. In the bitter fighting 60,000 had died and some Cheju islanders say that 60,000 died on each side, which seems rather improbable. Only 415,000 soldiers and civilians, after all, died on the southern side in the entire Korean War. The rifts caused by the bitter little conflict on the island are still felt today, however. No border, no frontier line, no armistice ever separated the warring factions down there once the battling was done; no hermetic seal was ever placed on the hatred between insurgent and conservative. And while thousands of Communists moved prudently across to Japan (many of the "North Koreans" who now live in Tokyo are in fact Cheju islanders who chose the wrong side in the island civil war), many of the collaborators and less visible members of the northern forces remain, occasionally to be uncovered, occasionally to be exposed. *Omertà* protects many; bitterness remains; it is an odd island, stranger than it might seem from the holiday brochures—a deep place, with long memories and peculiar secrets.

I trudged on through the city outskirts, past the ugly office blocks and the hotels, past the warehouses where the exporters store the oranges, kumquats, pineapples, tangerines, and bananas that Cheju sends to the rest of Korea. It would be idle to pretend that Cheju City is a pretty place; it looked as though it were made of gray Lego blocks, and a sooty haze of smoke from *yontan*, the powdered-coal briquettes used to warm the houses, hung over the place. The roads were wide, and there were few cars; the whole place had a strange sterility about it, an unnatural quietude. Perhaps it was the season. And there was something sinister about the way the airport suddenly loomed up, unmarked on any map (because of security, the authorities say) and surrounded on all sides by barbed wire and watchtowers. There had been fog, and no planes had landed at all that morning; but now the circling jets roared in one after another, and the place was a maelstrom of noise, an odd contrast to the silence of the town.

It was, in any case, a relief and a small pleasure to come down to the sea and to the rather raffish, rather seedy milieu of the coast. The honeymoon crowd were out in force here, down to see and, inevitably, to be photographed beside a strange contortion of basalt that was known as the Dragon Head Rock, or the *Yongduam*. A legend, of course, came attached, as so often in this legend-rich corner of the world—and woe betide any Korean who dares challenge its veracity. It seems that a servant of the Sea Dragon King was climbing Halla-san in search of some magic mushroom that holds the elixir of eternal life; the mountain gods were none too keen on an aquatic interloper finding such a thing and shot him dead. He was duly buried at sea, promptly turned into a dragon, and lo! His head reared up onto the beach and ascended thirty feet in the air, for the honeymooners' pleasure and delight.

Quick! Quick! shout the taxi drivers, and lead the poor brides—exhausted, quite shattered, and generally bewildered—to clamber up some knob or spire of rock or perch on some slimy crag. Here! Here! they beckon, and demand that the youngster, in the highly unsuitable combination of high heels and *chima chogori*, teeter to the edge of some precipice and pose with her bemused young husband. Click! go the Instamatics and hummm! go the Sony Video Plus 8s, and the record is there for all time and the elders.

There are a fair numbers of elders—unrelated, members of the *hyodo kwan guang* corps—gawking at this performance too. And there is an elderly and grumpy-looking horse, a tiny, shabby-coated Mongol nag that stands with infinite boredom by the top of a nearby cliff, and a queue of elders waits to mount him, briefly, for another picture-taking session. The ideal souvenir of a Korean journey to Cheju, then, would be a photograph of a frail, old, monkish fellow in gray *hangbok* and horsehair hat, sitting astride a barely living horse that by rights ought to be in the van for the glue factory, with the Dragon Head Rock in the background being clambered over by a cursing, spitting group of young brides busily laddering their stockings and breaking their heels but being too shy to cry out to their new husbands about the awfulness of it all. Koreans, in short, have not reached the most advanced level of tourism:

It is all done en masse, is very Confucian in its style and inhibitions, and cannot survive for long.

❖ ❖ ❖

I spent my final evening playing poker in a small house by the *Yongduam*, talking to a group of cheerful Irishmen to whom I had been mentioned by P. J. McGlinchey. They were missionaries, too—not all priests, mind you— and workers in a variety of fields: doctors, psychologists, social workers, accountants. Each Monday night they assembled in the little house in Cheju City and played poker and drank deep of Paddy until the small hours. There were copies of *The Listener* and *The Spectator* on the table, and we had boiled ham for dinner and ginger pudding and custard. I half expected to switch on the wireless and hear Liam Hourican reading the news on Radio Telefis Eireann, or hear the sweet tunes of The Dubliners or the tones of James Joyce. But the music, when I switched on the radio, was all in the same sad vein of Korea, and the announcer was saying his thank yous and farewells for another day of listening to Korean radio. *"Anyonghee kashipshiyo,"* he said. *"Kamsa hamnida."* Outside a stiff breeze blew in from the west, and there was the pungent sourness of strong *kimchi* from the house next door. Inside was a small oasis paved with the Ould Sod; beyond the thick walls of the house was the wild and mysterious Republic of Korea.

❖ ❖ ❖

Three hundred years ago the journey northward was more trying than mine would be. "They put us into four Boats with fetters on our feet, and one hand made fast to a block . . . on the north side of the island they call Sehesure is a bay, where several barques lye, and whence they sail for the continent, which is of very dangerous access to those that are unacquainted with it, because of several hidden rocks, and that there is but one place where ships can anchor. . . ."

For me it was a simple trek along the bay coast, taken at six the next morning. I bought a sailing ticket and, for the heck of it and in the hope of meeting someone interesting, a berth in a four-berth cabin. I showed my passport to the policeman, said my fond farewells to my poker companions of the night before, and boarded the Dongyang Express Ferry Number Two, waiting for its daily dawn departure for the port of Mokpo. A group of smiling attendants bowed, and one escorted me to the second deck and gave me the key to the cabin he had just opened, Number 169. A slim and exceptionally beautiful girl was sitting on a lower bunk, putting on her lipstick. *"Anyong,"* I said, with a smile, and put down my rucksack. *"Meeguk?"* she inquired. *"Anio, yong guk saram."* "Ah," she returned, with a smile. "An English gentleman. How are you?"

"In this Island there is a Mountain of vast Height, all cover'd with woods. . . ."
The Dutch sailors were impressed by Halla-san, the 6,397-foot volcano that
dominates Cheju and is Korea's tallest peak. It last erupted in the eleventh
century and is geologically similar to the Hawaiian peaks, with a summit crater
and lake. The British, in a fit of imperial eagerness, wanted to name it Mount
Auckland. But it has remained Mount Halla, a sacred place for Buddhists, a peak
whose summit all Koreans try to attain. A journey to and from the top—which is
swathed in cloud for three days out of four—takes a good five hours, and the
narrow pathways are invariably busy with Koreans of all ages trying to make
it. In midwinter, it is hazardous in the extreme.

Powerful matriarchies survive on the coasts and islands of the far south of Korea, where many women work—in this case as divers, gathering abalone and edible seaweeds—and leave the men at home with the children. Korean women are of legendary toughness: The southern-island *haenyo* can remain under water, even in midwinter, for four or five minutes. But farther north, Confucian rules demand she remains subservient to her spouse—a conflict that is becoming more of an irritant as Korean women's education and self-awareness continue to grow.

A few villages have, mercifully, withstood the modernizing zeal of recent Korean administrations, which have demanded that brick-and-tile houses replace those built with what they thought the world would regard as the "primitive" straw thatch and earthen walls. But such is the growing prosperity of Korea that even the most picturesque hamlets enjoy—or suffer from—full membership in the twentieth century, and on many a packed-mud floor will stand a Gold Star refrigerator, a Samsung television, and a Daewoo video recorder.

The "Pine Spreading Temple" of Songkwang-sa,
near the big southern city of Kwangju, is one of the
leading centers of Zen Buddhism in the country.
It dates from the twelfth century, though like all
wooden monasteries it has suffered grievously from
fire: The invading Japanese armies of Hideyoshi
destroyed parts of it in the sixteenth century, and
Communist guerrillas burned down the main hall in
a revolt in 1948. But, like Korea itself, the temples
always manage to recover from setbacks, and
Songkwang-sa is a fully active temple where several
foreign Buddhist priests and students come to
meditate. The covered bridges, reminiscent of New
England, are not seen elsewhere in the country.

Where the huge and strategically important Kum
River passes through the old Paekche capital city
of Puyo, it is called Paekma-gang—the White
Horse River. Like so many places in Korea, Puyo
is the setting for many tragic legends, the name
"white horse" coming from the equine-headed
dragon said to have been lured out of the stream
by the Chinese general who conquered the city in
A.D. 600. The best-known legend tells how all the
Paekche court women jumped to their deaths from
the cliffs to avoid capture and dishonor: Their
brightly colored dresses billowed up as they
tumbled downward, and the cliff is now known as
"the Rock of Falling Flowers."

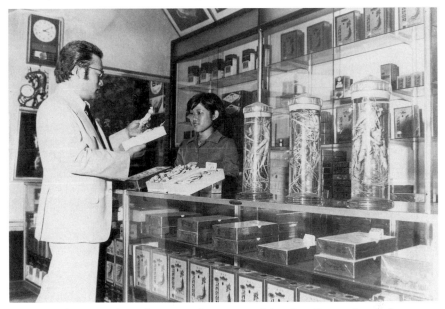

Ginseng—the curiously anthropomorphous root of the plant *Panax ginseng*, known to the Koreans as *insam*—is both a major Korean export and widely consumed at home. But it is expensive, in no small part because a good root takes six years to grow. Better-off Koreans eat thin slices of red ginseng root that have been dipped in heather honey; the ordinary worker will take it as an infusion—*insam-cha*—and trusts it will have much the same effect as that claimed for the pure root: the revival of a flagging libido, recovery of lost youth, a general feeling of well-being and clearheadedness. It is possible to buy ginseng chewing gum and shampoo and, though some might suspect a contradiction in terms, ginseng cigarettes.

Nighttime traffic swirls around Namdae-mun, the preserved and much-hallowed great south gate of the old city. The city walls have been dismantled to make way for the growth of a vast (9 million inhabitants), modern, and—it has to be said— spectacularly ugly metropolis. Most of urban Korea, constructed since the end of the Korean War in which so many cities were utterly ruined, has been rebuilt with an eye to efficiency rather than beauty. But the capital's lack of beauty does not inhibit its magnetism: "If you have a horse," counsels one old Korean saying, "send it to Cheju Island; if you have a son, send him to Seoul." Every bright and ambitious Korean wants to end up here—and what Seoul thus lacks in loveliness it makes up in energy and enthusiasm, the Korean miracle writ large in concrete and glass.

Seoul's Palace of Illustrious Virtue, the Changdok Palace, was where Hendrick Hamel and his fellow sailors from the *Sparrowhawk* were brought to be interviewed by King Hyojong in 1653. It still stands, providing refuge for the last surviving members of Korea's Yi Dynasty, who live in peace and quiet in the palace's Mansion of Joy and Goodness, the *Naksonjae*. Often, in May, the man who would be Korea's present king—had not his uncle, Sunjong, abdicated at the wishes of the Japanese in 1910—returns from the United States to take part in the elaborate Confucian rituals honoring the fallen members of the family—an occasion when one can imagine what life must have been like in one of the great courts of the Orient. Nowadays Changdok and its lovely secret garden, Piwon, are a shrine for tens of thousands of Korean visitors, whose pilgrimage suggests a relict fondness for the days of pomp and circumstance.

Koreans are eager to dress up in their traditional clothing—*hangbok*—whenever they have an excuse. Women and children invariably wear clothes that are vividly colorful, with lots of primary reds, yellows, and blues, and bright pinks and purples. The men, on the other hand, wear clothes made of gray and brown cotton and silk, very loose and baggy, and fastened with hasps and ribbons and bone buttons. Occasionally one sees men wearing tall horsehair top hats. Sadly, Korean cities are now filled by men and women wearing Western dress, except on major holidays, such as the May Festival, the Full Moon Festival, or the Buddha's birthday, when all the exotic clothes are brought up from basement storage and paraded in the streets.

Forty-five thousand American troops are stationed in Korea with the specific stated aim of protecting the republic from any hostile acts by the North Koreans. Most of these troops are stationed within easy reach of the DMZ, a massive barricade of barbed wire and minefields and artillery emplacements that snakes across the peninsula from the Yellow Sea to the Sea of Japan, keeping the two implacably opposed Koreas from resuming their bitter battles of three decades ago. South Koreans, too, are impressed into their own armed forces for long periods, and each year embark on massive joint exercises with the men and machines of the U.S. Eighth Army. Up on the DMZ, though, Korean and American troops work alongside each other all the time, keeping up their patrols along the most heavily defended piece of real estate in the world.

"Freedom House," this ornate but very modern pavilion, is at Panmunjom, on the South Korean side of the truce line that has divided the Korean Peninsula since 1953. A steady stream of visitors makes the thirty-five-mile journey from Seoul to the Demilitarized Zone and the tiny oasis, built on the site of the ruined village of Panmunjom, of the Joint Security Area—the one site along the frontier where North and South Koreans, together with Americans, Britons, and Chinese, can meet to discuss the endless troubles along the borderline. During their stay most visitors climb the steps of Freedom House to get a glimpse into North Korea—and are endlessly fascinated at the sight of unsmiling North Korean soldiers standing on their side of the Demarcation Line watching for any gesture, any facial expression on the part of the newcomers that might be construed as insulting and thus a cause for complaint.

CHAPTER

THREE

"There are in the Country abundance of Taverns and pleasure-houses, to which the Coresians resort to see common Women dance, sing and play on Musical Instruments. In Summer they take this Recreation in cool Groves under close shady Trees. They have no particular Houses to entertain Passengers and Travellers, but he who travels, goes and sits down, where Night overtakes him, near the Pales of the first House he comes at, where tho' it be not a great Man's House, they bring him boil'd Rice, and dressed Meat enough for his Supper. When he goes from thence, he may stop at another House, and at several. Yet on the great Road to Sior, there are Houses, where those that travel on Publick Affairs, have Lodging and Diet on the Publick Account."

—HENDRICK HAMEL,
1668

❖ ❖ ❖

T HE GREAT DEEP-OCEAN TRAWLER THAT, ON A
coincident track, lingered briefly alongside us as we rounded the south point
of the island of Chindo looked tired and weatherbeaten. She had long streaks
of rust staining her bright blue flanks, and the guard rails on her starboard side
were bent inward from the pounding of some tremendous storm. She was—I
pulled out my binoculars and could read her name on her transom—the trawler
77 Oyang, a thousand-tonner, one of the world's largest. She was quite well
known as one of the toughest and most adventurous of Korea's huge fleet of
deep-water fishing craft.

I had seen her some long while before at the fish quay in Inchon, when her
crew was readying her for a long trip in the Southern Ocean. The firm that
owned her was called the Oyang Susan, the Five Ocean Fishing Industries
Company, and they operated a fleet of boats that were usually scattered across
the seas from the Bering Strait to the waters off New Zealand. Now, after more
than a year of occupying her business in deep waters, this particular old lady,
the *77 Oyang*, was coming home to let her crewmen go to their families, to
let the owners inspect her, and to allow the maintenance men aboard to work
on her enormous engines. She had been fishing, as I recalled the skipper telling
me in a café in Inchon, in the waters off the Falkland Islands.

The prize, in such faraway waters, was something called the cold-water arrow
squid, which Koreans value with an intensity approaching worship. They dry
it and serve it up with peanut paste as a concoction known as *ojingoa*—you

can see hundreds of plastic packets of the stuff hanging from racks in the food shops—and it is said that Koreans consume half a million metric tons every year—twenty-five pounds of arrow squid for every man, woman, and child in the nation. Boats like the *77 Oyang* vanish for months at a time to hunt for it in the most distant corners of maritime geography.

Korea says she has no fewer that nine hundred deep-sea fishing vessels on her registers—almost the largest number in the world, comparable only to the deep-ocean fleets of Russia and Japan. The captain of this vessel was a man named Lee Hyun Wu, my notes remind me, and he once told me that his fuel tanks would allow him to stay at sea for three months at a time: He would make passage from Pusan or from Inchon to Wellington in New Zealand, a trip that would take twenty-four days. He would then refuel and pass eastabout in the Roaring Forties, below the Horn, and into Port Stanley, the Falklands' tiny capital. After a couple of days of relaxation and a chance to compare notes with the skippers of the other long-haulers, the Poles and the Japanese, he would take off for the fishing grounds, four days' steaming north. Here he would sit for the better part of two months—sweeping the seabed clean of its squid colonies, filling his holds with hundreds of tons of the tentacles and ink sacs and the white, fleshy muscles so favored by the folks back home. And then, his forty days in the wilderness completed, he would steer eastward yet again, pass below Capes Agulhas and Catastrophe, and return to New Zealand, and to the comforting womb of the Korean mother ship. He would do that three times before receiving his marching orders by radiogram from Seoul— invariably an instruction to return to base, interrupted only by a request to take a bellyful of some other kind of warm-water fish from the Saharan waters off Mauretania, where another factory ship was waiting. Forty days later, and he would be where I could see him on this windy March morning—butting through the swells of the Yellow Sea, with only a hundred miles to go before the lights and comforts of home.

Chindo, where we met him—and he disappeared over the northern horizon within half an hour, eager to get home before nightfall—is an island I had been to a few months before. It is in no sense a spectacular island, being merely a half-drowned range of low hills, about fifteen miles long and ten miles broad, and having just one scruffy county town and a handful of fishing villages. There are oddities about it, though, one of the more spectacular occurring each March when there is a great *tamasha*, widely attended by people from as far away as Seoul, for the "miracle" of the Parting of the Waters. Thanks to the mutual exertions of the gravitational fields of the sun and moon, a narrow finger of sea between Chindo and the tiny neighbor island of Modo dries up for a few hours; Koreans unversed in Newtonian mechanics believe various gods to have done the trick. Legends, not unnaturally, abound, and the island fills up for days beforehand as local shamans and other practitioners of the occult arrive to see the wondrous event. The hoteliers and the sellers of *ojingoa* make a good deal of money.

There is a more sober reason for taking note of this otherwise unremarkable place. On a bluff above a pretty little bay is a memorial, a large cross mounted— improbable though it may sound—on the back of an enormous turtle that stands in the middle of a shallow pool. The day I was there the turtle's gleaming white marble back was covered with thousands of red chilies, drying in the sun. But the farmer who placed them there would have meant no disrespect: Every Korean I met along my route spoke adoringly of the man for whom the memorial had been built—the man who was perhaps the country's greatest wartime hero and whose most celebrated battle took place in the waters off Chindo.

He was called Yi Sun-shin, and he was an admiral in the Royal Korean Navy of the sixteenth century. He is revered today as the man who, almost alone, administered a series of stunning defeats to the Japanese and proved that Koreans are capable of seeing off the ambitions of their most loathsome neighbors, if only they really try.

The Japanese made their first concerted attack on Korea in the spring of 1592, when the warlord Hideyoshi Toyotomi sent an army of 150,000 men storming through the peninsula on their way to China—Korea being thought of by the Japanese as merely a springboard or a convenient walkway for the acquisition of the larger prize. The invading troops had already been blooded in Japan during the Warring States period, and they were armed, moreover, with muskets, of which the Koreans were profoundly ignorant. Every Korean army encampment Hideyoshi encountered was routed in hours. He took Seoul within a fortnight and was leading his armies north of Pyongyang and heading for Manchuria within the month.

It was at this point that the then fleet commander of Left Cholla Province, Yi Sun-shin, began to display his brilliance—a brilliance that has led students of naval warfare the world over to compare him with Drake and Nelson and Halsey, as one of the great naval strategists of all time.

He was forty-seven years old; he had been in the navy for just sixteen years and had been appointed to his post, defending the southern sea frontier of his country, for just a year. It was an important job and one he had taken particularly seriously since discovering that, in his view, the coast was woefully badly defended. It was, he decided, sorely lacking in the kind of strong, fast, and well-armed capital ships that a country with so huge and vulnerable a coastline clearly needed.

So he set about building a new fleet. The core of the flotillas, he decided, should be a vessel of an extraordinary new design, although based on the crude, half-armored ships used a century before. The entire craft would have a roof built over it so that it resembled a floating house rather than a ship.

The roof would be made of thick wood covered with iron plates, and hundreds of sharp iron spikes would project from it. The gunwales would be solid, too, without the wide galleries from within which the guns could be trained to left and right, and that were so vulnerable to incoming shellfire. Admiral Yi's ships were built for maximum protection, and if that meant to aim a cannon the ship herself had to be turned by her steersmen, then so be it. His ships may have been clumsy, but they had enormous firepower, and they wouldn't sink. They were, in fact, the world's first truly ironclad battleships—built two centuries before the *Monitor*—and they utterly changed both the face and the tide of battle. The admiral called his craft *kobuk-son* (turtle ships), and the thick-shelled chelonian has been both his symbol, and the symbol of stubborn Korean resolve, ever since.

For his boats did the trick. His tiny but brilliantly organized squadrons set out from their bases hidden in the south coast fjords, and they stormed cheekily up to the huge Japanese imperial fleets. Each time he assaulted the enemy's wooden barques with his cannon fire, he crippled them; and each time the Japanese responded, their cannonballs bounced harmlessly off Yi's vessels and splashed into the sea. Even when the more adventurous and cunning Japanese vessels came close enough for their sailors to board the *kobuk-son*, the matelots found their passage frustrated by the iron spikes and beat a hasty retreat. One after another the Japanese forces were routed; at the great encounter of Hansan Bay only 14 ships survived of the total Japanese battle group of 73 capital vessels; and even when the Imperial Navy sent a further 500 ships across the Sea of Japan (the East Sea, to Koreans) to meet Admiral Yi in battle off Pusan, 130 of them were lost to a force of Korean ships barely one-third the size of the enemy's.

The results were catastrophic: Hideyoshi's army was by now in the far north of the peninsula, the supply line was three hundred miles long, and no reinforcements, no ammunition, and no food could be sent up for them. Moreover, Korean guerrillas were organizing themselves to make hit-and-run expeditions against the invading troop columns, and fifty thousand soldiers from the Ming relief army in China poured south to help. The tide was turned, and for the while the Japanese were forced to retreat, lick their wounds, and think again.

But they came back and tried once more. There had been all manner of jealousy and intrigue within the Korean court, and Admiral Yi, despite his victories (the more scholarly historical works published in Seoul refer to the Battle of Hansan Bay, perhaps not totally hyperbolically, as "the Salamis of Korea") had been demoted. An unknown sailor, one Admiral Won Kyun, took over, and was promptly and roundly trounced by the Japanese—so roundly, in fact, that Yi's painstakingly accumulated naval force was reduced at one stage to just a dozen ships.

The defeat made the bureaucrats in Seoul forget the palace intrigue for a while and discuss the dilemma. Inevitably the call went out: Get Yi! The admiral, a dignified Confucian whose personal life is said to have been utterly without blemish, agreed without demur to return to his old command and then fought his most glorious battle at the spot from which I had gazed from the turtle monument on Chindo. It was on a narrow neck of sea at a place named Myongnyang, and the official name of the turtle on which the farmer had set his red peppers to dry was the Myongnyang Great Victory Monument, commemorating the events of the afternoon of September 16, 1597.

The Japanese armada of 133 ships was heading west, bound for the Yellow Sea. Admiral Yi's dozen vessels made a ragged line across the strait, beneath the cliffs of Chindo and the long, low peninsula where the road, Route 18, now runs to the town of Haenam. It was a brave and brilliant maneuver—the ships came under a withering fusillade from the scores of Japanese craft but withstood it all and returned cannon fire as if all Korea depended on it. Thirty Japanese vessels were destroyed and either sank or were abandoned, burning, on the rockbound shores. The remaining ships then turned tail and fled, back to the protection of Japanese territorial waters. It was the beginning of the end of this particular attempt on the integrity of Korea, and there is no doubt—nor was there ever any—that Admiral Yi Sun-shin was the hero of the hour.

He died during his next battle—the campaign's last—at a place called Noryangjin. His strategy had already cost the Japanese two hundred ships when the fatal bullet struck him. His behavior in death had a more than passing similarity to that of Nelson on the *Victory*, two centuries later and many oceans away. He knew he had been mortally wounded, but he ordered his closest colleagues to prop him up so that none of his sailors would know he had been hit. Only when the battle was over and won did the officers involved in this final small conspiracy allow his body to slump to the deck. He was fifty-three years old, arguably the greatest of Korean heroes, the subject of heroic sculptures and paintings from one end of the country to the other. He is less well known abroad, of course, but among naval historians, who have studied the details of battles that he so carefully documented in his diaries (themselves preserved at his gravesite, some sixty miles south of Seoul), he is regarded with awe.

And there is a third reason for my having taken a more-than-cursory interest in Chindo as the island slipped further astern and as the Dongyang Express Number Two growled ever nearer the mainland. It all had to do with a dog—a chowlike animal with a short, off-white coat, an arched tail with a splash of ocher along its inner edge, and a face of great friendliness, determination, and, dare one say it, chutzpah. The *Chindo-kae*, the only dog wholly peculiar to Korea, is a remarkable beast—and that, the government has decreed, is official.

The decree is something I found rather more interesting than the dog. Ever since Korea was a Japanese colony there has been a frantic desire, by government officials with nothing better to do, to classify almost anything of value as a "national asset" and, moreover, to give it a number. I was already dimly aware of having seen such things: the tomb of a long-dead king somewhere in the deep southeast had been styled National Asset Number 38, I remember, and a library of Buddhist books in a mountain monastery was National Treasure Number 32. It all smacked of rather too much organization, I thought, and anyway, I didn't believe the numbers. I assumed they had been given randomly to make visitors think that Korea had a lot of whatever the things were—at least thirty-seven other tombs and thirteen other libraries, for instance. But when I met my first *Chindo-kae,* and the little devil came wagging and yelping across to me, and its mistress informed me sternly that I was about to offer a bowl of Purina Puppy Chow to Natural Protected Resource Number 225, I started to take the classification system more seriously.

The supreme orders of classification are included in a trinity known as the Objects and Sites with Historic and Artistic Value. The first of these are the *kukbo,* the National Treasures, of which at last count there were 206—castles, palaces, Buddhas, tombs, and memorials, all of the very best quality and the most venerable antiquity. Next, rather more prosaic sounding, are the *pomul,* the Treasured Things, of which there were 734 listed in the 1958 reclassification—old village guardian stones, pots and pans of various dynasties and kingdoms, and temple bells and celadon vases. Third, there are the *sajok,* the Historic Sites—battlefields (such as where Admiral Yi was killed at Noryangjin), landing places (such as where MacArthur came ashore at Inchon), the grounds of old palace complexes, and long-ruined temples.

Below this esteemed series come five lesser levels. There are 5 Scenic Sites; there are 120 items officially designated as Folklore Material; there are 12 Historic Places of Beauty; and there are 72 Intangible Cultural Assets and Living National Treasures—my own favorite classification, which includes aged but nonetheless indisputably living men like Mr. Kim Tong-yon, who, in a "culturally intangible" way, makes bamboo baskets in Tamyang town. He has a number, which he will show you on request, and he is delighted to have been informed that he cannot be done away with (because he is an Intangible Cultural Asset) except on the specific instructions of the government. (Mr. Kim's baskets belong later in the story: They are remarkably pretty and complicated affairs, which he has been making for sixty years. He doubtless deserves his status and the popular adulation it brings in its train.)

The final category, which brings the total number of cultural assets in Korea to well over a thousand, is the one that holds the 235 Natural Protected Resources. Trees, flowers, birds, and wild animals (of which there are precious few in Korea, for reasons I will discuss later) are on the list in huge numbers, and so is one domesticated animal—the *Chindo-kae.*

To the stranger who happens across one of the many breeding kennels on Chindo, the Chindo dog may just seem a pretty little animal, a feisty, protective little ball of fur and teeth. But it would be unwise to forget that it is Natural Protected Resource Number 225, and thus subject to the rigors of the law. In order to protect the dog from itself (which means, of course, from its ever forging meaningful relationships with dogs of less impeccable family backgrounds and with sullied gene pools) and to protect it from Koreans (who, as like as not, would boil the dog up in a stew and serve it with onions and garlic—of which, too, more later), one is expressly forbidden to take any dog off the island.

The Chindo Great Bridge (built by Hyundai, a small-scale version of that mighty Korean-built bridge that links Penang Island with the Malaysian mainland) has armed guards at both ends. Their ostensible purpose is to prevent any North Korean spies getting on or off the island, but when they open the trunk of your car and peer into the boxes on the back seat, they'll tell you with a grin that they are actually out hunting for contraband *Chindo-kae*, and woe betide you if you happen to have smuggled one out. I had once entertained a pleasant fantasy of walking the length of Korea with a little off-white dog by my side and was saddened to learn of the restriction and that my dream was not to be.

❖   ❖   ❖

We arrived at Mokpo with a rush. The ferryboat rounded a headland, scattered some small fishing boats, bumped through a white-capped tide race, and there, suddenly, like a new slide flashed onto the screen, was the town, a cluster of houses ranged at the base of a steep little mountain. It looked to me exactly like a little Greenland town called Sükkertoppen, a dusting of sugary white crystals on the hill, a village of little dockyard cranes and bobbing masts down at sea level, a fresco of small old houses hugging the contours in between. I half expected to see Greenland fishermen—indeed, the Koreans were none too different in appearance, and those in oilskins looked, at first glance, as though they could well do their fishing in Disko Bay or the Davis Strait. An anthropologist could have made more of the connection; for me it simply offered a powerful blast of déjà vu.

Seagulls mewed and wheeled in the sky above the nets; the streets were lined with small fish tanks from which old women sold the smaller fry from the boats; the ground, when I stepped off the ferry, was slippery with fish oil and guts and scales. The whole place smelled of cold halibut oil and *yontan* smoke, and there was a gritty dust in the wind. I snapped on my pack, said my farewells to the honeymoon couple—the poor girl could barely keep her eyes open—and strode off to the north.

The town thinned out, and away from the sea and out of the wind it grew pleasantly warm. The sun came out, lighting up the meadows and the little lakes, putting everyone in a good mood. Koreans are very quick to change their moods, I had always found (dangerously quick, one might say in other circumstances); today they waved and smiled at me, and every car that passed, and particularly every bus, honked its horn, gave the double-finger V-for-victory sign—the Korean equivalent of thumbs-up—and cheered at my strange but apparently praiseworthy effort. Quite a few cars going the same way stopped and offered me a lift. I learned the polite rote: *"Gwen chan sumnida!"* I would wave back (No thanks!), *"Panmunjom kkaji goro kamnida"* (I prefer to walk all the way to Panmunjom). And they would whistle with amazement, *"Panmun-jom, chong mul?!"* and offer sweets and chocolate, anything they had, to help me on my way. (The gift that came most often was a small can of mandarin orange juice called Sac Sac, a most peculiar drink full of the uncrushed sacs of juice that the drivers seemed to think would most refresh a perspiring *yang-nom*, as the Koreans rather impolitely call a Westerner. I became positively addicted to the stuff as the journey progressed.) That day, in the sunshine, it seemed that there were no more hospitable people on earth.

I was making for a village called Illo, and for a Korean family that my friend Oh Kyoung-sook had said were distant friends of hers and would be sure to put up a stranger for a night. I was a little apprehensive: Father McGlinchey had also given me a string of Irish addresses, of people he knew in the province of Chol-lanam-do, where I would be walking for the next few days. "Cholla people have the reputation of being absolute *bastards,*" he had said. "They say the Cholla people are lazy, parochial, and boring—and not at all hospitable either. I don't say that, other Koreans do. See if you like them. I always find them okay, although they absolutely hate the government in Seoul. They're a bolshy lot, as far as the government is concerned. But don't let me put you off. If you like them, fine. If not, have these addresses. They'll look after you, for sure."

But, tempting as it might have been to spend time with the Irish, I did actually want to meet Cholla people, obstinate and inhospitable though they might well be. So I dug out the address of Mr. Kim Jung Jin and quickened my pace a little to be sure of arriving well before dark.

The two Cholla provinces are the rice centers of Korea, and here, on this warm, early spring day, the farmers were out ploughing or planting the paddy. Last year's stalks peeked above the water like thousands of mustaches neatly trimmed by the autumn harvesters. This year's new plants—transplanted from smaller seedling beds—were being dibbled into the thick mud by small posses of women, each woman bent double, her skirts hitched up around her waist, her feet and legs quite bare, and a straw hat jammed on her head to protect her from the glare of the sun. The men—bare armed, bare legged, and splattered with mud—worked the ploughs, the oxen pulling the single share of fire-hardened wood and the new earth almost bursting from beneath the old with exuberant ease. Now that the last frosts had gone, the earth seemed to *need* to be worked—maybe it was the energy and might of the oxen, maybe it was the eagerness of the farmers to get on with their growing season—but everything here seemed to be happening so fast, so enthusiastically. In other countries where I had seen people plant and harvest rice—India, northern Luzon, Burma, China—there was always a sense of laziness to the rhythm, a comfortable sense of languor, as though everyone knew the sun and rain would do the trick, the rice would grow, the granaries would fill, and no hurry was required. Here in Chollanam-do, there was a factorylike urgency to it all: Pull that plough! Turn that wheel! Plant that seedling! Dig that furrow! I found it almost exhausting to watch.

I had been on National Route Number 1 ever since I left Mokpo, but now, as the sun began to slant down behind the poplars on my left, I had to leave it for the country road that my map said went to Illo. I crossed the railway line a couple of times—smart-looking diesel trains hurtled past me, the blue one bound for local destinations, the red-and-white ones bound for the big cities of the North. (National Route 1, which I planned to follow intermittently, led all the way to Seoul and beyond, to Pyongyang and the Manchurian border. Three hundred miles north of where I stood, at this junction with the lesser road, it would be cut by a pair of fences, the most impregnable and most heavily defended in the world.)

It was late afternoon when I reached the turning to Illo Town. Two motorcycle policemen were waiting there, directing traffic to stop for a caravan of long black limousines that shot along the highway and turned up to a government building on the skyline. Local government leaders, the police explained. I asked for directions to Saint Gertrude's Church, beside which Mr. Kim and his family were said to live. The usual inquiry: Was I American? No, English, and a broad beam spread across the policeman's face. "I am take you," he said with immense pride, and pointed to his pillion seat. It was an order rather than an offer. I got aboard with some difficulty; my pack weighed innumerable pounds and my standing on one leg trying to wrestle the other over the back of the motorcycle turned into a performance that would have won me a place in the Royal Ballet. But eventually I was on, whereupon the policeman turned on his blue flashing light and we roared off down into town, scattering people and chickens on every side.

I found the house—small, two storied, with a bright blue roof, and a balcony. It was deserted and neighbors pointed to the number seven on my wristwatch; by seven, it seemed clear, the Kims would arrive home. There was nothing for it but to wait, and so I contented myself sitting on the steps of the nearby church, eating strawberries in the early evening sun and watching two middle-aged Korean men playing tennis. They were, I soon realized, excellent players. They hit hard and true, and their brown arms and legs, muscles taut as hawser wire, gleamed with fine sweat. They never said a word to each other. They just grunted with their exertion as they played, machinelike in their accuracy and speed, absolutely matched in their excellence. I became more fascinated as their game went on, rally after rally, never a ball lost or a shot missed, the net unmoved, the fault lines untouched, exchange after exchange after exchange. Their excellence was hypnotic—boring even, since there were no spectacular errors or misjudgments to upset the balance of their play.

Having seen the rice planters working so hard earlier in the day, and now watching these tennis players competing in so deadly a fashion and with such silent, bloodless determination, I found myself thinking—tangential though the thought might at first seem—about the extraordinary success of every one of Korea's recent ambitions. How triumphant the country had become from utter ruin in the 1950s to the world's fastest-growing economy in the 1980s! And much of that success, I fancied, had come about because of the sheer willpower and concentrated effort that the Korean people apply to any venture they undertake—they play tennis hard, well, and to win; they build ships night and day, at lower prices and in greater numbers to beat the competition; they work their fields at an exhausting pace to make quite certain their fellow people want for nothing in their diet, and so that the nation has to import nothing—no food, anyway—from abroad.

My mind, lulled by the long metronomic thuds of the players' rallies, pursued the thought a little further. A year or so before I had been saying my farewells to a friend who was changing trains in Irkutsk, in Siberia. It was well after lunch on a bleak day in deepest midwinter, bitterly cold and snowing hard. The express from Novosibirsk to Khabarovsk arrived exactly on time, rumbling out of the grayish gloom, snowflakes glistening in the yellow glare of its headlight. As it creaked to a halt amid a sudden smell of hot iron and warm oil and steam, a dozen burly women rushed from a hut beside the rails and, using heavy iron crowbars six feet long, set about prying the enormous blocks of accumulated gray ice from between the bogies of the carriages. With huge crashes like the calving of small glaciers, the ice fell away and the wheels, hitherto hidden in the ice, looked like wheels again, ready to convey the express on to its next Siberian city.

The women, all smoking tiny, sweet-smelling Russian cigarettes, finished their task just at the moment the guard waved his flag and blew his whistle, and the train began to move on eastward once again. Not a second had been lost; with great efficiency and zeal the huge trans-Siberian monster had been kept in running order, kept well greased and fueled and equipped to do battle with the worst weather the world can hurl at any means of transport anywhere. And I thought back then to Nikita Khrushchev, and the bullying remark he once made to the then American vice president, Richard Nixon: We will bury you, he had said. We will bury you. And now, looking at this simple Siberian scene, with its mixture of great determination, of absolute obedience to duty no matter how irksome and difficult, of oblivion to difficulty, to cold, to pain— I thought: My God, they will, you know. These Russians—and I realized, of course, that I was making a none-too-reasonable and even sentimental judgment on all Russians merely on the evidence presented by a dozen Siberian laborers—these Russians have the capacity and the ability to do *anything they wish.* Nothing can stop a people as determined as this. No strikes. No argument. No grumbling unwillingness to work. Utter ruthlessness, obstinacy and obduracy and willpower, all directed to the good of the state. They can bury anyone they want.

And as with Russia—thus went my thoughts a year or more later, on this spring evening in the tiny town of Illo—so with the Koreans. With such determination—in the fields, in such factories as I had seen, in the fishing boats, or on the tennis court baseline—how could they lose? Maybe they would not win today, not immediately, not for some years. But one day they would be up with the masters—one of the big boys, one of the kings of the world, and make no mistake about it.

"Are you an English-speaker, sir, by any chance?" A very pretty girl had tapped me on the shoulder, starting me from my reverie. She was smiling broadly, her finely chiseled features glowing in the warm twilight. "You are? Why are you here? We see very few foreign people in Illo." I explained that I was waiting to see a Mr. Kim from the house beside Saint Gertrude's and that I had a letter, written in *hangul*, that would explain. I pulled out and gave to her the crumpled note of introduction Kyoung-sook had written for me at Sogwipo, whereupon the girl gave a cry of sheer delight: "We are friends, she and me! I was at school with her! I am the daughter of the house. You must come in. Come on in!"

The family—or the three then in Illo, members of what I later learned was the total family of five—had been out for an afternoon stroll. The parents were sitting on the floor of their living room when Ae-ri (as she introduced herself— "A most lovely name, don't you think?" she giggled) brought me in, and there was some confusion as they put down teacups and bottles of O.B. beer, and struggled to their feet to greet the newcomer.

Mr. Kim, the father of the house, was tall, well tanned, a fit-looking man in his early sixties who spoke some English, and after a hurried consultation with Ae-ri said he would be "very happy indeed" if I would stay to dinner and then sleep there for the night. "We have a Western bed, you know," he said proudly. He introduced me to a small, curly-haired lady with shiny red cheeks and a ready smile: "This is Kyu-Hwan *eum-ma*," he said, meaning, literally, "This is the mother of Kyu-Hwan." His wife.

Korean protocol can on occasion be cumbersome and confusing—this occasion being one such. The lady that Mr. Kim was introducing to me was the person that a Westerner would probably call Mrs. Kim. Her actual name, the one she would use if she was introducing herself to a shopkeeper, say, was, Ae-ri explained to me later, Mrs. Choe—Choe Mi-young. But to Mr. Kim she was neither Mrs. Kim nor Mrs. Choe. She was, instead, the mother of the family's eldest son. And since the eldest son was called Kim Kyu-Hwan, then Mr. Kim's wife was introduced as "Kyu-Hwan *eum-ma*," Kyu-Hwan's mother.

The system, for all its apparent clumsiness, does have some advantages, even for me. The moment I heard Mr. Kim's phrase I knew first that this woman was Mrs. Kim; second that Ae-ri was not the only child of the union;

third, that there was a son somewhere; and fourth, that he was called Kyu-Hwan. The modest sentence of introduction thus gave me a considerable amount of information about the Kim family—rather more than a Mr. Smith at a cocktail party might give me by introducing his female companion as "my wife, Mary."

Mr. Kim, who was dressed in baggy silk trousers and a gray silk blouse tied with ribbons and toggles made of bone, settled himself back onto the floor, crossed his legs, and pushed a royal blue silk cushion across to me. He asked me to sit, apologizing for the lack of chairs but noting rather grandly that "we don't like to use chairs—they take up so much room." He made a signal, and his wife and daughter left silently through the sliding paper-windowed door, presumably to find some more tea. Once they had gone Mr. Kim, without any ceremony or shyness, proceeded to ask me my age—an important first step in the forging of any relationship, I was later to discover, between Koreans and the rest of mankind. I told him ("You are a Monkey!" he said, when he worked out that I had been born in 1944. "Very—how shall I say?—very tricky!"), whereupon he immediately began to gush forth facts and statistics about his family.

He was sixty-four. (That is to say he was sixty-three, to the Western way of counting. In much of the Orient, Korea included, a child is reckoned to be one the moment it is born.) He had been born in Mokpo and had grown up in the bewildering atmosphere of Japanese colonialism—he had been given a Japanese name at school, he had been forced to learn to speak Japanese, he had been impressed into the Japanese militia, and he had been given a job guarding prisoners of war from Singapore. "You will never understand, no matter how long you stay, how bad the Japanese times were. They tried to strip away everything from us. They tried to destroy all that was Korea. But we stood up to them. We rejoiced when they were defeated. I have never spoken a word of Japanese again—and I never will." He shuddered with distaste as he said this, though Ae-ri, when she brought in more beer, rolled her eyes heavenward and tutted at her father, who had clearly given this little speech many times before. "Why don't you forget it? It is so long ago. We need the Japanese. We must be their friends again."

His wife was fifty-nine, he went on. He had three children—Kyu-Hwan, who was thirty-nine, an engineer in Seoul; Sung-Hwan, who had been born after the end of the Korean War, in 1954, and was now working with the police in Taegu; and Ae-ri, who had gone to Soodo Women's University in Seoul (to study Japanese, her father later admitted, with evident distaste; it was at the university that she had made friends with Kyoung-sook, who had studied Japanese too) and was now working in Seoul as a ticketing agent for Korean Airlines. There had, I gathered, been some trouble with her marriage, and she was now back in Illo "getting over it." But it was made clear to me, despite all the degrees of intimacy of the conversation thus far, that I was to know little about it and that it would be impolite to ask for further details, since the family had already lost a considerable amount of face over the whole incident.

Mr. Kim had worked for so much of his early career in Seoul—the children had all been born and brought up in the capital, where most ambitious Koreans eventually migrate–but had ended up as a foreman at a steel factory on the east coast. He had retired four years ago and had used his final bonus—a month's pay for every one of the twenty years he had worked—to buy this modest house in Illo. He now spent his days walking, his evenings reading or talking. He was very interested in the outside world, never having been beyond the shores of Korea, nor ever likely to. His last real holiday had been a trip to Cheju-do two years before, and he talked delightedly about the beauty of the diving women, and laughed happily when I warned him that the *haenyo* were in fact rather more beautiful in retrospect than they actually were at the time.

But his most powerful memories were, as one might suspect, of the Korean War. Once our modest dinner had been cleared away—we ate alone, the women bringing us soup and rice and a small dish of meat with perhaps eight side dishes of pickles and marinated fish—he brought out a map, demanded more beer, and showed me where he had seen action.

He had been twenty-six when the North Korean Army invaded on that wet June Sunday in 1950. He was immediately impressed into service—the standing southern army at the time of the invasion was a mere 95,000 men, with eight divisions, some mortars and some artillery pieces, but no tanks. With immense assistance from the Americans an army was hurriedly formed, trained, and sent into war. Kim Jung Jin was a recruit, an infantryman of no particular distinction—a "grunt," he would have been called in that later war as tragically pointless as the one in Korea, and fought so nearby, and between such similar enemies.

Private Kim had been busy in his war. He had also been lucky. He had fought his way through the length and breadth of the peninsula for nearly the entire three dismal years that followed and was neither captured nor hurt, "not even a scratch."

He pulled a blurred old sepia picture from his wallet, showing him, or so he said—it could just as well have been Audie Murphy, so blurred was the picture—"on the road near Taejon, some time in the summer of 1951." The image was a pathetic one: It was of a young soldier, barefoot, with baggy trousers and a camouflage shirt tattered beyond repair, shuffling along a dusty road alone. He carried one boot—his only boot, so far as I could see—in his right hand, and an elderly rifle was slung across his left shoulder. He looked more like a gamekeeper on a rather decrepit Yorkshire estate, and the thought that he had wandered through Korea like this for three years, being shot at by the fanatically trained soldiers of the Korean People's Army, or by the "volunteers" of the Chinese People's Liberation Army, seemed barely believable. "It was very cold in winter," he said, brightly. "This picture was taken in the summer."

He knew his war backward and inside out. He knew all the dates, all the men, all the battles, all the decisions, all the victories, and all the defeats. He was, in fact, a walking encyclopedia of the Korean War, and we talked of it late into the night, over yet more beers and with many small bottles of that powerful firewater known as *soju*, the drinking protocols of which require each drinker to fill the other's glass so that there is always something to drink and no possible way of avoiding the drunkenness that follows.

So my recollection of his conversation is a hazy one, although I see from my notebook that I managed somehow to write down a fairly complete chronology of the war on the day after the one I spent in Illo, so at some moment during the day's hung-over walk I must have recalled it all.

He remembered (according to these notes) all the strange arcana of the times. He knew that Yugoslavia, India, and Egypt had abstained from the Security Council resolution naming Douglas MacArthur as commander of the UN forces. He knew that MacArthur's landing at Inchon was code-named Operation Chromite, and he could recite the names of other American operations, the actual or the merely planned—operations with names like Big Switch and Little Switch; Killer, Ripper, and Strangle; Piledriver and Roundup and Thunderbolt (which latter was General Matthew Ridgway's celebrated attack on the Chinese defenses of the Han River in that bitter winter of early 1951).

He knew of the pointless ebb and flow of battle, how Seoul fell to the Communists, was retaken by MacArthur, was taken again by the Reds and then once more by Ridgway's men, and how similar tidal races had raged up and down rivers and ranges of hills and impenetrable valleys and fjords and coastal plains and paddy fields. He remembered the cold; of being entrained and marched or crammed into swaying trucks to every corner of the old kingdom; he remembered the trenches, and the C-rations and the packs of Lucky Strike cigarettes, and the occasional and much-valued comradeship with those few Americans who actually tried to talk to the soldiers of the ROK armies.

He knew of all the friends and foes, of the armies and navies and air forces of the Americans and South Koreans, of the Chinese and North Koreans, and of the battle groups made up of such improbable allies as Ethiopians and South Africans, Frenchmen and Dutchmen, Filipinos and Turks, Thais and Belgians, Australians and Colombians, Canadians and Greeks, and that little contingent of infantrymen from Luxembourg, all of whom were waging war under the UN flag.

And Mr. Kim knew of the British, too, and of the Glorious Glosters, and their defense of Hill 235, just south of the Imjin River. "Ah yes, the Glosters," he breathed admiringly. "The only unit in your army allowed to wear its cap badge on the back as well as on the front." (I later looked it up. He was quite right. The Gloucesters (as they were properly known) had fought the French in the Battle of Alexandria in 1801 and were attacked both from the front and the rear. The rear rank promptly faced about and dealt with the situation—the honor of having successfully fought "back to back" never being forgotten and thus memorialized on the uniform beret.)

I knew only the schoolboy tales of the Glosters' stand on Hill 235, of the massive casualties they sustained, of their heroism, of the Victoria Cross they won, and of the commendation from the Eighth Army's Commanding General, James Van Fleet, proclaiming that theirs was "the most outstanding example of unit bravery in modern warfare." But I was able to tell old Mr. Kim something I had learned in Northern Ireland that he did not know. One of the generals dealing with that grubby little war in Ireland was Anthony Farrar-Hockley, who had been with the Glosters in Korea, and he told many stories of the time.

Back then he was a captain, and adjutant to the battalion CO, Lieutenant Colonel James Carne. When the Chinese began their final assault on Hill 235 they did a most peculiar, psychologically devastating thing: They blew hundreds upon hundreds of bugles, making a vast, discordant, strangely triumphal sound that echoed all around the war-scarred hills above the Imjin River. But Captain Farrar-Hockley refused to be intimidated by this weird music, and he ordered the battalion bugles to return the salute. There was only one instrument remaining, in the care of one Drummer Eagles, who gave it to the sergeant-major to play. And play it he did, giving the Chinese every tune and call and fanfare known to a British Army bandsman, with the single omission of the call "Retreat."

But finally, as the attacks went on and it became all too obvious that the Chinese would overrun the Glosters' position, and there was no option but for the British to leave, Drummer Eagles made a final gesture. He blew his bugle apart with one of his own grenades, making sure that no British bugle would ever fall into enemy hands. I told Mr. Kim this story, and he was so well oiled with *soju* and beer that he laughed quite helplessly for five minutes before suddenly appearing to sober up and suggesting that I go along the corridor to where my bed—a real Western bed, a legacy of his army days, he said—had been readied for me.

I slept dreamlessly until the middle of the morning, by which time Mr. Kim had gone out on some business, and it was left to Ae-ri to make me breakfast (she found some bacon and an egg and a glass of mango juice) and show me the way out of town. I was feeling quite dreadful and hoisted my pack to my back with no certainty that I could carry it much farther than I could throw it. *Soju* is powerful medicine, I decided. Never again.

Before I left Illo I looked in at the local Catholic church, to see if any of the missionary fathers whose names I had been given back in Cheju were around. But they were away. All I found was a book, a history of the mission-aries in Korea; my eye was immediately caught by the story of two of their number who suffered horribly. I jotted it in my notebook, and since it follows my memories of Mr. Kim's remarkable chronology of the war, it seems proper to include it here. The book, *The Splendid Cause,* tells of the fate that befell Monsignor Patrick Brennan and Fathers John O'Brien and Tom Cusack, who happened to be in Mokpo, Mr. Kim's hometown, on the day the Communists arrived on July 24, 1950 (exactly a month after the beginning of the invasion). The three priests were arrested and taken off by North Korean troops to the prison in Kwangju. A young American lieutenant, Alexander Makaroumis, found them there, and later wrote:

> It was a cold night for August, and there were no blankets for us in the cell. There were only three blankets in all, but these were im-mediately shared by three missionaries. It was the first of the many acts of kindness and consideration the priests were to show us during the dreadful days we were to go through. . . .
>
> When we first met the priests they had been prisoners for about five weeks. As the meals consisted of only a small bowl of barley with a slice of pickled turnip, the priests all lost a great deal of weight.
>
> Monsignor Brennan and Father Cusack were wearing black trou-sers and black shoes. The Monsignor had on a black suit; Father Cusack a blue one. Father O'Brien was all in white; he had a white collar, a white tee-shirt and a white cassock. They kept their cassocks rolled up and out of the way most of the time—I guess they didn't want to use them.
>
> It would be hard to tell you what these guys did for our morale— they boosted it by at least 500 percent! Monsignor, for instance, would stand at the cell window and listen to the birds chirping mer-rily outside, then he'd turn and cheer us by telling us a singing bird was a messenger of hope. . . .
>
> At other times he'd encourage Father O'Brien to sing us a song and do one of his Irish jigs. Father O'Brien had a good voice and the way he sang "Faraway Places" sort of made you forget you were cooped up in a prison cell, and sent you flying back home. . . .

The priests were sent off to another prison near Seoul. Makaroumis went, too.

> In preparation for the journey the priests' hands were tied with ropes. The hands of the military people were fastened with hand-irons and ropes. We traveled only at night to escape allied bombers. . . .

We were on this truck for three nights straight and then, when we were approaching the city of Taejon, the truck broke down for good. We were told to get off and walk. . . . It was a sad procession.

When we got to Taejon we were made to sit out in the open for about thirty minutes while a Korean with a small camera took pictures of us. We were put on display for about two hours while hundreds of North Koreans, army people and others, came in to look at us. For us, the story of the missionaries ends in the prison of Taejon. We do not know what happened after we were taken from the cell. But wherever they are I shall always remember them for the comfort, cheerfulness, kindness and courage they somehow communicated to us when they were no better off themselves.

The next news of the three Columbans came from the wife of a South Korean judge. She had been confined in the same room as the three in the old Franciscan monastery in Taejon and heard that on the afternoon of September 24, when the Communists were preparing to hurry north to avoid a huge party of advancing UN troops, there was a massacre of all remaining prisoners:

> Later no one could recognize any of the Columbans among more than a thousand corpses piled up in the monastery garden. The bodies were so decomposed and swollen . . . a well in the garden was filled with bodies that no one had a chance to inspect . . . in the archives of the society of St. Columba, Monsignor Brennan, Fathers O'Brien and Cusack are recorded as having died in the massacre of September 24, 1950. Thus the matter rests today, but a beautiful new church in the city which they served now honors their brave fidelity.

I left shortly before lunch, having read that morning's *Korea Times*, which had come down from Seoul on the milk train. How close that made me feel to journey's end, and yet I wasn't even halfway through! Ae-ri came with me for the first half mile, apologizing (though I kept insisting that no apology was needed) for her father's loquacity, his stories of the war. "I just wish he'd forget—and forget all this nonsense about the Japanese," she said.

It was market day in Illo—once every five days the country people stream into Illo to buy and sell each other's wares—and the town was crowded. Most people seemed to be selling huge bundles of leaves to each other—the makings of some form of *kimchi*, Ae-ri said, and innocuous enough—but there was one distressing scene when a huge dog, just sold for some unspecified and unimaginable end use, was being pushed into a plastic bag for the journey back home to its fate.

It was a large beast, spotted like a Dalmatian, and it had no intention at all of going into the bag. It wanted to spend the rest of its life, no matter how attenuated, leaping about. But the customer had bought it and, for reasons that may have had something to do with squeamishness, was not about to walk his dinner (for that is what I imagined the dog to be) home on a leash. He wanted it in the bag. So he and the seller grabbed the shrieking animal's rear legs and thrust and pushed them and tail into the bag and then gave their attention to the forelegs—whereupon the animal flexed its rear legs and leaped out of the bag like a jack-in-the-box. Under any other circumstances the business might have been comic—if the dog was being bundled up to go on holiday, for instance—but the fact that I supposed he was going to be rendered into *poshin-tang*, the famous Korean dog soup, made it rather ghastly. So I left the three protagonists at it and walked steadily away without turning, until the shrieking of the terrified animal faded away. (Later a specialist on canine cuisine informed me gravely that this dog was not for the pot: Only medium-size yellow dogs go into *poshin-tang*, and they are hung up at least a week before their appearance on the dining table. This may simply have been a very belligerent pet.)

I did eat a dog in Korea once, and quite bearable it was. I was in Seoul, and a friend named Park Choon-sil had urged me to try it, since in her view to write about Korea without trying dogmeat would be to write about England without eating roast beef. "Both are rituals, are they not?" Now I am the owner of two exceptionally stupid but very endearing dogs—an elderly beagle named Biggles and a Jack Russell terrier called Tusker—and I have to confess I felt no shame in tucking into their colleagues, just once, for the sole purpose of better understanding the nature of those who eat them.

The victim-dog—a big yellow mutt specially bred for the table—was served up in medallions on a bed of onions and lettuce (and then served again as *poshin-tang*), and it tasted quite reasonable—very strong, very rich, and with a background flavor of kidney. The restaurateur, a fat and kindly woman, came up to me as I took the first forkful—as I was wondering how Biggles would react if ever he came to know, by smelling it on my breath, for instance. "Very good, *poshin-tang*, for"—and as the entire café collapsed in helpless laughter, she pointed at a spot some six inches below my navel—"good for stamina!"

And that was, and still remains, the core of my understanding. There's nothing in all this guff about dogs keeping you warm in winter and cool in the summer. Hardly anyone can be found who ever likes these more weird breeds of food. They all eat them to prove the axiom that the more disgusting it is, the more good it will do the libido. So Korean men tuck into dogs for the same reason the Cantonese eat snake and the Thais eat the brains of still-living monkeys and the Filipinos crunch up the entire embryos of ducks—they all labor under the apprehension that by so doing their sexual drive and ability will be immeasurably enhanced, their erections will last longer, their performances will be of a more virtuoso nature, and their children will be more numerous. Tired? Jaded? Listless? A little dog'll do ya.

I walked eastward, dazzled by the high sun. Ae-ri turned back, a little sadly I thought. She had given me a telephone number in Seoul. I stumped along the railway line as she had advised. I could have taken the road, and crossed the Yongsang River by the bridge, but that would have taken the best part of a day and a half. By taking the railway line—a modest illegality with which the police apparently did not bother—I would save eight hours' walking. I would have to cross the river by boat. Sure enough, after an hour of trying to work out why railway sleepers the world over are all placed in such a way that it is impossible to walk along them, and after dodging perhaps a dozen trains that hurtled by, I arrived at the river. A bridge is to be built, the locals say; but for now it was a short ride on an old ferry, with six old men, one blubbery old hog, and a motorcycle and a payment of 250 *won*. I fetched up on the eastern side at a place called Okchong-ri and started along a dusty, unpaved road toward the town of Naju.

(Korean administrative districts range from the *-do*, the largest, as in Cheju-do, Chollanam-do, Chungchongbuk-do; to the smallest, the *-pan*, which is roughly equivalent in size to the city block. In between are the *-dongs*, the *-ris*, the *-myuns*, the *-shis*, the *-ups*, and the *-guns*, the latter being the name of the county. So the full address of the person I was planning to visit in Naju, for example, might well be: Mr. Kim Young Sam, Song-pan 24, Ilsa-dong, Uichang-ri, Simban-myun, Yangwon-up, Naju-shi, Naju-gun, Chollanam-do, South Korea. And if pedantry be your game, then it should be added that the name of Korea is, to Koreans, not Korea at all, but Daehan Minguk, which is what you will see on Korean stamps. North Korea, which uses the same *-pan* to *-do* system, is giving the portmanteau name of Chosun Minchu-chui Inmin Konghwa-guk.)

From here it was a good long slog. The sun was out, I was feeling well rested and healthy, and I strode along contentedly mile after mile. First it was pine forests and lakes; then, down in the lowlands again, apple orchards and some of the old and gnarled blossom trees that would soon produce another crop of the pears for which Naju is rightly famous; then uplands again, and a long haul up a mountainside. Occasionally jet fighter planes would roar past, streaking down the valleys, hugging the contours. Team Spirit was on, the huge annual springtime exercise staged by the American and Korean troops to prove that they could work well together in war; I assumed the aerial activity had something to do with that. I cursed the planes for spoiling the silence. So did the farmers: I saw one gaze up at the sky after one particularly low-flying plane had startled the beast that was pulling his plough, and though he stopped short of shaking his fist, he looked extremely displeased. Team Spirit, as I have no doubt its organizers know, is not much of a public relations exercise, whatever else it may be.

I had been going for perhaps half an hour when I was suddenly aware of someone behind me. I stopped, and the someone crashed painfully into my rucksack. *"Mian hamnida!"* came a strangled voice, and a young man, a fellow I remembered having seen waiting by a bridge five miles or so back, picked himself up, dusted himself off, and continued to apologize.

He said he wanted nothing more than to talk. He was a member of the Pine Tree Club, he explained, an English conversation group that met every week in a hall in Illo. What was my name? He was Mr. Lee. He was seventeen years old. What was I doing? Did I like Korea? His English was execrable. He could barely speak a word. And worst of all, after the pleasantries, the questions and phrases I had come to anticipate, he then proceeded to go quite mad. He embarked on a number of theories, all of which related the inexplicable nuances of Korean history and their relationship to geomorphology.

The only theory I felt I could understand was his strange belief about how the hills in Chollanam-do were, in the view of Confucian scholars, of entirely the wrong shape—they all looked like tortoises, and not like the more favored lions and tigers—and that was the reason why the old Koryo kings of Korea (those who gave the country its name) had never liked the Cholla people. "They think we bastards!" he kept saying. "They think we bastards." He gave me an apple and talked a little more about his various theories—I think I would have found them hard enough to understand had they been announced on the BBC—and then, with no more warning than a cheery wave, he turned off onto a country road and in seconds had vanished among the pine trees.

What on earth! Had he been for real? I wondered. And then I remembered someone in Seoul warning me. "Watch out for the *angibu*," he had said. The secret police, the tappers of phones and followers of dissidents and beaters-up of radicals, they would be bound to be on my trail. Watch out for them. But had this young fellow been from the *angibu*? I frankly doubted it—he had seemed too peculiar, too mad. A member of the Pine Tree Club if ever there was one, I concluded, and with a shrug, walked on.

It grew cloudy for the rest of the afternoon and was pouring with rain as I passed between the huge stone guardian lions of Naju, and so, not thinking I was cheating too seriously, flagged down a taxi. *"Cho-un hoteru odi isumnikka?"* I said, wondering if that was indeed the way to ask for a good hotel, but he replied with *"nay,"* which, confusingly for Westerners, is the Korean word for yes (*"anio"* being no), and we lurched off into the rain. Five minutes later, as we passed under the shadow of an enormous tobacco factory, we came to a mess of tiny streets and a large and gloomy hotel. There was a room, for about $10 a night—it was huge, with a massive Victorian bed and three clocks. I squeezed the water from my socks, put my boots on the radiator, took a bath, clambered into bed, and fell asleep. I woke in total darkness, hungry as hell.

It was about nine o'clock, cold, still raining, and the people of Naju had clearly seen very few foreigners. I was stared at from every doorway. People would nudge each other and point at me. Girls would squeal and put the palms of their hands to their mouths, the classic expression of shy terror and bewilderment. It was not a cruel or mocking curiosity: The people who saw me, and who had never seen such a lumbering and hairy creature before—a head taller than most Koreans, pale and ghostly skinned, and covered with a primeval fur—were amazed. They had seen such creatures on television; now here was a real live one, and in their town, too. (Having said that, it has been reported that Koreans with blue eyes and light-colored hair have been seen in both Namwon and Sunchon, cities where Hendrick Hamel and his party of shipwrecked Dutch sailors spent some years. Naju was one of the towns in which they had spent time en route to Seoul—my journey through Korea, it may be remembered, was designed to follow their approximate route—and it is entirely possible that genetic relics of the Dutchmen's passage may still be found. I had imagined that a man who was a little taller than normal and had blue eyes and sandy hair might be living in Naju somewhere; but the locals' reaction to me suggested that such a signal was totally alien—the collapse, I realized, of my small theory. The Dutchmen must have behaved themselves, or else their stock was too insubstantial and has vanished in the wash of the twelve generations since their wreck.)

But it turned out I was not the only Westerner in town, anyway. I was mooching along a lane, looking for a *bulgoki-jip*, a restaurant serving the barbecued beef for which this part of the peninsula is famous, when I glanced into a bookshop. There, standing at the back in animated conversation with the owner, were two white men in long raincoats. I opened the door, and they looked up at the jangling of the bell, their faces portraits of blank astonishment. "What . . . !" they both spluttered, and then I told them what I was doing, and we all marched off to dinner. "Simon," said the taller of the pair, "my name is Elder Harper and this"—he pointed to his friend, a small, blond boy who looked about eighteen—"is Elder Cran." They were both missionaries of the Church of Jesus Christ of Latter-Day Saints. Mormons.

With no disrespect meant to its followers, I have never been able to be terribly enthusiastic about the Mormon church. Logically I have to suppose there is not much to choose between prophets being crucified and rising from the dead in Palestine, sitting under trees and gaining self-knowledge in northern India, or finding golden plates at the top of hills in upstate New York and then urging followers to walk across America to found Salt Lake City. Faith—in matters like these and in leaders like these—is what powers a religion along; a moral code, having precious little to do with legend or leadership, is what actually makes it worthwhile; and Mormon's moral code is certainly not to be sneezed at, even if it is a trifle too strict for many tastes.

Mormon leaders I have come to know in Hong Kong in recent years have suggested their church is making a "big push" in the Orient; the effort that Elders Harper (Eric, from Arizona) and Cran (Michael, from New York) were making in Naju was presumably part of the push. They were the foot soldiers of a new battle for converts being directed from Salt Lake City, and like all foot soldiers, they were having to suffer for victory.

We sat on the floor of a small café, eating *bulgoki* and *kimchi* and rice and most of the about twenty side dishes this particular café had to offer, and I drank a large bottle of O.B. beer, and listened to them talk. They had been together in Naju for the last month. Eric Harper was the elder, at twenty-three. Michael Cran, who looked no more than a child, was twenty-one. Both wore identical blue suits and white shirts; each had his name and station in the church on a plastic tag on his lapel. They lived in the Mormon House on the outskirts of town with one other American—the leader of their little cell—and a Korean, to help with the language.

"I was sent out here to do missionary work ten months ago. I learned a little Korean at headquarters in Salt Lake, then I came out to Taegu to polish it up, then I was assigned here." Elder Harper exuded doctrinal self-confidence, like the better kind of car salesman. "I'd sure love to have you come over to the Mormon House. But we don't allow any strangers to come in. I'm really sorry about that. You've been staying with the Catholics? They're much easier, aren't they? I sometimes envy them. They make life so easy. But then a hard life can mean better rewards, can't it?"

Elder Cran seemed not quite so convinced. He had only been in town for four weeks, spoke very little Korean, and was a little homesick. "It's been three months since I left home. We aren't allowed to see any newspapers or magazines. Tell me what's been going on back home. I saw the cover of a copy of *Time* magazine the other day. But the church doesn't like us to get distracted by the news. I miss it, I must say.

"Still, we must be doing a good thing. We were in that store trying to persuade them to take copies of the Book of Mormon and stock it. We've had it printed in *hangul,* you know. He wasn't too keen. It's a challenge, all right. How many converts have I made? Well, that's difficult to answer. Not many, that's for sure. How do I tell if I've had a good day? Well, I guess if it feels good, it must be good.

"But I like Korea, that's for sure. I always wanted to come to a country like this. South Africa, that's the kind of country I like. Strong, knows what it wants, good police and troops. Korea's like that. They like American power. They're pretty conservative. Strong regimes are just what I like. So Korea's a good place."

We talked in this vein, Harper the self-assured, Cran the uncertain, for a couple of hours. "Sure wish I could join you in a beer. Not allowed. No coffee or tea either." The church hierarchy hadn't taken a position on the acceptability of the two types of tea offered in all Korean restaurants—the *poricha*, or toasted-barley tea, and the *oksusucha*, made from corn—glasses of which are set down without asking the moment you walk in. "So we stick with water. No stimulants. That's the word around here."

We left, and as the pair walked me back to my hotel I came to the uncomfortable realization that we—the café, the hotel, and the lanes in between—were right in the middle of a red-light area. Scores of dingy little bars, all with English names and the strange tautology "Room-Salon" in neon above the door, beckoned to us. Girls licked their lips and pouted and I, eager to see what it was all about, hastened back to where I could drop the elders off. "Disgusting, this," said Elder Cran, the man who liked conservative regimes. "So debased. Surprising, I find it. Do you have this sort of thing in London? I guess you do."

The pair left when I turned into my hotel doorway. "We'll be back tomorrow to go to the *mogyoktang*. You have one in your hotel. It's the one we always use. We have to come—no choice—there aren't any baths in our house." And they pointed to the door of the public bathhouse, steam pouring from it into the cold night air and a few pinkish Koreans walking out, hurrying home before they caught cold.

I waited until they had gone, then walked quickly back up the road to the Room-Salon with what I thought were the prettiest pair of girls. They were all in pairs, usually one standing at the doorway, the other sitting at a table, her short skirt pulled as high up along her thigh as the law and decency allowed. I found one pair that seemed particularly seductive and went inside. The door was slid shut behind me, and one of the girls asked simply: "*Maekju?*" and when I said yes, three large bottles of O.B., and a plate of peanuts and toasted seaweed squares were placed on the table, and the girls got down to business.

It was a brothel, of course, of the very coarsest kind. The girls, on close inspection, were slatternly, but they giggled a lot and had fun trying to teach me some Korean. I liked the phrase "*I shipaloma,*" which has to do with carnality and whoredom, but in which order I could not be sure. I was told never to use it in polite society. I told them one or two choicer phrases in English and then went hard at it trying to convince them that Texas was not in England. Yet it was, they kept saying. "Diana. Queen in Texas. Texas *yong guk.*" Then, it being quite hot in the airless little room, I took off my windcheater, whereupon one of the girls, the perkier of the two, started, with beguiling gentleness, to pluck at the hairs on my forearm, saying all the while to her companion, "Gorilla! Gorilla!" and laughing. She had never seen anything quite like it. Her friend, who was rather thin, laughed a lot and slopped more beer into the glasses. My girlfriend, who had long hair and a degree of buxomness rarely seen in Korea, turned up the cassette recorder, pulled down the blinds, and asked me to dance with her. Sheena Easton, a pretty girl herself who I remembered came from Glasgow and had been turned into a star on the BBC, belted out some dire song, and the Korean girl, who said her name was Anna, danced slowly around the floor, pressing her body tightly against mine and after a minute took my hand and pressed it to her back to prove that she was not wearing any panties.

Then, in quick succession, three things happened. Anna, emboldened by the beer, or perhaps overcome with the doubtful magic of dancing with a gorilla, thrust her hand down the front of my shirt and felt every last detail of my chest. I, emboldened by the beer, and perhaps overcome by dancing with a girl who had wanted me to know she wasn't wearing any panties, thrust my hand down the front of her dress. She was not wearing a bra, and I had a glorious moment feeling her very substantial breasts and feeling their nipples stiffen to my touch.

And then a man walked in. I took my hand away. She took hers away. There were some ill-tempered words muttered by all three of the Koreans in the room, and from somewhere a bill appeared under my nose, and I was asked to pay about twenty American dollars—six or so for the beer and fourteen or so for the seaweed. *Anju, anju,* the girl kept saying, explaining as best she could—and through tears, for she seemed to know she was in some kind of trouble—that the *anju,* the salty appetizers that always come with beer in Korea, were very expensive. And then the doors were opened, and it was suggested that I might like to leave. The cold air pierced me like a knife, and I staggered, somewhat morose and bad-tempered, back to my bed, alone.

❖   ❖   ❖

The following morning I was up at dawn, having slept like a log. The sun was rising into a sky of the clearest eggshell blue. My socks were quite dry. My pack felt lighter than it had for days. I stopped at a stall and bought oranges, chocolate, and a carton of milk and stepped out for the long haul to the city of Kwangju, the capital of the province of South Cholla, and a place that will always be linked—not merely in Korea, but all around the politically conscious world—with the memory of a most savage tragedy. The city of Kwangju, where the face of modern Korean politics was changed for all time by the most terrible of massacres.

CHAPTER

FOUR

"Justice is severely executed among the Coresians, and particularly upon criminals. He that rebels against the King, is destroy'd with all his Race, his Houses are thrown down, and no Man does ever rebuild them, all his Goods forfeited, and sometimes given to some private person. When the King has once made a Decree, if any man is so presumptuous as to make any Objection to it, nothing can protect him from severe Punishment, as we have often seen it executed.

"Among other particulars I remember, that the King being inform'd that his Brother's Wife made great Curiosities at Needlework; he desir'd of her, that she would embroider him a Vest; but that Princess bearing him a mortal Hatred in her Heart, she stich'd in betwixt the Lining and the Out-side some Charms and Characters of such nature, that the King could enjoy no pleasure, nor take any rest while he had that Garment on.

"After he had long study'd to find what might be the cause of it, at last he guess'd at it. He had the Vest rip'd, and found out the cause of his trouble and uneasiness. There was not much time spent in trying that wretched Woman. The King condemn'd her to be shut up in a Room, the Floor whereof was of Brass, and order'd a great Fire to be lighted under it, the Heat whereof tormented her till she dy'd.

"The News of this Sentence being spread abroad through all the Provinces, a near Kinsman of this unhappy Woman, who was Governour of a Town, and in good Esteem at Court for his Birth and good Qualities, ventur'd to write to the King, representing, That a Woman, who had been so highly honour'd as to marry his Majesty's Brother, ought not to die so cruel a Death, and that more Favour should be shown to that Sex.

"The King, incens'd at this Courtier's Boldness, sent for him immediately, and after causing 20 strokes to be given to his Shin-bones, order'd his Head to be cut off."

—HENDRICK HAMEL,
1668

❖ ❖ ❖

Dusk was coming on when I arrived on the outskirts of Kwangju. The warm, still air was drenched with the scent of early jasmine, and the sky was alive with flights of early swallows. But it was far from being a scene of total pastoral peace: Every ninety seconds—I timed the intervals when they seemed so regular—the whole earth shook, the magnolias and cherry trees trembled, and a thick, pounding roar sounded from off to the west. Artillery practice, someone said.

And then the swallows vanished from the sky, and fighter planes screamed low overhead, deafening and maddening all life below. Army trucks, endless convoys of heavy green monsters with their headlights on and with helmeted, masked, and rifle-carrying soldiers standing alert on the back, growled slowly along the roads. The booming of the artillery was endless. Kwangju seemed like a city on the edge of war.

I should have had some early clue as I walked there, through the brilliant morning and the warm, sultry afternoon. Within five miles of Naju the road suddenly widened to perhaps five times its normal width and stretched straight as an arrow for three full miles, with yellow markings and arrows painted on its surface. It was an emergency airfield runway. There are many such in Korea, just as there are in Switzerland, which—like Korea also—has secreted high explosive charges deep inside its bridges and tunnels to protect itself against invasion and the threat of war. Korea's emergency airfields are used regularly, often to the intense chagrin of motorists: Only the day before I had read an announcement in a newspaper saying that the main Seoul-to-Pusan expressway would be closed the next day for six hours so that air force fighters could use it as a landing site. In the interests of national security, the traffic that normally thunders along the country's main artery would have to do as best it could on the country roads.

This runway had clearly been used the night before. Uniformed men were clearing any strings of landing lights from the cabbage fields on either side of the field; and scores of massive steel barricades, the black-and-yellow tiger-striped objects that, as I have said before, have unwittingly become one symbol of modern Korea, were being wheeled back onto the taxiways, closing off the strip to unfriendly craft. I suddenly felt quite insignificantly tiny, walking across this huge frozen ocean of concrete. The sun reflected up from the cement, glaring hotly. I found I had to stop every mile to eat a biscuit and drink a sip of water; perhaps, as a result of my frolic in the Room-Salon, I had become spectacularly unfit, or else an airfield runway is a deceptively exhausting thing along which to walk. Either way, it was a trying couple of hours, especially since passing police cars eyed me oddly, and I wondered if I was not, in fact, allowed to be there at all.

It was altogether much more comfortable to be back on the old road—still Route 1, my diversion now being complete—no matter its narrowness and its congestion. The drivers were still friendly, often stopping to encourage me or offering me lifts (which I feel bound to say I declined, though on steep hillsides I did so with very marked reluctance) and food and drink.

It might perhaps seem, in view of their immense hospitality, rather churlish to remark critically on Koreans' driving. But my strong impression then on the road to Kwangju—and it was an impression that didn't alter very much en route—was that the Korean driver is a very dangerous animal indeed, a beast totally without understanding of speed, pathologically incapable of steering, utterly ignorant of the width of his vehicle, and eternally forgetful of such luxuries as the brakes and mirrors with which his car is invariably equipped. He knows only one device, and that is the horn, on which he seems to spend most of his time sitting, if not standing.

So a Korean road is a noisy place: Horns blare, tires screech, car bodies carom and richochet off each other with wild abandon. On my first day I watched two buses sideswipe each other; between Naju and Kwangju I watched a truck overcook a bend and shed at least a hundred thousand bottles of Coca-Cola, all of which shattered, fertilizing half a dozen *pyong* of grass verge with their strange chemistry; and every day I would see wrecked cars nestling down ravines, in culverts, up trees, and halfway through bridge abutments; and ambulances raced this way and that, sirens sounding, bells ringing. I had seen similarly execrable driving once before, in Turkey; and once in Iran I came upon two buses that had collided head-on and watched forty bodies being carried out onto the sand. But those, in a way, were one-off spectaculars: Here in Korea, the sound of wrenching metal and splintering glass was like a bass continuo, and if you managed your day without getting or giving a dent, or at least a fright, then you were both lucky and statistically unusual.

(I have hired cars on four occasions in Korea. None has been a great success. Once, on Cheju Island, two tires blew out in the first half hour, and the car, duly retreaded, would only steer to the left and insisted on describing large counterclockwise circles in the road. Another time, in Kyongju, a farmer drove his tractor—a three-wheeled microtractor that disrespectful souls call a "rice rocket"—into the side of my car while I was parked and demolished both doors and windows. On a third occasion thick black smoke poured out of the steering column, and when I tried to remove the key the plastic surrounding had melted, welding the engine permanently on. And with the last car, we went over a bump at modest speed, and a door opened and flew off. Having detailed that I am no great fan of the Korean driver, nor of the cars that are given to rental companies, at the risk of diverting from the main topic, it is only fair to add for the record the peculiarly Korean style of Article 2 of the General Principles of Our Company, as written on the back of the form from one of the firms from whom I had rented a car: ". . . we shall operate this business on the principle of *Kindness,* and shall make our best Efforts to provide Safety and Convenience to the Renter, with the Service devoted to the Renter in the Spirit of Trust and Sincerity."

This was on the form handed to me by the pretty girl whose car had smoke pouring from its steering column. She seemed near tears when I told her of the vehicle's fate, and she bowed many times and then offered to pay for the whole thing herself.)

Route 1 turned north after the runway and crossed a range of hills that were higher and longer than any I had crossed so far. By now it was a hot day, and I was exhausted when I reached the top. I sat down to rest by a railway embankment overlooking the next valley. The peace was profound and quite lovely. I had come well away from the road, and the only sounds I could hear were birdsong and the distant desperation of a baby goat crying for its mother. The earth was warm, the grass was moist and fresh and the palest of greens, the embankment was covered with newly blooming forsythia and wild cherry. Down in the valley below, the roofs of the houses presented a many-colored checkerboard, orange and blue and yellow, above the whitewash of the walls. Once in a while a small local train hummed past—for this was not the main line but a branch line to places like Hwasun and Polgyo, a line for the nearby farmers and smallholders, not for the businessmen bound between Seoul and Pusan—and its passengers waved pleasantly at me. I lay back in the sweet-smelling grass, serenely pleased with life, and slept contentedly for a while in the afternoon sun.

Most of the rest of the journey was downhill. I could see another runway off to my left, and a cloud of air force jets, tiny as gnats, were wheeling above it. In the first village through which I passed an elderly woman was trying in vain to get a sack of potatoes up onto her head and asked me for help. Once I had settled it—and it must have weighed fifty pounds, at least—on the small plait of straw that served as a cushion between scalp and spuds, she stood erect and tripped along quite merrily, singing to herself and waving her thanks. If I had seemed foreign to her, she clearly had not minded in the slightest. Nor had she seemed to mind the burden, which would have broken the backs of most healthy adult males.

Her village was a pretty little place, twenty or so cottages grouped round a dusty little square, each one home to a family of hardscrabble farmers who eked a living from the nearby rice fields or in the apple orchards. One aspect of the village was unusual, though it made it prettier still: Many of the houses had thatched roofs, thick mats of straw curled over the gable ends, tied down with twine, and weighted with stones. President Park Chung-hee, who did more than most Korean presidents to raise the national morale and self-esteem, decreed that thatched roofs were a stigma of underdevelopment and ordered a nationwide campaign to replace thatch with tile. In the rest of the country most thatch has gone; but here, down in Cholla, where they are said to loathe the government with vigor and venom, a lot of it has stayed, both as a defiant symbol of Cholla independence and because it is warm, cheap, and handsome. And it provides a home for harvest mice, which Koreans regard with affection and as a sign of good luck.

The night before I had been listening to the BBC World Service, and through the scratchy reception—sunspots, as usual!—had listened to a documentary—a radio portrait, it had been called—about Korea. It was nothing very substantial—a thirty-minute recital of political problems and assorted economic miracles. I didn't remember much, although one statistic stood out: By the end of the century, one of those interviewed had said, every Korean would enjoy a standard of living equivalent to that of the British middle classes today (an achievement that some cynical Britons would find rather less than staggering). I was in the old lady's village when I remembered this remark, and I noted in my book that I doubted it very much.

I doubted it because of a strong impression I had been forming from all my visits to Korea, and particularly from my visits to the countryside. The life of the urban Korean was changing with unprecedented rapidity, without a doubt; but out here, far from the influences of city life, the ancient, Confucian rhythms were being preserved—and the economic simplicities that went with them. Poor villages—no one ever hungry but no one with a compact-disc player, either—are strung along the length and breadth of Korea, and within them are hundreds of thousands of ordinary Koreans for whom the goal of middle-class British life is not only unattainable but also profoundly undesirable. It would be condescending to say that the Koreans are a people who admire what some writers about India call the "dignity of poverty." Quite the

reverse: The Koreans are an ambitious, hardworking people, perhaps more hardworking than any I have ever encountered and ever will. They want to improve their lot. They want, desperately, to improve their children's lot. They will work all the hours God gives them to provide a good education for their offspring—no sacrifice is too much for a Korean father to make, no hours too long for a Korean mother to work, if only the child is well educated, is given a better chance, a better series of opportunities.

But at the same time there are those Koreans, both old and young—and the fact that young Koreans are included is important—who have as a conscious ambition a desire to preserve the essence of their lives and are thoughtful enough to care to resist the seductive charms of change. I mentioned that when I arrived in Mokpo, it reminded me of a small Greenland fishing village I had once seen. It reminded me in more ways than one. It was in that Arctic town, ten years or so ago, that I first encountered the keenness of young Greenlanders to resist the devilry of the modern and preserve the simpler delights of the old. The Koreans—not all of them, by a long chalk, but many— seem to feel the same way. They know that Seoul is only a few hours away and that there are chromium and glass and glitter and money and power there, and they appreciate the magnetism of it all. But they know also that what they have in these small villages—and yes, they also have electricity and direct-dial telephones, and I know one man in a thatched cottage who keeps a facsimile machine next to his kimchi pots—is as worth preserving as the modern world is worth exploring. Perhaps, I thought, I would meet someone along the road who would explain it more succinctly. For now, all I knew was that a laudable—if barely audible—radio documentary purporting to present the nature of a country's soul had inadvertently succeeded in missing its very essence.

As I left the village I saw a clothesline strung between two of the gently uptilted gable ends. It was a perfectly ordinary clothesline, hung with perfectly ordinary clothes—until I looked a little more closely. Hanging from it, from left to right, were, according to my notes, "Shirt, trousers (blue), shirt, fish, vest, underpants, two fish, skirt, trousers (brown), fish, octopus, vest, shirt, fish, vest, vest."

And then I hauled up another long hill, and there, smoking gently in the evening sun, was the great southwestern city of Kwangju.

The Dutch sailors had not bothered to call at Kwangju; they spent the fourth night of their odyssey twenty miles to the west, in Changsong (that, at least, seems to be the town nearest in pronunciation to the place Hamel calls "Sang-siang"). Today's guidebooks do not exactly paint an alluring portrait of Kwangju: "Kwangju . . . is a low-key city," reports one; "the entire area is remote . . . the city boasts two universities, three newspapers and three radio stations," is all that can be found in another. The fifth-largest city in Korea, a sprawling, roughhewn giant of a place, it remains perhaps one of the better-known Korean cities outside the capital. And I felt compelled to walk there,

even though the sailors had not, because of its unique standing in the country's modern history.

The reason for its fame or, more properly, its notoriety, stems from a week of events that started on the evening of Saturday, May 17, 1980, on the campus of Chonnam University, which nestles in the shadow of a mighty range of hills on the north side of town.

It is worth remarking on the context. Six months before, on October 26, 1979, President Park Chung-hee had been assassinated in a *kisaeng* house in Seoul by his Director of Central Intelligence, Kim Tae-kyu. (There had been a famously lovely singer at the *kisaeng* house—the Korean equivalent of, though rather less proper than, the geisha house—that night, performing for President Park. But after the sudden interruption to her cabaret she mysteriously vanished from the city, and when she reappeared six months later, she had, unaccountably, no memory of where she had been nor any recollection of the events that were said to have taken place during her last performance. There was talk about brainwashing, and the girl became something of a cult singer for a while.)

The assassin Kim, who was later executed, said he killed Park because he opposed the crackdown on dissent that the president had ordered some months before—dissent that had erupted after the world rise in oil prices had started to cause serious economic difficulties in Korea and had stimulated popular protests. A swingeing set of martial law regulations was immediately promulgated throughout much of the country—regulations that effectively gave plenary powers to the army commanders and led directly to the quasi-military dictatorship that exists in Korea today.

From the morning after the assassination the National Assembly was dissolved; all political meetings and activities were banned in designated areas; there were to be no assemblies of any kinds other than weddings, funerals, ancestral rituals, and religious ceremonies—and in the case of those four exceptions, no political statements of any kind were to be made. All press and television and radio broadcasts were to be rigorously censored. All colleges and universities were shut down; strikes and unexcused absences from work were forbidden; the spreading of rumors was banned; and there was to be no defamation or slander of any present or past officials of the Korean government.

During the early part of the winter the political atmosphere inside Korea, despite the withering power of these regulations, became strangely effervescent. A stand-in president, a civilian, was in power. He had made speeches promising to return the country to democracy. There was much excited discussion over glasses of *soju* and tumblers of *makkoli* about the possibility of a return to Korea's old civilian constitution and the likelihood of Korea weaning itself from its apparent love affair with political brutality. And, as if they

sensed the public mood, the military commanders who had been so much in evidence during Park's reign slipped briefly into the shadows.

But only briefly. In a move in mid-December that was to have lasting significance in modern Korean history, General Chun Doo-Hwan, commander of the Army Security Command and the man appointed to investigate Park's assassination, took a step that guaranteed him a reputation for dangerous unpredictability: He ordered a number of frontline battalions and special forces units from the Ninth Infantry Division to come off their border duties (to the anger of the American general who was the titular commander of the country's military) and march down to Seoul. There, after a spectacular shoot-out, Chun arrested thirty generals as well as no less a figure than the army chief of staff and, to the amazement of everyone concerned, charged him and his brother officers with complicity in Park's murder. From that moment on, General Chun, a balding, bespectacled, even rather gentle-looking man, effectively ran Korea, and the civilian president was president in name alone. It has been the same ever since, with generals and colonels in mufti running the country under the guise of a civilian democracy.

Those who had been so optimistic about a return to a democratic constitution—the country's intellectuals and students and trade unionists—were bitterly disappointed and later enraged. They staged demonstrations that were put down with great ferocity. The government extended martial law to the entire country and made it clear it would tolerate no further dissent. On the evening of Saturday, May 17, in line with its policy of rooting out all sources of discontent, squads of police and militia raided the homes of student leaders and known organizers of the democratic movement at Chonnam *Taehakkyo*, one of the two Kwangju universities. They did not know it at the time, but they had caught a tiger by its tail.

The students reacted; the government brought in fresh troops, and paratroopers; the entire population of Kwangju—people who in ordinary circumstances would never have considered taking to the streets—embarked on a rebellion, and for the best part of a week the city was run by its very own communards, a law unto itself. And then the troops retook Kwangju, and there was even more bloodshed. Four distinct incidents—the student riots, the troops' reaction, the people's rebellion, and the official revenge—are now welded into one. What you call it depends on where you stand in Korean politics. It is either the Kwangju uprising, the Kwangju massacre, the Kwangju rebellion, or the Kwangju incident. Whatever the semantics, the events of those seven days in May have left scars on the Korean psyche like no event since the 1950 war.

I was not present at the Kwangju incident, of course. But many of the people who offered me their hospitality were, and they remember with great sadness, and often great anger, the small tesserae of tragedy that they witnessed: "I was coming home from shopping that Saturday afternoon, and I saw a great commotion. I went up to the crowd, and I saw a number of paratroopers getting on and off a stopped bus. After a while I realized what they were doing. They were looking up and down the bus aisle, searching for anyone under about thirty. The moment they saw such a person, they'd haul him off the bus, frogmarch him down the aisle, kicking and abusing him. Then they'd throw him off the bus into the hands of other soldiers, who would beat him and tie his hands behind his back—with barbed wire! After a while they'd get everyone they wanted off the bus, and they'd let it go and then stop the next one. The students would be beaten and kicked, and then they were put into an unmarked truck, and taken off—goodness knows where.''

I heard dozens of reports like that, and I heard of dozens of killings, too, of youngsters brought into hospitals bearing evidence of the most appalling violence. But my stay in Kwangju, fascinating though it was, did not give me a good enough overall picture of what was, in fact, a very complicated event. I am thus quoting verbatim from a report which I believe to be accurate, and which my Kwangju hosts believe to be a fair distillation, too. It was written by a group of Americans from the Washington-based organization Asia Watch and was published five years after the dust had settled on a city that can fairly be described as Korea's Sharpeville (or Amritsar or Londonderry or, for the more romantic souls, Concord Bridge).

On May 19 more trouble started when a crowd estimated at three to five thousand filled the downtown streets and clashed with police. The demonstrators threw stones, Molotov cocktails and sticks, and the police responded with tear and pepper gas. Then at 10:30 in the morning about a thousand Special Forces troops were brought in. They repeated the same actions as the day before, beating, stabbing and mutilating unarmed civilians, including children, young girls, and aged grandmothers. They forced both men and women to strip naked, made others lie flat on the ground and kicked them. Several sources tell of soldiers stabbing or cutting off the breasts of naked girls; one murdered student was found disemboweled, another with an X carved in his back. About twenty high school girls were reported killed at Central High School. The paratroopers carried out searches in side streets, firing randomly into crowds, carted off the bodies in trucks, and piled them in the bus terminal. They even took the wounded out of hospitals. Ten high school students were killed in front of the Kaerim police box. The troopers chased two hundred students into the Catholic Center and then invaded the building and killed over a hundred. They had virtually declared open season on anyone under thirty, arresting and beating any they found on the streets. A dozen students were killed on the roof of the Kumyong building and thrown off. A student was roped to a personnel carrier and dragged through the streets.

When a mother protested the teasing of her daughter by troops, both were shot dead on the spot. Eleven persons were killed in front of the Hyundai theater. In one famous case, the troops killed four taxi drivers for transporting students throughout the city (the drivers' union then joined the demonstrations). They even threatened and beat ordinary police who were trying to help the injured lying bleeding and unconscious on the streets. One police officer urged people over a megaphone to return home lest the martial law troops catch and kill them.

The violence only served to inflame the feelings of the people . . . and sometime during May 20 the students and citizens of Kwangju began to seize weapons from abandoned police stations to defend themselves against the troops, and the sound of rifle fire was heard throughout the city. The state of insurrection continued throughout the evening as demonstrators succeeded in taking over Kwangju City Hall, smashing the equipment of the KBS broadcasting station, setting fire to the MBC television station, and occupying a number of police boxes, police and fire stations. While clashes were continuing downtown the troops divided up and conducted house-to-house searches, beating and killing even more people. One account estimated several dozen killed and a hundred wounded at Chonnam University alone; another source estimated 200 dead and a thousand injured throughout the city; one reporter personally counted 200 bodies himself, so the death rate was undoubtedly higher: many estimates now put the death toll at 2,000. The reporter who saw the bodies was told by a captured paratrooper that these troops had been hardened for three days by food deprivation, and just prior to their arrival had been given drugged liquor. Officers told these men they were putting down a communist uprising, and chose only those from Kyongsang province as if to give license to discriminatory violence against the Cholla people on the basis of traditional regional prejudice.

[And so it continues, horror piled upon horror.] At about 1 P.M. on May 21, riot troops began firing into thousands of demonstrators marching towards the provincial administration building . . . urban warfare broke out at 6:30 in the evening . . . students mounted a machine gun on the roof of the Chonnam University medical school . . . two regiments of special forces troops from the Twentieth Division were moved from the front lines on the demilitarized zone to engage in the fighting.

It was the decision to move forces south from the DMZ that was to leave one of the greatest legacies of bitterness. The American commander in chief would have been bound, it is assumed, to have given permission to General Chun to withdraw men from the frontline defense of the realm and send them to help "clean up" Kwangju. By giving his permission the American commander, and by association his government, became knowing accomplices in the tragedy. The American government has consistently denied any foreknowledge of the events in Kwangju and has said with certainty that its task is to protect Korea from external threat and that it would never be directly involved in dealing with a civil matter. As to whether it did, despite this caveat, become involved in Kwangju, spokesmen have always offered rather ambiguous explanations. Korean radicals have never believed the Americans, and the growing anti-American sentiment in South Korea—a phenomenon I was to encounter a number of times during the coming days—largely stems from their somewhat questionable role in the mournful events of May 1980.

❖ ❖ ❖

An attractive young woman named Ki Hwe Ran showed me around Kwangju one Saturday morning. She had been eighteen at the time of the insurrection and remembered it well. She would point at this building, and down that street, at that memorial, and into that hall, and talk graphically of what she remembered. "The bodies they piled in here!" she said, as we pushed open the doors of a large gymnasium, where a horde of small boys in white cotton suits were performing the balletic steps of a *taekwon-do* lesson. "They rolled back the mats, and lay at least a hundred in here. On the Monday, it was. The blood was all over the floor." It seemed hard to believe—or at least, it did until the chilling moment when the boys in the class, in unison and at a barked command from their instructor, suddenly adopted the *palsae*, the "picking fortress out" fighting posture, and the air of Saturday morning gave way briefly to one of martial menace. Then, it suddenly seemed, the Koreans were quite capable of any beastliness imaginable.

"They're so like the Irish," someone had said to me back in Cheju. "They're sweet and sentimental. They're sad. They sing songs, and sad songs, too. But if you get them angry, you'll be terrified. They have a kind of anger that is unforgettable. They completely lose control of themselves. They've no idea what they are doing. It's a frightening sight. Never make a Korean angry. You'll come off worse if you do."

Miss Ki was going off that Saturday afternoon, taking the bus to Seoul to go shopping (another depressing indication of how quickly I could be back in the capital if only I would abandon this lunacy of walking). "But I want to show you their graves," she said, and we hailed a taxi and took off for the municipal cemetery.

The driver was none too eager to go. It was a long way out of town and besides, he whined, only troublemakers went there. Nonsense, said the plucky Miss Ki (and time and again it seemed to be the Korean women who displayed the pluck and initiative—a uniquely liberated group, when tradition permits them to be). Nonsense, she said. This foreign traveler, this stranger, had heard about Kwangju, and had heard the cemetery was beautiful, and wanted to see it. Why not, indeed? The driver slumped his shoulders in resignation, for to be impolite to a foreigner was, in pre-Olympic years, simply not done. He demanded *man won*—*man* being ten thousand—for the journey, and set off to the north and miles out into the countryside.

The cemetery was majestically sited in a bowl-shaped depression in the hills. To the south was Mudung Mountain, which Buddhist monks regard as blessed, and where they grow a special tea that is scented with persimmons and that they steam and dry nine times, but only in the very early morning when the dew is on the grass and the valleys are hidden by mist. The graves—thousands upon thousands, the ranks of neat, identical stones marching along the neat grass like a cemetery for the dead of war—are thus ideally placed, on holy ground and in especially fragrant air.

But only a very few of the graves belonged to the youngsters killed in the incident, and we wanted to see them. An elderly sexton, looking suitably miserable and suspicious, shuffled up from his hut. Miss Ki asked him where the students were buried. What students? We have no students. Miss Ki reminded him. He recalled, if vaguely. Why did we want to see such things? We were not relatives, were we? Miss Ki put her foot down. We had come a long way. The Westerner was interested in history. What happened in Kwangju was history, was it not? And so, under the combination of persuasive bludgeon and cajoling bastinado, the sexton eventually concurred and led us to a small patch of raised ground in a far corner of the cemetery. At this point another man, who seemed to have been hiding behind a tree, came up and asked Miss Ki a number of questions, which ended with her agreeing to give her identity card number and my passport number. "So they can make sure we don't have any more trouble," she explained, winsomely, not believing a word of it.

The graves of the massacred students were no different from the others—the same eighteen-inch-high tablets of gray granite, carved with Chinese characters and set a precise two feet apart. There were 124 of them, and the only oddity appeared when I managed to transliterate the dates. Most of the dead had been born in the late 1950s. But all had died on the same day, May 24, 1980. That was the Saturday when the troops retook the town, and General Chun was able to say that the "Communist uprising"—for that was how all Seoul, and all Korea, first remembered it—was over.

No one knows, or ever will know, how many died. Lurid rumors still circulate about hidden graves, lime pits, quarries that have long since been cemented over. It is commonly believed that the 1980 bills of mortality for Kwangju show 2,600 deaths—2,000 more than the average. It is therefore commonly believed that 2,000 people died during the insurrection, and whether or not the exact numbers matter very much, the thought that the government saw fit to lie about them compounds, in the eyes of most critics, the felony.

(And numbers really do not matter: The facts that 2,000 Indians probably died in the Jallianwalla Bagh, and 60 black South Africans died at Sharpeville, and just 13 Northern Irish Catholics died in the Bogside are unimportant as mere statistics. The places became symbols of tragedy and political change—and so has Kwangju, whether the 191 officially admitted to have died is the correct figure or whether it is 1,000 or 2,000 or half the civilian population. Kwangju is a part of Korean history, just like Panmunjom and Inchon and Pusan and the Yalu River, and the memory of what happened there may evolve and transmute into legend, but will never be rubbed away.)

Miss Ki and I drove back to town, and I put her on a bus for the capital and promised to write. "England is my fantasy," she said. "I will not forget you." And I went back to the hostel where I had put up and switched on the television and watched the news on AFKN, the U.S. armed forces network.

My notebook records the first item that amused me. President Chun—the General Chun of Kwangju, the man who ordered the troopers in—had that afternoon been visiting an American army base "somewhere in Korea" (the announcers never say where). There were many pictures of the president looking intently at artillery pieces and air defense radars and self-propelled howitzers, and then there was an interview with an American GI. His name was Private Bradley Hackenburger, and he solemnly intoned the thought that "it is a great day for U.S.–Korea relations when the president of this country shows such an interest in American technology." It all sounded very droll.

❖   ❖   ❖

If Kwangju effected a profound change on the face of Korean politics—by halting the slow return to democracy and reinstalling, at least for the time being, military officers in positions of near-absolute power—it also concealed the seeds of what seems likely to be an even more profound change in the nation's body politic. For the incident made a world-class hero—or an anti-hero, depending upon your point of view—of a middle-aged opposition politician, hitherto little known beyond the shores of Korea, named Kim Dae Jung.

Kim Dae Jung was from the Korean southwest—one of Father McGlinchey's "absolute bastards" of Cholla, an obstinate, fiery, argumentative firebrand of a man, a spellbinding orator, who very nearly toppled President Park when he ran against him in the national election of 1971 and had been marked down as a troublemaker ever since. The Korean Central Intelligence Agency and the secret police, the *angibu,* had their eyes firmly trained upon him, and in 1973, while he was touring through Japan attempting to solicit support for the restoration of democracy in his country, they kidnapped him.

The incident, so spectacularly similar to the kind of madness perpetrated by agents of North Korea, and thus, one might say, so typically Korean, has passed into legend. Agents of the KCIA burst into his Tokyo hotel, blindfolded and gagged Kim with a chunk of wood, put him aboard a small boat, and took him out to sea. He probably would have been murdered, except that there was worldwide uproar. His captors evidently had a change of orders: The boat put about and landed Kim in Korea; the men escorted him to his house and let him go.

In spite of this extraordinary experience, Kim, who is a persistent and courageous man, remained a thorn in the government's side. He spoke out vehemently when, in the wake of Park's assassination, it became clear that General Chun was wresting power away from the civilian presidency. It was thus not altogether surprising that in the aftermath of the Kwangju tragedy, General Chun ordered Kim—whose political power base was in and around the city—to be arrested and charged with fomenting the uprising. Kim, the general's prosecutors said, had links with the North Korean regime, was himself the next best thing to an active Communist, and had organized the rebellion at Kwangju in an effort to bring down the entire South Korean government.

The trial was a farce. Alleged co-conspirators were tortured to extract "confessions." Kim was accused of bribing men to become his followers, of having medals struck with his image on the obverse, of handing out ballpoint pens inscribed with his name, "of behaving as if he were a head of state." Old records, claiming his involvement in subversive activities in the 1940s (though he was never charged) were paraded before the members of the martial law tribunal; his remark that he supported a federal solution to the problems of the divided Korean Peninsula was used to support the contention that he was a die-hard Communist—simply because Kim Il Sung, the North Korean leader, was a federalist as well. He was accused of fomenting the trouble in Kwangju, of paying the student leaders and persuading them to demonstrate and riot, and—worst of all, considering that his supposed allegation has since been manifestly proven as the truth—of putting around the story that Chun's paratroops in Kwangju had mutilated the bodies of women they had killed.

The verdict was a foregone conclusion. The martial law tribunal found Kim guilty, and the soldiers sentenced him to death. And so the man about whom the world was largely ignorant came to enjoy, almost overnight, the semi-mythic status of a Nelson Mandela or a Ninoy Aquino—a status, cynics would later say, that bore little relation to the actual character of the man.

The realities of global politics intervened, and Kim Dae Jung was not executed. Just before President Chun left for an official tour of the United States in January 1981, the sentence—which the American government had bitterly criticized—was commuted to life imprisonment and then commuted again to twenty years. Finally, just before Christmas 1982, and after intense negotiations between Washington and Seoul, Kim was freed and "permitted" to go to the United States for "medical treatment"—his sentence remaining in force and liable to reinstatement should he transgress once again. Other defendants in the Kwangju conspiracy trial and 1,158 ordinary criminals were freed as well— all part of a determined attempt by President Chun to give liberal credibility to a regime that, it was widely acknowledged, had further stained Korea's ugly reputation around the world. Economic miracle-state though it might be, the public perception of Korea and its leadership was just as the villain Oddjob was personified in the James Bond films—a cruel, harsh, and ruthless country and people, utterly merciless in their corporate pursuit of wealth, power, and national pride.

The reputation was hardly enhanced when Kim Dae Jung returned from America in February 1985, four days before a general election (in which Kim could not, since he was banned from politics, participate). He did not suffer, as some had feared, the fate of Senator Aquino, who was murdered at Manila Airport, probably by agents of then-President Marcos; but heavily armed goons from the KCIA barged aside the official welcoming party, including senior American officials, and rushed him home and into house arrest. The goons' purpose was plain: They wanted to deny the thousands who had come to greet Kim the opportunity of seeing him and of voicing their support for his politics and their opposition to those of the coterie of generals who ran the country from Seoul's highly fortified and ruthlessly protected Blue House.

And so for a while Kim lapsed into the kind of notorious obscurity that is the natural corollary of house arrest. His elegant little villa in a lane in central Seoul was constantly surrounded by secret policemen, and anyone entering or leaving was photographed. I was: I went to see him on a number of occasions, as did many foreign visitors to Seoul. I have pleasant memories of slightly bizarre interviews, conducted over breakfasts of seaweed soup and *kimchi*, while his beloved Chihuahua dogs fought each other noisily under the table and took small chunks out of my toes. Kim would talk, as Mrs. Aquino (whom Kim knew—they had met in the United States) would talk at about the same time down in the Philippines, of the possibilities of restoring democracy in Korea; and he would issue pleas for the world to stay away from the Olympic Games or to take a more active interest in the menacing behavior of the Chun regime.

Often he would lead me downstairs to his study—thousands of books, many in English, a catholic collection indeed, from John Stuart Mill to Bertrand Russell, Henry Kissinger to Mencius, and C. S. Lewis to Arthur Schlesinger, Jr.—and write a calligraphical souvenir of my visit. He would write my name and the date—"early summer, 1986"—and then ask me to choose from a card with suitable aphorisms such as, "There is no freedom without a free press" and "No greater love have I than a love of free speech." Whichever I had selected he would then write on the card. My abiding memory is of Kim swathed in gray Korean silks, hunched over his calligraphy table, writing quickly with a thick black brush that he occasionally dipped into a puddle of heavy ink on its obsidian palette. It was always a rather charming moment, though rather contrived—good for public relations, perhaps, but a gesture that was more transparent than might be suitable for a really great politician.

But whether he is a transparent politician or not, Kim's time may yet come. The anniversary of the Kwangju uprising in mid-May has invariably, in past years, triggered serious trouble for the Korean security forces: Riots and protest marches were always staged in the dead students' memories, though Kim himself was never allowed to attend. In May 1987, however, shortly after I had walked through the town, there was an eruption of violence on a scale never experienced before, and it spread through the country like a forest fire.

The ostensible reason for this quite extraordinary inferno of protest—beyond, that is, the simple and almost routine commemoration of Kwangju—was that President Chun had refused to make even the most elementary concessions to popular demands for democratic reform, and had named General Roh Tae Woo, one of his army colleagues (and another figure notorious for his own involvement in putting down the Kwangju uprising), as his successor for the presidency.

The furor that resulted turned out to be uncontainable. No matter how many tons of tear gas were hurled about, no matter how many and how violent were the baton charges, and no matter how many thousands were arrested, the Chun regime's forces could not hold the ring. (They could have shot to kill, of course, but the world's television cameras, hurried up from their semipermanent firebases in Manila, were relaying the horrors to Trinitrons and Zeniths across the face of the earth, and Korea's public image was already taking a terrible hammering.)

In midsummer the generals blinked. The new presidential nominee himself, outflanking General Chun, announced a massive and unprecedented package of reforms: There would be free elections in 1987, before the Olympic Games; the press would be unshackled to report as it liked; and, most important in this context, the activities of Mr. Kim Dae Jung could be fully reported in these papers (up to then he went almost unreported, an officially decreed nonperson) and, should his supporters so desire, he could be a candidate in the polls.

And so Kim, the modest little man (as his supporters would have it) whom Presidents Park and Chun had had variously kidnapped, arrested, sentenced to death, exiled, placed for many months under house arrest, and discredited as a Communist, an agent of Kim Il Sung, and a corrupt, base, and venal crook—this Mr. Kim was now in the lists at last. One day, some thought, he might well lead the country, and all, historians will be sure to note, because of the tragic events—and Kim's alleged role in organizing them—that took place in May 1980 in this rather ugly and undistinguished southern city of Kwangju.

❖   ❖   ❖

My host during my stay in the city was a psychiatrist, an Irishman whom I shall call O'Neill, a small, birdlike man and a very voluble one. "I've analyzed this country *exactly*," he declared within minutes of my arrival, after he had me sitting in front of his fire with a cup of tea. "Tell me, do you know Maslow?" I confessed I did not, although I muttered something about having gone to Oxford with someone named that, only to remember his name was Masri, and he was one of a pair of Lebanese twins. O'Neill—everyone addressed him thus, and I never heard his first name or any title—explained, probably writing me off as a fool as he did so. Apparently someone named Abraham Maslow had written a book, a work of biblical authority in the dark world of psychiatry, on the hierarchical needs of man. It illustrated the condition of Korea perfectly, O'Neill went on.

"The needs are these. First, a baby has a *physiological* need. He needs food, he needs milk. Then he realizes he needs something to hold on to—he needs *security*. Following me? Next, when he becomes a teenager, he needs *love*. Then he needs *self-esteem*—that's when he becomes ambitious, tries to accumulate things that make him feel good about himself. And then he needs *growth*—he must expand his family, his interest, his influence on the world. Do you see?"

I wasn't exactly sure that I did, thinking that maybe it all sounded too neatly tied up, but for the sake of O'Neill's theory—and because I knew nothing about the mysteries of this new science of national psychiatry—I held my tongue. The fire chuckled in the grate. Other doctors came in, then heard O'Neill in midpropounding and fell silent or hid behind their month-old copies of the English papers.

"It's just the same with Korea. First, after the war, she needed *physiological* things. She had to feed her people, keep them warm. So it was all rice, imported wheat, getting the coal mines open again, getting the *yontan* factories back into production. Next—see how this all works?—she wanted to fix up her *security*, build up the army, make sure the Communists could never surprise them again. Okay, on we go—then it was *love*, the *love needs*, I call them. It's building hospitals and schools and universities—not luxuries, not essentials, but things to show that the state, or society, call it what you will, loves the people—things that make the people love the society.

"Now we're into the *self-esteem* phase of Korea's needs. She wants to feel good about herself. So she gets the Asian Games here. She gets the Olympics. She sends her cars to America. She exports TV sets to Britain. She feels proud, she has a sense of swaggering about a bit. A long way from the war, eh?

"And then, once the self-esteem is all in the bag, she'll go for *growth*. She'll consolidate what she's got and build on it, making herself richer and more stable, so that she can have any of the other things as and when she wants them. If she wants to build a hospital or raise a regiment or stage a motorcycling race, she can. But she needs to grow to be sure she can.

"That's it. That's the theory. What do you think? Good, eh? Countries just like humans. Q.E.D."

A few moments later O'Neill went on to quote, approvingly, Patrick Pearse's comment that education was "the murder machine." He was an unconventionalist, at the very least.

He has run his psychiatric clinic—it is funded by donations from abroad—for the last twenty years. He was in consequence utterly absorbed by the nature of the Oriental mind and how society dealt with it when it went awry. "There's been so little study of the mind here. Do you know how many psychiatrists there are? Just three hundred, and that in a country of more than forty million. That's nothing. They were developing a healthy interest until the Japanese came. They crushed it totally, and it hasn't recovered yet.

"Okay, I can hear you saying that they don't need psychiatry because they're mentally healthy people. Well they're not, not as healthy as you might like to think. They don't have the tensions that the Westerners do, that's true. But as things get more modern, they have problems, and they have no way at all to deal with them. It's all tied up with face, this ghastly Oriental thing that hamstrings everything. Face—they mustn't lose it. No public shame. No embarrassment. And that means—in my field, anyway—that if you've someone in your family who's got a problem, a mental problem, you just don't admit it exists. You lock it away somehow. Literally—you lock a mentally ill person in his room and pretend he doesn't exist. Oh sure, sometimes they have to come here, because they are really so sick, and people know we exist and think we might be able to do the trick. But I have seen them dumped on our doorsteps, trussed up in ropes, tied up like parcels. They used to think mental illness was the curse of the devil—what am I saying, used to? They still think so. They either dismiss it totally—you simply aren't allowed to be depressed, you aren't allowed to have neuroses—or else they get terribly hostile about it and think it brings shame and a loss of face to the whole family, and they reject it. That's when it lands on my doorstep, trussed up like a chicken. And that's if they're lucky. I know many parents of girls who have problems, and they tell them they've got to kill themselves rather than bring shame on the family. I tell you, face is a terrible thing."

John Gunther, when he wrote his essays about the East for American audiences half a century ago, used to grumble about face. He once wrote an article about Shanghai and the certainty that the Chinese would have problems if they threw the foreigners out (the revolutionary breeze was blowing then, and Gunther could feel it and knew what damage it might do). They suffered from many disadvantages, he thought, but the most exasperating of all was face. Face meant you'd never take a risk, never take an intellectual gamble, a stab in the dark, since by failing you would lose your face and suffer shame and ridicule. So, if the tenets of the revolution forced them to reject all foreign influence, there would never be a Chinese Thomas Edison or a Chinese Henry Ford or a Chinese Albert Einstein. And as with China, so with Korea.

How many times have I heard in conversation: ". . . and then he made me lose my face"? To a Korean, there can be no greater anguish. The young woman with whom I had argued so strenuously back on Cheju Island had lost her face—her *myonmok*—in the exchange. The fact of losing the argument was of no consequence by comparison. If you see a Korean on a golf course, do not approach him, no matter how dreadful his play might be, and advise him on how he might improve matters; he would be deeply offended, and you would be deeply wrong. "To lose face is bad," Confucius is supposed to have said. "To make someone lose face is unforgivable."

The Confucian deal, in a society like Korea's where Confucianism is still widely followed, is a simple one: If people will agree to forget their individuality and concentrate on their duties, then they can be guaranteed that they will be treated with respect and kindness by all. Self-abnegation is bargained, in other words, for universal respect. Happiness is to be gained through human things, coming to terms with oneself, one's family, one's community.

The modern world, which has Korea firmly in its grasp, offers a very different deal. Self-abnegation has been replaced by self-assertion. Human relationships, respect for elders, certainty of place in society—all these things are being overlooked today, and Koreans, like the rest of us, search for happiness through the purchase of goods and services, the quest for material pleasure and success.

The two systems, the material and the Confucian, sit uneasily together. The assaults on Confucian values result in many more frequent tribulations among those who still cling to traditional ways—and deep within themselves most Koreans do, for a myriad of reasons—because of their upbringing, their fondness for their country, and for reasons of sentiment and faith. "He made me lose my face" is heard more often these days simply *because* of the disharmonies between the two systems. We hear of cases—O'Neill had a number of them as patients—of what is called *maum sang hada*: a state of mental anguish over the loss of face that can make its victim want to give up, to throw in the towel, to retreat from society and hide in shame. You hear tales of people wasting away and dying, so severe is their shame.

Which, then, is the better of the two systems? Is a life of self-abnegation, respect for others, a sense of duty, and correct behavior more worthy than a life of self-assertion, of total freedom, of "looking out for Number One"? Or, put another way, is a society that is liberally stuffed with Edisons and Fords and Einsteins, and with depressives and murderers and alcoholics—is that approaching the ideal? Or do we have a more fulfilled society when all is carefully structured social harmony, where the *jen* and the *yi*, the *yin* and the *yang*, are in near-perfect equilibrium, where no one raises his voice, and every parent is revered by every child, where the elders are cared for, children are adored, imagination and innovation and invention are feared rather than favored, and the individual is forgotten?

There is no easy answer, for both systems have their attractions and both their ugliness. I had a letter waiting for me in Kwangju, from an English friend, a bright diplomat who had been fond of Korea for many years. "I am now seriously hoping," he wrote, "that I can retire to Cheju-do and live out my life in studied Confucian idleness." I could see what he meant. Others would opt for a compromise, and yet compromise, too, is fraught with complication. It is too easy simply to advocate the middle way, to hope for an eventual mixture of Western and Confucian values. The experiences of men like O'Neill would suggest that the two simply do not mix and that to impose Western material values on societies, on human beings, that have become adjusted over generations to wholly different sets of values, is to court danger. The clinical cases that O'Neill and his fellow doctors see in the hospitals and clinics in Kwangju are, they say, the tiniest indications of a deeper malaise, a sickness deeply rooted in a society that is perhaps rather more unhappy within itself than it might at first appear.

❖   ❖   ❖

On my final day in Kwangju one of the doctors who was making a house call dropped me at the front gates of the American air force base that lies eight miles west of town. I had left messages at the U.S. military headquarters in Seoul, saying that I might well pitch up at one of the bases along the route, and before I reached the big one, the huge fighter base at Kunsan, I wanted to make sure the system worked. So I coughed politely in front of an enormous American sentry, mentioned my name, and asked whether the base enjoyed the luxury of a full-time information officer, and if so, whether he could see me. The sentry's face creased into a broad smile.

"Hey, man, you must be the Limey who's walking here? Good to see you. Hey, Brad, look at this fucker!—oh! begging your pardon, sir—he's the guy I was telling you about. Walking all the way to the north. Isn't that right?"

The system did indeed work, and very well. One phone call, two signatures, and five minutes later a Chevrolet pickup had arrived, and I was in the hands of one First Lieutenant Mitchell Norton from Tennessee, inspecting what turned out to be "the biggest store of war reserve matériel in the whole of the Pacific Ocean." "Think of it as one great military version of Sears," he said. "Everything is here, ready to be delivered, ready to go."

He handed me a leaflet: Welcome to the 6171st Air Base Squadron, Kwang Ju, Republic of Korea. "Read it while we drive. It'll save you asking a lot of damn fool questions."

The world according to the United States Air Force was a rather different place from the one I had come to know with O'Neill and his friends: "Welcome to Korea, 'Land of Morning Calm,' and to Kwang Ju Air Base. The base is located about eight miles southwest of Kwang Ju city—a bustling and rapidly growing metropolis, it is known in Korea as Education City. The name Kwang Ju translates to 'bright valley' . . . the village of Yong Bo Ri is located outside the gate and has a population of 1,800. The village consists mainly of stores, teahouses and other entertainment facilities catering to American servicemen." Or brothels, as they are known elsewhere.

The military men were still enjoying their Team Spirit exercise when I arrived at the base, and this normally peaceful out-station of American might (it is officially listed as a contingency base, kept on permanent standby in case of war) was busy and very noisy. The runway (which is also shared by the civil airport: Passengers arriving on Korean Air Lines planes are ordered to pull down their blinds so that they can't see anything) was crowded with jostling little fighters bidding for take off. I was surprised to see how frail and insectlike these fighters were. They were F-15s, state-of-the-art, high-technology, huge firepower, all-weather wonders, and they had come here to Korea from the Kadena base on Okinawa. They might pack mighty punches, but from beside the flight line they had delicacy and grace about them, as though a hefty gust of wind would blow them away and send them tumbling over the grass.

Each few seconds a pair would take off, their jet engines screaming, gobbets of fire trailing from their tails. And every ten minutes or so a huge transport plane would follow, its propellers chewing hungrily at the air, its body swaying back and forth on its springs, until it reached enough speed to haul itself up into the air. A vast C-5 Starlifter took off, too—it eased its way painfully slowly along the runway until, at what looked like walking pace, and just as I was convinced it would plough into the chain-link fences at the edge, it just managed to get itself off the ground and staggered slowly above the hedges and the perimeter trees. Not until it was a good mile clear and felt itself freed from the gluey magnetism of home base did it start to arc into the sky, and then it diminished quickly to a dot in the blue, heading east for home with two hundred men and scores of tons of their gear.

There was one curiosity at Kwang Ju, brought in by a Starlifter the week before. The 354th Tactical Field Hospital—motto: Mercy. Readiness. Honor—had come in a few dozen wooden crates all the way from Myrtle Beach in South Carolina. Now, unpacked, it stood in a compound a hundred yards from the fighter flight line—a half-dozen khaki tents with treatment rooms, a dentist's chair and drills, a drugstore, a physiotherapy unit, a collapsible operating theater in which two operations could be performed in tandem, and a couple of armored ambulances. "What you see before you, sir, is the finest example of mobile medical technology anywhere in the free world," said Captain Randy Hartley. He was standing beside a crudely lettered signboard, of the type much loved by Americans abroad, that indicated the mileage to the nodal points in the outside world. Myrtle Beach was at the top of the list; then Fayetteville,

San Francisco, Honolulu, and the DMZ. "We need that there," said Captain Hartley, "to give our boys a handle on where they are, how far we are from home."

He took me around the tents, showed me the operating theater, the anesthetic bottles, and the cases of scalpels. "Basically we can see our first patients thirty minutes after we hit the dirt. In battle our gear comes down on 'chutes, and we've tried it. We can have the first tents up in half an hour, we can do a fairly standard operation in ninety minutes. The whole hospital is fully operational in six hours."

And then he took me into the ward. It was empty, except for one sleeping airman who had come all the way from Oklahoma and had then tried to pick up a bomb and strained his back. There was one nurse in charge of him, a handsome blond woman named Rose Layman, a lieutenant from California. She grinned as I was introduced. "Winchester? You don' say. Then call me Hoolihan. Hot Lips Hoolihan!" and everybody in the tent laughed. The Okie in bed wasn't asleep either, and he turned over and yelled " 'M*A*S*H*'— I don't believe it! Is this 'Candid Camera,' or what?" And of course, everything was there, right from television. Korea. A mobile hospital (though this was air force, Hawkeye's was army). A blond chief nurse. And a dude with a funny voice, hardly any hair, name of Winchester. It all seemed too good to be true, and Lieutenant Norton insisted on taking me for a drink to celebrate. "Hey guys, this Limey's called Winchester. Stars in 'M*A*S*H*.' Buy him a beer!"

It was with some difficulty that I escaped a couple of hours later. But a young officer rescued me and put me into his jeep and drove me back into town. He had a sticker on his back bumper that identified him as belonging to an ordnance company. There was a drawing of an almighty explosion and in fluorescent yellow lettering the motto: We Leave Smoking Holes.

The following morning I went across to see the last of the Irish priests whose name had been given to me on Cheju Island: Con Cleary, a chubby man in his late forties who lived in a tiny parish about five miles out of the city. He, like the rest, had been in Korea for most of his life, though after the Kwangju incident, which he saw and remembers in graphic detail, he went back to Ireland, shocked and horrified. "I had to go home, to work things out, to think about what I had seen, what it meant. For those of us who were there that week, it was unforgettably awful."

His cook made me lunch, and then we examined the maps, and then Con took me in his rusty old car to the road junction about a mile from home, away from the congestion of his parish. It was a little after two on a boiling hot afternoon. I was over the mountains now, on the northern side, and the only evidence of the city of Kwangju was a vague streak of pollution that seeped out along the valley toward the river. I would probably never go back again, but I would remember the place always. It was a city that had staged an event that Con Cleary, and all his friends, and half Kwangju, and half Korea, and half the world remembers—an event that, as Con had said, had been unforgettably awful—an event that had changed Korea forever.

And then, with my pack on my back, my stick in my hand, and the unfamiliar tightness of my boots back on my feet again, I stepped out for the north. The map told me to proceed for a mile or two along beside the river. I was in a meadow strewn with wild cosmos flowers and the first daffodils of spring. Ahead, some twenty miles off, a vague blue line on the far horizon, were the Naejang Mountains. I glanced at my watch and quickened my pace: 120 paces a minute, 3.6 miles an hour, an unvarying pace I had managed to sustain all these miles so far. I had to hurry, for I had a dinner appointment in the foothills—a dinner appointment with a Buddhist monk.

CHAPTER

FIVE

"*The Religious Men offer Perfumes before an Idol twice a Day, and on Festivals; all the Religious of a House make a Noise with Drums, Basons and Kettles. The Monasteries and Temples, which the Kingdom swarms with, are for the most part on the Mountains, each under the liberty of some Town. There are Monasteries of 5 or 600 Religious Men, and at least 4,000 of them within the Liberties of some Towns. They are divided into Companies of 10, 20 and sometimes 30, and the eldest Governs, and if any one does not do his Duty, he may cause the others to punish him with 20 or 30 Strokes on the Buttocks. It being lawful for any Man to become a Religious, all the Country of Corea is full of them. . . . *"

—HENDRICK HAMEL,
1668

❖ ❖ ❖

HIS NAME WAS HAEDARNG, HE WAS SOMETHING OF A
Shakespearean scholar, and I had met him a fortnight before near the summit
of Halla-san. He passed me, coming down the hillside with a pair of companions. He was large, verging on the corpulent, though his figure was somewhat
disguised by his gray, buttonless robes of a Chogye Buddhist monk. His head
was perfectly shaven. "A very good afternoon, sir!" he shouted as he strode
past. His English was perfect, almost unaccented. I replied. He stopped. "Allow me to introduce myself. I am Haedarng, and I am a monk. Do you speak
English?"

And once he knew that not only did I speak it but that I was English, he
called over his companions to shake my hand, and he kept saying, again and
again, what a *very great honor* it was to meet me, how *very wonderful* it was
that I had traveled all the way from my home to visit his humble country, and
though he possessed nothing that I might consider suitable, he would be *more
than happy* to offer whatever he had. After two minutes of this he stood back,
breathing hard and sweating a little. I expressed my gratitude, and told him
that I might in fact see him later on, and told him of my plan. He was ecstatic.
"You really must come, dear sir. I live in a house that is *terribly humble, terribly
humble*. But it is on your way, in the mountains between Kwangju and Chonju.
Please, sir, please do me the honor of coming to see my humble home. I will
tell you about my Shakespeare project, you would be very interested. I would
try to give you a wonderful time. You must *promise* that you will come."

101

And I did so promise, and he wrote his name and address, in English, in my Alwych book: "Haedarng, Monk—Chonnam, Darmyarng Kun, Soobuk Myun, Oh Jung Ri." He added his telephone number and the name of his monastery—Kumta-sa. I said I would do my best to get there, in about two weeks' time. He blessed me profusely and went on down the mountain bowing and pressing his hands together in gestures of farewell.

It took a while to translate his address into something approximating the words I found on my map (although there were few enough romanized words on the map—most words were in Chinese characters, a few were in *hangul*, which all made map reading even more difficult than usual). "Chonnam," I realized after staring at it for a good ten minutes, was a compression of the word "Chollanam-do," or South Cholla Province. It was then clear he had written his address backward, as many old-fashioned Koreans still do. The next word, "Darmyarng-kun," stumped me, until someone suggested that the monk, like many older Koreans, was employing a system of romanization called the Ministry of Education System, which was now hopelessly out of date. It had been replaced, since 1983, by the internationally accepted McCune-Reischauer System, and if I wanted to decode Haedarng's language I had to substitute Ts for Ds, Ks for Gs, kick out all the superfluous Rs, stir the whole thing around a bit and, with luck, a real, recognizable word might emerge.

I did this, and, hey presto! for "Darmyarng-kun," I read "Tamyang-gun," and promptly found it on the map and in the gazetteer—a small country town twenty miles north of Kwangju, the bamboo-growing capital of Korea. I never did find Soobuk-myun, and I thought I might well miss his *ri*, his village of Ojung. But I now knew roughly where it was, and so, once I got near Tamyang town I planned to ask directions. This was not as easy as I thought: When I approached farmers and rice planters and schoolchildren with the inquiry: "*Ojung-ri odi isumnikka?*" they may have wanted to help but clearly had never heard of the place and ended up making me more confused than ever. I quickly realized that salvation would come only if I was brave enough to try to read the *hangul* on the road signs. If I continued to shy away from any words that were written in King Sejong's modish linguistic invention, I would never reach Ojung-ri, and a cold and uncomfortable night would be in store for me. So, with the sense of desperation I remembered as a schoolboy when told to stand up in class and translate a paragraph of *Civil War, Book Three* that I had omitted to read in homework the night before—with desperation much akin to that, knowing the consequences of failure, I set about trying to read every little granite road sign and marker I could find.

❖   ❖   ❖

The Koreans are quite possibly the only people in the world who have a national holiday to celebrate the invention of their system of writing. (There is, so far as I am aware, no Cyrillic Day, no Devanagri Week, nor anything to celebrate Arabic, or Roman, or Katakana, or Chinese.) Shortly after the defeat of the Japanese in 1945, a decree providing for such a day was handed down from Seoul. In essence, the declaration read as follows: Since during the entire time of the Japanese occupation, the use of *hangul* has been banned, and since with the defeat of the Japanese it will be possible for *hangul* to be used once again, then the date of October 9, the anniversary of the first promulgation of our national writing system in 1446, shall henceforward be called *Hangul* Day, and shall be a national holiday for all the people of our country.

It is a system well deserving of a day of celebration. Its invention has helped foster Korea's remarkable sense of national unity, and it has helped make sure that nearly all of the Korean population, for the last two centuries at least, has been able to read. The astonishing advances in Korea's economic standing in recent years are, of course, principally the result of hard work, determination, and shrewdness. But the fact of near 100 percent literacy, and the fact of an almost wholly unified sense of national purpose (*pace*, of course, the young radicals' loathing for the policies of the present government) must have contributed: King Sejong is well worthy of the reverence accorded to him and to his invention.

He began work on a replacement writing system in 1420. His reasoning was simple. Korean didn't exist in written form at all; there was a very rich language being spoken out there, but no one could read or write in it because there was nothing to read or write it in. Those few people who could write had opted, some centuries before, to use Chinese characters—characters that, as a writing system for the Korean language, were entirely unsuitable.

The two tongues are wholly unrelated: Korean is a Ural-Altaic language, linguistically connected (though only rather vaguely) to Turkish, Mongolian, Finnish, and Magyar. Chinese, on the other hand, is a Sino-Tibetan tongue, with ties to Burmese and Thai and Tibetan. Using Chinese characters to express Korean sounds would be like using Chinese characters to express English—it is technically possible, but is also clumsy, useless, and philosophically out of whack. Chinese characters couldn't begin to express the sounds and subtleties of Korean, and besides, whether or not they could, the Korean people just couldn't begin to understand Chinese script.

It just didn't make any sense to them; the thought of using up to thirty-two brushstrokes to form a single character, and having to learn as many as fifty thousand characters that had appeared to have precious little logic behind their construction was anathema to most ordinary Koreans. The *yangban* and the scholar classes made an effort to learn classical Chinese script with which to communicate to each other, and, indeed, all literature and official prose was written using it. But the ordinary people had nothing. A simplified version of Chinese was introduced in the seventh century—it was called *Idu*, or "clerk writing"—but it was still regarded as far too complicated, an unneccessary pile of artistic baggage with which to express the meaning of a beautifully simple language. So King Sejong, who was the fourth king of the Yi Dynasty (the dynasty that reigned until the Japanese extinguished it in 1910), decided that a new system was needed. He devoted all his efforts, and those of a scholarly body known as the College of Assembled Worthies, to the invention of one.

On Christmas Day 1443—though of course no Christmas was celebrated in Korea, since no Christian missionaries had yet reached Korea—the new script was unveiled. It was to be known, the great Sejong had decided, as *Hun min chong um*—"The Correct Sounds for the Instruction of the People." (An odd title for a supposedly simple script: He changed it three years later to *hangul*, which means "the Korean Writing.")

"Being distinct from Chinese," Sejong wrote, in the introduction to his proclamation (which was written in Chinese), "the Korean language is not confluent with Chinese characters. Hence, those having something to put into words are unable to express their feelings. To overcome such distressing circumstances I have designed twenty-eight letters that everyone may learn with ease and use with convenience for his daily life. Talented persons will learn *hangul* in a single morning, and even foolish persons will understand it in ten days."

The king, who was forty-seven years old when his alphabet was completed, devised a system with seventeen consonants and eleven vowels. It was elegant, it encompassed all the sounds uttered by the Korean tongue, and it had its roots—like no other system known—in human physiology. Thus the consonant letters were designed actually to look approximately like the organs of speech. The letter ㄱ, for example, which represents the sounds of our letter *k*, was meant to show the shape of the back of the tongue blocking the throat while the *k* sound was being made. The shape of the tongue reaching up and touching the inner ridge of the gums, ㄴ, is the *hangul* symbol for our sound *n*, which is made in precisely that way. The simple squared-off circle, ㅁ, the script for our letter *m*, is said to represent the shape of the lips as the *m* is being uttered. And while I, as one of Sejong's "foolish persons," cannot boast of having learned it in a morning, I can say in common with almost all others who stay in Korea for longer than a week, that *hangul* is a delightfully easy script to learn. It may not be possible to understand what you have read, but to read it and to come out with an utterance Koreans will recognize, is easily possible after only a couple of days' practice.

There was some resistance to the introduction of what the Confucian elders called "the Vulgar script." To create a new script "is to discard China and identify ourselves with the barbarians. This is what is called 'throwing away the fragrance of storax and choosing the bullet of the praying mantis.'" Sejong was unmoved by so withering an onslaught; both he and his son Sejo were determined to broadcast the good word, in concert with the Buddhism that the pair so ardently followed. There were setbacks, both for *hangul* and for the Buddhists, but within a century the script had taken a firm hold, and it was not until the Japanese tried to suppress it that its purpose briefly faltered.

It was simplified in 1933, when one of the vowels and three of the conso-nants were officially dropped. Essentially, though, the system that survives today has remained untouched, and enormously popular, for more than five centuries. Its popularity stems only partly from its simple elegance; more than anything, it represents to the Korean something that is *his very own*, an illus-tration of his cultural and linguistic uniqueness, a device that sets him apart from the Chinese, the Mongols, and the Japanese who, for reasons good or ill, so often have occupied their peninsula and attempted to subdue, suppress, and subjugate these more independent of Asian people. *Hangul* is a real and living symbol of the cussedness of the Koreans, of their unquenchable spirit, of their unwillingness to be subsumed by their mightier neighbor-nations.

(One problem unforeseen by King Sejong was the difficulty of writing *hangul* on a typewriter. The various syllables of Korean words—the first consonant, say, then the vowel, and then the third consonant—are grouped together in a specifically stylized manner. The first part of the word *kamsa hamnida*—"thank you"—is broken up into the syllables *kam* and *sa*; the syllable *kam* is made up of the first consonant, *k*, ㄱ, which is written on the left; the vowel, *a*, ㅏ, which is put to the immediate right of the ㄱ; and the final consonant, *m*, ㅁ, which is put below the first two: 감. *Sa* is similarly done, and easily, thus 사. The other syllables are constructed likewise, but with one very confusing difference, in that *ham* is actually written *hap*, 합, but the *p* is pronounced like an *m*. *Ni* and *da* are less complicated because of their being made up of only two letters. The final version of the word is thus 감사합니다. As you can see, to type the syllable *kam*, 감, involves both lowering the font and backspacing; in the one word this operation has to be performed twice. In some words—such as the word "telescope," *man won gyon*, or 만원경 — every syllable is constructed with three letters, with the last and sometimes the intermediate ones positioned in a way that is highly inconvenient for the typist. There is no suggestion it is more complicated than Chinese; but when compared with Devanagri, or Urdu (despite its being written from right to left), with the knittinglike Burmese or the spaghettilike Tamil, Korean is very trying. The benevolent king, whose statue sits in benign invigilation over the Toksu Palace in Seoul, on a *hangul* covered plinth, could not have been ex-pected to know the trouble he would cause for the Remingtons and Olivettis of this world.)

❖ ❖ ❖

And thus armed with my smattering of *hangul* I scanned the road signs. I was dreadfully slow at first, but was nonetheless determined to keep walking while I tried to read. In the early afternoon the frustrations were enormous: By the

time I had managed to twist my eyes and brain around the complexities of a
Sokwang-ju or a Ssangtae-ri, the junctions by which I might have reached
these villages was long past. But slowly I managed some degree of fluency. And
as the sun began to slope down toward the hills—a welcome relief, for it had
been a very hot day, and sweat was running from beneath my hat and down
my neck—I saw the name I wanted. I recognized the 오 as O; I just managed
to get the 정 as *jung;* and I had by now become accustomed to 리, or *ri.*
Ojung-ri, carved on a granite post, and a number 5. Five kilometers, I guessed,
up this stony path that led through the paddies and the groves of young bamboo, and into the mountains proper.

The path entered a small copse of pine trees where the sunlight was split
into thin shafts of dusty air. It became much cooler. The air was fresh with
the clean, crisp smell of resin. A tiny stream burbled somewhere in the deeper
gloom. The birdsong, bright and cheerful out in the warmer air, was muffled.
I walked steadily for ten minutes, always slightly uphill, until I came to a small
clearing, strewn with old pine needles. A small obelisk, inscribed with Chinese
characters, stood on a mound; it was probably a gravestone or a village guardian designed by the local shaman to keep away unfriendly spirits. I stood still
for a while, lingering over this tranquil spot. And then I became aware of
someone else also standing in the shadows. It was a man dressed in a neat
blue suit and well-shined brown shoes. He hadn't seen me and was just standing stock still, gazing up toward the patches of blue sky. I watched him for a
few minutes and coughed to let him know I was there. He turned round, and
his face broke into a broad smile.

"Good afternoon," he said, and in impeccable English added, "What is
your name?"

I told him and said how sorry I was for spoiling his reverie. "Oh no!" he
replied. "It is so nice to have company. I was just looking for somewhere for
my parents to live. They will be retiring soon; she is seventy, you know, a
wonderful woman, and she and my father have always said they would like to
retire to a peaceful place in the hills. I told them I would look out for somewhere. It is Saturday, I had time off, so here I am. What about you; why are
you here?"

I told him of my walk, and he chuckled approvingly. It was so unusual, he
said, to see people in Korea doing things alone. The Confucian spirit, he said,
laid great emphasis on the group, on togetherness. "Solitude is not a Korean
pleasure," he said. "You and me, we like it. We shall be friends, I think."

We walked slowly together across the mossy floor of the woods, while he
told me a little of his life. He worked as a manager of a tire factory in Kwangju.
He had been a teacher until three years before, but he had left his job. There
had been some trouble. In fact he would tell me about it. It was a strange
little story. I might find it amusing.

"You will know we have a president in power who is not very well liked down in these parts. Well, even if we like him or not, it is part of our way of life that we give him great respect. Not everyone does—the students up in Seoul do not, for instance—but most of the older people, like myself, we do. And of course the young children are in awe of him and his position.

"Well, some years ago we were told that he was coming down to our town and that he would visit a local school. There was great excitement. The security people wouldn't say exactly when he was coming, but they told the school to go ahead and make all the preparations to greet him properly. So they did just that: They arranged a big ceremony, and as one of the ways of welcoming him, they made a huge portrait of him, broken up into hundreds of pieces on the back of colored cards. When the children held the cards up one way, they made a pretty pattern. When they turned the cards over, there was the president's face.

"The day arrived, and we were told when he would be arriving. The children were ready, everyone very nervous. Then one of the children asked permission to go to the bathroom. His teacher said that would be fine, but hurry. Well, you can guess what happened; while the boy was in the bathroom the president arrived, and the security people wouldn't let the boy back onto the field. So the celebrations went on, the children did their dances with the cards and turned this way and that, and then, all together, turned them over.

"The president's face was there all right—except it was missing a left eyebrow. The official people went crazy! The president himself didn't say anything of course, but after the party had gone the education department had the master in and fired him on the spot. The headmaster was in trouble. I even heard they visited the parents of the child and warned them of the consequences. And then an instruction went out. If ever there was a demonstration of loyalty like that held again, the children had to be told if they wanted to pee, they peed where they stood. Understand?

"I got to hear that there was another demonstration some weeks later, and the president was late, and the children were waiting for several hours. And they did as they were told. And when it was all over the children, particularly the girls, went back to their mothers, terribly upset by it all. It had been a bad experience for them all. So it was then that I decided to leave. I just didn't seem to be in the right job. Tires are not much fun, but out in the commercial world I'm not so much a part of the machine. I feel better now, although I miss the children. I miss teaching."

I have no way of knowing whether his story was true or not. It is about a microcosmically unimportant event, but one that nonetheless somehow illustrates the way that authority occasionally works in today's Korea. There is no way of finding out if what my tire maker alleged had indeed happened or whether it was the fanciful invention of a man who loathed the regime. I did, though, mention it to a doctor in Kwangju and to another in Seoul, and both said they had heard the tale and believed it to be true. So my initial nervousness about including the tale evaporated: Even if it is not literally accurate, and even if my guide had a somewhat selective memory, it represents the kind of assumptions that are made these days about the behavior of governments, and as such it has a purpose. The beginning of the tale was amusing enough, anyway, and Mr. Shin—as he later introduced himself—was an excellent story-teller.

But he had no idea where Kumta-sa might be, and when we reached the next hamlet we asked, and no one knew. Then I remembered that most Buddhist monks were called *Sunim*—whether that was a title or not I wasn't really sure—and so I tossed that word around a little, and sure enough a small boy, bright-eyed and smiling, said yes, he knew where a *sunim* lived, and pointed up through a grove of bamboo higher still up the mountainside. "Haedarng," I heard him say, and suddenly there was a murmur of agreement, and everyone started nodding and grinning and pointing up into the hills. My friend was no stranger, thank heavens.

The child—one of those curious mop-headed youngsters whose sex is quite indeterminate, to themselves as well as to everyone else—offered to lead the way and skipped ahead down the rough track. She—for that is what I came to think the child was—wanted to try to carry my rucksack, and so I gave it to her: She promptly fell over into a ditch, giggling. *"Mukkop-ta!"* she said, and I had to agree that it was very heavy, but the brief respite from the never-ending pressure of the shoulder straps was a great relief.

It was a half mile, through bamboo thickets, past a field with a pair of tumuli—old graves, probably for a husband and wife—across a mountain stream, before we came to a wall, pierced by a green gate. I rang an electric doorbell—the Korean government manages to insert electricity into the deepest recesses of the country—and lo! there was Haedarng, beaming genially. "My friend! You came! What a *great honor* it is for me. A great, great honor. Come, both of you, Mister Simon and your friend. Please enter my humble house. I am so sorry. This really is *most inconvenient*, I must be honest with you. A *very* inconvenient time to visit. But you must come and stay. I am so happy. So happy." And thus, trilling like a little fat bird, he led the way through the vegetable garden and sat us down on the floor in his room. "Welcome!" he beamed, and in shuffled a middle-aged woman with a tray on which were three small glasses of tea and a plate of sliced apples.

I started to protest at the inconvenience of our call, but Haedarng would have none of it. He was an honest man, he said, and didn't want us to think that we had called at the most propitious of moments. It was not that we weren't welcome, it was simply that there was nowhere to sleep because that very afternoon his mother had traveled down from Seoul, and she had naturally occupied the only other room. "So I am just thinking. Tonight you and me, Mister Simon, we will have to sleep together. Tonight I will not sleep with my wife."

Wife? I had supposed Buddhists to be monogamous and celibate. In fact, I learned later, the whole question of monastic celibacy had caused a furious debate in Korea, and only thirty years before. The Japanese colonial masters had introduced the notion of married monks to Korea; it was all part of the Japanese grand design to do all they could to lessen the cultural and religious differences between the two countries, as part of their moral rationale for having carried out their annexation. By the time World War II ended, and the Americans and the Russians had thrown the defeated Japanese out, several hundred monks had married and had started families. Indeed, many monasteries were run by married "monks," if the phrase doesn't sound too oxymoronic.

The consequences of this development, however, were dire. Not only did it reduce the number of traditional-minded lay supporters of Buddhism (though it did not increase the number of more liberal-minded ones—they, presumably, were more tempted by the proselytizing of the Christians), but it also squeezed the monasteries of funds, which were needed to provide for wives and families. The Chogye sect, who were (and still are) the largest of the various major groups in Korean Buddhism, argued vociferously against permitting married monks; the hierarchy in Seoul dismissed married men from their positions in many temples; two factions, bitterly opposed, grew up. The situation became almost grave, threatening Buddhism's classically nonbelligerent attitudes, and it was to deal with this emergency that President Syngman Rhee had to intervene in 1954, calming down the Chogye elders, insisting on a compromise.

But even today the row smolders on, the actual fact of monastery marriage being probably rather less obnoxious than its symbolism as a relic of the habits of the Japanese.

Anyway, the middle-aged lady who brought us the sliced apples and tea was in fact Haedarng's wife, though in the customary ways of the Korean family, I only saw her that first evening when she brought food or took away the dishes, playing the role of serving wench.

Since it became clear very quickly that Mr. Shin was going to have to leave, Haedarng invited him to tell his story—why he had fetched up at such an obscure hamlet as Ojung-ri. As Mr. Shin explained, telling us again how he was searching for somewhere peaceful where he could build a cottage to which his parents could retire, the monk's face beamed, until it was illuminated by a kind of radiance. "You see!" he turned to me. "What a *good man* this is. All this trouble he goes to for his old parents. He should be very proud. I hope you will tell such stories in your home. Do people in your country do such things?" And then Mr. Shin did leave, and a lot of deep bowing went on, the two men clearly deeply respectful of each other. I was mildly pleased at having played catalyst to what might be the beginnings of a friendship.

Haedarng had come up here to this sweet-smelling retreat just two years before, when he had completed four years of training and had been accepted as a monk. He had been a teacher before that in Kwangju for fifteen years, cramming physics and English down the throats of youngsters whose eagerness to learn impressed him still. The coincidence of dates was interesting, and I asked him if there was any connection.

"Yes, of course! Of course! I saw the whole thing, the whole awful massacre! I saw bodies being slung off the back of army trucks like so many pigs. I saw terrible things. I couldn't stand thinking about it. I went into deep meditation almost immediately after it was all over. It affected me very deeply. I decided then and there to give my life over entirely to the Lord Buddha. Will you, perhaps, excuse me while I give the evening rite to him?"

And he slid the paper doors back quietly and left the room for another next door. In a few moments I heard the clacking of the hollow wooden clapper known as the *moktak,* and I heard the faint, pleasantly relaxing notes of his sutra, which he chanted slowly before the image of the man whose life he now followed.

I looked about his room. The floor, as in most Korean houses, was quite bare, was covered with a pale-yellow-lacquered paper, and was very warm. It was a typical *ondol* floor, much used in today's Korea (except in modern apartment buildings, which find it difficult to arrange the necessary pipework). I find the *ondol* one of the most comforting aspects of a Korean house, but Henry Savage Landor, whose book *Corea—The Land of Morning Calm* is one of the more amusing late Victorian accounts of the country, thought otherwise:

> The Corean process of heating the houses is somewhat original. It is a process used in a great part of Eastern Asia—and, to my mind, it is the only thoroughly barbaric custom which the Corean natives have retained. The flooring of the rooms consists of slabs of stone, under which is a large oven of the same extent as the room overhead, which oven, during the winter, is filled with a burning wood fire, which is kept up day and night. What happens is generally this: The coolie whose duty it is to look after this oven, to avoid trouble fills it with wood and dried leaves up to the very neck, and sets these on fire and then goes to sleep; by which means the stone slabs get heated to such an extent that, sometimes, notwithstanding the thick oil-paper which covers them, one cannot stand on them with bare feet.

These days there is no subterranean room to house a fire but a series of flues that carry the hot gases from the kitchen range beneath the floor. It is a very cheap and efficient system: The cylindrical *yontan* briquettes that heat the cooker cost 200 *won* apiece—25 cents—and each lasts for eight hours: One will boil the cabbage and steam the fish and roast the beef, and heat the floor of the living room, too. The system is still used in Afghanistan—many's the deep winter night I have spent out on the ice-cold deserts there, snug on the floor of a tiny inn, the baked earth yielding up the kitchen warmth to the frozen bones of the travelers. But elsewhere locally—Japan, for instance—they don't seem to use *ondol,* and more's the pity.

The price to be paid for such a system, though, would be considered steep by most Westerners. In the older and poorer Korean houses, only one room is usually used by all the family for living, eating, and sleeping. This was certainly the case in Haedarng's tiny house. During the daytime the room was almost empty of furniture—chairs are quite unknown, and when a meal was to be served small black lacquer tables were brought in from the kitchen and taken away when everyone was done. A large cupboard stood at one side of the room, and inside it, piled in colorful bundles, were the silk-lined mattresses and coverlets that would be brought out at night. Mr. Landor (whose other work, *Alone with the Hairy Ainu,* is, I suspect, a classic of its kind) shows that little has changed in ninety years:

> The Corean custom is to sleep on the ground in the padded clothes, using a wooden block as a pillow. The better classes, however, use also small, thin mattresses, covered with silk, which they spread out at night, and keep rolled up in the daytime. As the people sleep on the ground, it often happens that the floor gets so hot as to almost roast them, but the easy-going inhabitant of Cho-sen does not seem to object to this roasting process—on the contrary, he seems almost to revel in it, and when well broiled on one side he will turn over to the other, so as to level matters. While admiring the Coreans much for this proceeding, I found it extremely inconvenient to imitate them. I recollect well the first experience which I had of the use of the "kan," which is the native name of the oven. On that occasion it was "made so hot" for me, that I began to think I had made a mistake, and that I had entered a crematory oven instead of a sleeping room. Putting my fist through one of the paper windows to get a little air only made matters ten times worse, for half of my body continued to undergo the roasting process, while the other half was getting unpleasantly frozen. To this day it has always been a marvel to me, and an unexplainable fact that those who use the "kan" do not "wake up—dead" in the morning!

It is rather more comfortable now. As soon as the sun went down, and as soon as we had a frugal supper of soup and rice, *kimchi* and strawberries and *poricha,* and as soon as I had washed (out in the open, an upended *kimchi* jar as my washstand), Haedarng spread out the mattress, the *yo* (he gave me two "because I suspect the English backside is not used to sleeping on the floor—am I right?"), and the *ibul* (the coverlet) and the *pegae,* or cornhusk pillow.

He gave himself a hard wooden block, African-style, on which he rested his neck. Within seconds he was asleep, and snoring hard. I fiddled around, trying to avoid the hot spots on the floor—the flue connected directly to the *yontan* nozzle seemed to surface wherever I planted my hipbone—and in a matter of moments was asleep. The next thing I knew, daylight was filtering in through the paper screens and Haedarng was up, off to give the Buddha his morning rite. Would I care to come?

Buddha was seated next door, in a tiny, darkened, fragrant, and slightly smoky cell. He was about three feet high, white and gold, and was seated in the classic position of the mendicant pauper. The smell and the smoke came from a tiny sheaf of incense sticks that smoldered in front of him. A prayer mat, with a small bell and the *moktak*, lay before him, and it was on this that the barefoot Haedarng now stood and motioned to me to be silent and follow what he did. He knelt, in what I now know (but learned only with some pain) to be the classically acceptable Buddhist kneel: I had to bend my toes (stiff from my first eighty miles of walking) and kneel on the mat, then straighten my toes and sit back on the soles of my feet, then bend my back forward until my forehead touched the mat, and finally bring my hands over my head and lay my hands, palms uppermost, on the mat beside my ears.

That was quite tricky enough for someone fit and perfectly sober to do without falling over, but then it had to be reversed. Without—and this is the killer—without being allowed to use my arms as support, I had to stand up, essentially only using my toe muscles to help me do so. The first time I tried it I stumbled wildly in the dark, pitched into the impassive figure of Haedarng (who managed these movements with enormous grace, the Nureyev of the elephant world) and nearly brought the whole proceeding to an undignified halt. And it wasn't as though a Buddhist morning rite has just one episode of genuflection: I must have gone down on my knees thirty times in the following thirty minutes, sometimes at such a pace that I began to have a sort of nightmare that I was in the gymnasium back at school, with whoever had so signally failed to teach me phys. ed.

I would like to say that the morning prayer was an exercise in serenity and beauty. But my nerves and my strained muscles made it descend into something perilously close to farce. Haedarng didn't seem to mind. He was evidently thinking of other things, for as we left and emerged once more into the sunlight—and the cloying smell of the incense was replaced by the crisp tang of balsam firs—he asked, rather chirpily, "Have I told you about my theories about your William Shakespeare?"

He then began to rattle off lines from memory and to ask questions I wished I could answer more readily. " ' 'Tis in ourselves that we are thus,' " he said. "Do you know it? 'Our bodies are our gardens, to which our wills are gardeners; so that if we will plant nettles or sow lettuce, set hyssop and weed up thyme . . .' What exactly is hyssop, Mister Simon?

" 'The expedition of my violent love outran the pauser, reason. Here lay Duncan . . .' Tell me what you think of Duncan, please." He would ask his questions with great deliberation, and I could see him note down the replies on a mental notepad. I was lamentable and told him of my shame. "Do not be ashamed, Mister Simon. It is my great study. My life's work. I shall be honored to give you a copy of my recent paper." And from a chest he pulled a slim, yellow paperback volume—a book that, for me at least, proved somewhat difficult to comprehend: *Shakespearean Tragedies Illuminated by Buddhism; or, Around the Philosophy of Retribution of Cause and Effect, Thoughts of Dhyana, and Matters of Ignorance.* It had been privately printed and was written in a confusing mixture of Chinese characters, *hangul*, and rather fractured English. The nub of Haedarng's theory—which he had propounded after "years of intense study" of the five tragedies, *Othello, Hamlet, Julius Caesar, Macbeth,* and *Romeo and Juliet*—was that Shakespeare and the Lord Buddha were both able to recognize the causes of tragedy (the ultimate being human ignorance) and their effects (death, sin, and misery), but that only Buddhas bothered to try to do something about them:

> One thing I would like to say is why Shakespeare did not tell us the way to get rid of the causes of human tragedy. I expected to find out it in the five works of his tragedies because it could be the fruit of his philosophy concerning human beings. We Buddhists understand that is the emphatic core of Buddha's teachings. . . .
>
> In conclusion, Shakespeare showed up the cause and effect of human tragedy so dramatically in his masterpieces, and Buddha told us the way to avoid human tragedy and attain the Pure Land through his whole life of over eighty years.

Or, put another way, William Shakespeare may have been a wise old bird, but he couldn't hold a feather to Buddha, who had wisdom in unrivaled abundance. Haedarng's paper was, I suppose, an essentially chauvinistic document, the kind of thing one might expect from a very enthusiastic convert to a new religion. And he had been an English teacher, so, West meets East, and the East wins. I felt briefly tempted to ask him if he was now thinking of reviewing the General Theory of Relativity in relation to the Buddha's teaching but then thought better of it and held my tongue.

Cars began to arrive. Haedarng looked up, and exclaimed: "Ah! I regret we must stop this most interesting discussion. It is my wayward family! They have come for the birthday party." Mother, it transpired, was sixty-three years old this April Sunday, and her children were gathering about her for a morning celebration of the occasion. (A Korean is counted as being born at age one; the sixty-third birthday of a Korean thus equated to the sixty-second birthday of a Westerner.)

The most notable of Haedarng's relations to appear was his younger brother Hwang Chi-Woo—the monk Haedarng actually being a Mr. Hwang in his teaching days, before he converted to Buddhism and took a sacred name. Chi-Woo, who had driven down from Seoul the night before with his wife and two children, is a celebrated poet, a former aesthetics student at Seoul National University. "Korea's Oxford," he said proudly. "I have to tell you we are not a very popular family with the government," he explained. "One of us has become a monk because of the Kwangju massacre. Another is a school-teacher. Here am I, well known as an antigovernment poet. And the fourth is a trade union organizer in Inchon, and he is in hiding. He has been on the run from the police for most of the last two years. So you have picked yourself dangerous company."

By the time the last couple had arrived—a mother and child whose role in the family was never explained—mother emerged from wherever she had been hiding these past hours, and a lacquer table was brought in with scores of steel and china dishes balanced precariously on it. It was ten in the morning. This was a birthday brunch, I supposed. Haedarng leaned over to me. "Forgive me, Mister Simon, but you will see *meat* on this table. I do assure you it is only there because mother is still a Christian, and so is my—indeed, so is everyone at this table, as are you, I think, yes? I decided that even though I am sworn not to eat meat, we shall have it today in mother's honor. I have asked the Lord Buddha, and he has said it will be all right."

It was quite a party. Had I been here three years before—when mother turned sixty—it would have been even more so. A sixtieth birthday is a special thing in all those countries that have come under the maternal influence of old China, Korea very much included. The body is then deemed to have passed through the five twelve-year zodiacal cycles—the *yukgap*, as the sixty-year period is known—that constitute the proper life span of the human being. Once someone has successfully completed the span—as old mother Hwang had done three years before—then all time beyond is regarded as a marvelous bonus: You retire from active life, take your respected ease as an elder, let your children make you as comfortable as they can, and let filial piety take over the reins of your life.

To celebrate this turning point (the only other points so celebrated are the second—or, in Western terms, first—birthday and the hundredth day from birth, when thanks are offered for the child having made it thus far) a great party is staged. It is known as the *hwan-gap* and has become such big business in modern Korea that special *hwan-gap* halls have been built in most big cities—places where families can entertain their elders in a style of which Confucius would have approved.

The old man or old woman at the center of the occasion sits, dressed in silks and satins and bows and furbelows, on a huge pile of multicolored silk cushions, like a large-scale Pekingese dog in a Barbara Cartland romance. Before him or her are ranks of gleaming candelabra and castles of sweetmeats—biscuits, *ttok* (rice cakes), apples, oranges, almonds, toffees—and beyond them an unceasing tide of youngsters who kowtow and in a myriad of other ways display their undying respect and affection for the Honored One. (In the commercial *hwan-gap* halls the amount of the food on display that you are allowed to eat depends, not unreasonably, on the amount of cash you have decided to pay up front. The rest of the food stays right on the table, all wrapped in plastic to keep it fresh looking for the next celebrants on the day's schedule.)

After an hour or so of homage has been paid a party gets under way; there is music (cassettes in the *hwan-gap* halls, unless you pay a great deal for a live band; a friend on the drums and the zither if you're out in the countryside); there is dancing; and there is a great deal of drink. Koreans are an unashamedly bibulous people, and no stigma will attach to those (unless they are Buddhist monks, of course) who stagger away from the *hwan-gap* several sheets to the wind.

This celebration may have been a relatively muted affair, but it was a gastronomic triumph. There were dishes of rice (plain and glutinous) and many kinds of roasted meat; there were nine different types of *kimchi* (for Haedarng's wife was celebrated all along the valley for the strength and piquancy and variety of her pickled vegetables, which—like most country people—she buried from November in the strong brown earthenware jars designed for *kimchi* manufacture); there were oysters, quails' eggs bedded in straw, cloves of raw white garlic, yellow turnips, great scarlet radishes, gleaming piles of silvery whitebait, seaweed (in pressed and toasted squares, as well as in wild untidy masses); neat chunks of tofu, pink and shivering shrimps, various sauces and condiments of every color imaginable, chilies (red and green); and strawberries, apples, pine kernels, and pears. If any dish was emptied, the monk's wife scuttled off for more. Rice was consumed in prodigious amounts—the children fattening up before my eyes—so that after an hour of spooning the stuff in (and flattish spoons are provided, as are two pairs of chopsticks, one steel, the other wooden) their bellies were as hard and distended as drums. There was a great deal of contented belching, and legs moved beneath the table in a constant dance as everyone—all seated on the floor—squirmed for more space and more comfort as the meal progressed.

Then a birthday cake, Western in appearance, was brought in, with a circle of twelve dark candles (for the completion of the *yukgap*) and the additional three in the center. The old lady blew the candles out, there was much applause, and then the cake was put neatly back into its box to be taken back to Seoul. A huge crystal decanter was brought carefully into the room: It held a colorless liquid and a huge ginseng root that, with pinkish arms and legs attached to its thick and wrinkled trunk, looked like a headless little man floating in preserving fluid. The root was so huge, and the decanter's neck so small, that I began to try to puzzle out how the one got into the other, but it took only about ten minutes for the *soju* (for that is what the liquid turned out to be—the grain-spirit firewater with a taste varying between paint thinner and formalin) to take effect, and I forgot my inquiry until the next day.

Confucian drinking habits—and there is an organization known as the Korean Young Men's Confucian Association that issues directives on how to drink properly—are exceptionally tough on unseasoned skulls. Koreans often drink with the specific objective of becoming drunk, and what might pass for extreme courtesy at table is simply an elegant way of ensuring that this happens. Basically it involves giving a glass (with both hands; everything in Korea is offered with both hands, indicating that no hand is free to aim a blow or draw a sword) to your friend at table and filling it to the brim with liquor. He will drain it at one draught, then pass it back to you and fill it for you, whereupon you drain it, and offer it back to him. You never fill your own cup; you never refuse drink offered to you; you will always be offered drink; you will get drunk very quickly; you will remember very little of the proceedings; and you will (especially if you drink *soju*) have the mother and father of all hangovers.

All I recall is, very soon after lunch, when the rest of the household was sliding into hazy slumber, that I insisted on getting going again. They didn't want to let me go, nor did I much want to leave; but eventually I was given a crumpled piece of paper with an address scrawled on it—the address of another monk who lived at a monastery in the Naejang Mountains. "He helped to tutor me," said Haedarng as he and I stumbled along the pathway from his little one-man monastery. "He will look after you. A good man. Anyway, it was an *honor*, a real honor. I wanted to tell you one thing: I am reminded of our great cartographer, Kim Chong-ho. He walked through Korea many times and made the first real map of Korea. It was in 1861—a date many of us remember with pride. You are like Kim Chong-ho, in my mind. So thank you for coming. And thank you for sharing in our little birthday. My mother was honored too. I hope you like my theory. You will keep in touch with me, yes? There is so much more to say." Then he giggled and belched and turned very red in the face. "Farewell, my friend. The Lord Buddha will watch over you. Farewell." He turned and in an instant was gone, swallowed up in the shadows of the balsam firs, a good and remarkable man in a good and remarkable place.

❖ ❖ ❖

I wound my way on tiny country lanes up and through the eastern edge of the range of hills. It was warm and hazy, there were a few puffs of pure white cloud, and the countryside and the smell of warm greenery made me think of a late spring day in Kent or Suffolk. Had I been in England there would have been the first practice games of cricket on the village greens, and a few energetic gardeners would be edging their lawns or out on their hands and knees bedding in the summer's roses. It was a Sunday, and all would be quiet. But here a bright blue cement truck rocketed past me, throwing a trail of stones and dust in its wake. It bumped noisily up the hill to a distant site where I could see a drainage culvert being built. Here everyone was working: There were the silhouettes of the planters, bent double and moving slowly like huge black snails across the glistening plates of the paddy; *chige* men, with their ancient wooden A-frame carriers strapped to their backs with thick baling twine, staggered past carrying their loads of green leaves or vast bundles of twigs; two roadmen were sitting in the shade, waiting for a fresh load of gravel to pour onto the tar—they offered me a drink from their jug of milk white *makkoli* and handfuls of rice. Nowhere in this immense Sunday panorama did I see a single Korean taking his ease, enjoying the warmth and the pleasant sights and sounds of the season, taking pleasure in doing nothing.

I startled a snake—or rather, we startled each other as I nearly stepped on it and shot about six inches into the air. It was a green beast about four feet long, not, I hoped, a specimen of something called *Agkistroden halys pallas*, which is the only local snake with a potentially fatal bite. Had I been a Korean I probably—even if it had been A. *halys*—would have given chase, caught it, whirled it around my head and smacked it against the ground, cut off its head, unzipped its skin, and boiled it up for soup. Snake potions—for treatment of neuralgia and TB (vipers are favored for these ailments), for longevity (albino snakes are said to help here), and as cures for everything, with yellow python being the favored generalist—are expensive and highly regarded; and in the better restaurants *paem tang*, or snake soup, and *paem sul*, or snake wine, are taken for pleasure too, like dog soup and ginseng tea.

Back on the metaled road I did eventually come across Koreans who were trying to enjoy their Sunday off. But even they were working at enjoyment rather than indulging in the "creative loafing" that grips the West (and that indeed is the title of a magazine in Atlanta devoted to the more mellow pursuits). So, in large groups, they cycled or walked past me (cheerily, always waving, even the fellow who rode straight into me and knocked himself and a half-dozen others to the ground) or they went off to rock climb. In every case they were kitted up in brand-new expensive gear so that they all looked the part, even if they didn't particularly care for the sport for which they had dressed themselves. ("The rules for mountain climbing," one writer on Korea noted, "demand not that you climb a mountain, but that you dress up in heavy boots, alpine hat, colored jacket, and have a knapsack or pack over your shoulder. If you are thus equipped you are 'mountain climbing,' even if you get on the wrong bus and end up at the seaside.")

It was a long afternoon, and I had to fight off the effects of the morning *soju* session as I marched on northward. I sat for ten minutes in the sun outside a small shop, but so many people came up to me and wanted to shake my hand, denying me the very peace I craved, that I gave up and marched on. But by seven, when the sun was sliding down behind yet another range of hills, I was at my destination, the Zen Buddhist temple of Paekyang-sa, where

I was to meet the man whose name was on Haedarng's piece of crumpled paper.

The setting was near perfection. I had been walking into a deep valley in the Inner Sanctum Hills, the Naejang-san, the slopes on either side covered with maple and oak and cherry trees, with thick clouds of pink-and-white blossom and pale green early leaves. The river beside me was full and rushed over the stones loudly. The roadway was thronged with walkers streaming out of the national park after the holiday—so this is where they had all been going—and when I came to the gate I found myself the only person wanting to go in, and the park officials very confused.

"Nine hundred won," a man demanded. I tried to explain that I was to be a guest at Paekyang-sa temple, but when I mentioned the word for sleep—cha-da—he pointed to a hotel sited just outside the gates. No, I said, I wished to go inside. "Nine hundred won," he said. I was about to pay when I thought to mention the magic word sunim, the word that had worked so well in finding Haedarng's home. There was a chorus of relieved sounds and nodding heads, the gate slid open for me, and I went through—the remaining walkers now dribbling out looking at me very curiously.

By the time I reached the temple itself all the remaining visitors had gone and the place was silent and empty. A placid lake—the river had been dammed by logs—reflected the long curving roofs of the temple buildings beyond the high walls; smoke curled lazily from one of the buildings; the faint sound of chanting could be heard from within. I crossed an old, moss-covered bridge, then passed beneath the entrance gate and its traditional four enormous statues of the guardian kings—their eyes bulging, their piglike nostrils flaring, their faces a strange mixture of menace and benignity. A fence of red palings kept them at bay; but in any case they let me pass unmolested, their purpose being only to halt the passage of the foes of the Buddhist faith. (They have been tested only twice in the thirteen centuries since Paekyang-sa was built in A.D. 632, and on both occasions they failed. The temple was sacked twice by invaders and was destroyed on two other occasions by fire.) The buildings now grouped beside the lake and beneath the vast exposed cliff of White Mountain were built in 1917 by a Zen master—the temple being a classic Zen structure of the Chogye sect. A single bo tree—a ficus tree under which the Lord Buddha meditated and found enlightenment—stands in the temple courtyard, having seen many of the buildings' previous incarnations and listened to the striking of the temple's bell and gongs.

Do Yaun Sunim, tall, shaven-headed, about thirty years old, and with a face of immense kindness and sagacity, stood near the entrance, his long gray robes stirring in the evening breeze. His trousers ended in what resembled old army gaiters, and he had on thick gray socks and slippers. He seemed very pleased that I had found him.

"Haedarng telephoned me. He said you were walking here, so I knew what time you would arrive. You are right on time. I hope I may walk with you when you leave. You will be staying, of course?"

He took me to his rooms—two small *ondol*-floored cells, with paper screens and, in his work room, a desk and a chair. Books on Buddhism were piled on his desk and by his dressing table. He sat me down, took my bag, and began slicing an apple. "We will eat after prayers. But you might like this to start with?" I chomped hungrily on the apple: He took down his prayer robes, his cowl, his belt—all of the same gray woolen cloth, all perfectly clean, impeccably folded—and one by one put them on, tying the ribbons that fastened them, aligning belts and straps with a precision born of habit and intense training. (I once met an English Buddhist in training at a monastery in Hong Kong; he had spent several days learning the exact way—the Zen way, the meditative, pleasurable, meaningful way—of folding his scarf.)

Outside a young monk was beginning the sounding of the temple bell—an enormous, acorn-shaped iron bell, ornately carved and chased—that stood on a covered podium by the entrance gates. The monk drew back the four-foot striker that hung beside the ball suspended on thick ropes; he looked at his watch; he looked at the sky; he muttered a soothing sutra or two, and struck the bell with all the force and weight of two hundredweight of wood.

The sound was huge, a great roaring gong sound that cannoned across many octaves and twined itself into many harmonies. It filled the air with vibrations, it echoed around the hills, it cascaded from within the bellhouse itself, and then, just as it was beginning to fade away, the young monk struck at the metal lips again and another layer of perfect clean sound overtook the now dying notes, and the old echoes were supplanted by new ones, and new harmonies came and went with a strange and beautiful but slightly unsettling effect. The temple bell had been booming out its evening call here for centuries; it was almost as much a part of the mountains as the rocks and the streams themselves.

When Do Yaun was ready we went to the main Buddha Hall, the central Buddha glimmering in the candlelit gloom with his two attendant Bodhisattvas, the deities who, the teaching has it, postponed their own enlightenment so they could help novices on their way to nirvana. The hall was huge: At one end there were perhaps twenty monks, including Do Yaun, who stood, tapping on their wooden *moktak* clappers and chanting sutras to the time of the slow bell beat. Now that I had had some practice, I found the kneeling rituals less of a problem, though climbing socks on a freshly waxed wooden floor do not make for great adhesion, and I stumbled my way through some of the faster changes. A disciple noticed my clumsiness, and placed a silk kneeling mat on the floor for me, which made at least the impact a little softer.

Dinner was simple—two bowls of rice, tofu soup, and an apple—there is a strict rule in Buddhist temples that not a grain of rice can be left in a bowl nor a drop of water in a glass. A large and cheerful woman was on hand to do the washing up.

And then, it being all of eight o'clock, Do Yaun suggested sleep. He unrolled the *yo* and the *ibul*, gave me a proper pillow in place of the wooden brick on which he, too, chose to rest his neck, and he turned in and was sleeping like a child within minutes. It took me a little more time, but the creak of the trees in the wind, and the cry of a distant owl, and the occasional clap of a *moktak* from some cell where private devotionals were taking place set me drifting off. All my muscles ached pleasantly—it had been a long and strenuous walk—and no matter how hard the floor (and tonight there was but a single *yo* on the *ondol* floor, Zen concessions to Western needs only going so far) it was wonderfully good to relax and let consciousness fade slowly away.

The alarm jangled tinnily. I looked at my watch. It was 2:45 A.M. and Do Yaun was dressing, as quietly as he could. He saw me awake. "Sorry," he shushed. "Meditation time. You will hear the bell, I am afraid. But try to sleep."

Zen meditation in Korea is said to be very different from Japanese Buddhist meditation—though both aim to produce the same end result, the enlightenment that goes hand in hand with attaining a near-unattainable state of Buddhahood. In Japan the common practice is for the disciple to meditate by "just sitting" (and being beaten on the base of the spine by patrolling disciplinarians who can see if the back is becoming bowed by the intense pain) or attempting by deep thinking to answer a *koan*, a riddle set by the Zen Master. In Korea the *koan*'s essence only is studied—a single, outwardly simple though bafflingly pointless question known in the calling as a *hwadu*. The *hwadu* may be the expression "No!" or the question "What is this?" or "What is this mind?"

(One of the more famous Zen masters in Korea was Hyobong, who was a judge during the Japanese occupation—in fact, the first Korean ever to be allowed to sit on the bench. But after having to sentence a man to death, he became suddenly disenchanted with the whole idea of colonial justice, resigned, and became an itinerant toffee seller, during which time he thought deeply about how he could best lead a decent life. He finally decided to become a Buddhist monk and to start proper meditation.

He then chose the *hwadu* "No!" and in 1931—though it might be difficult to accept this kind of thing happening so recently, so much does it sound the stuff of legend—had himself walled into a tiny hermitage, with only a tiny hole for food to be passed in and out. He stayed there for eighteen months, until one day in 1933 he realized that all of his doubts had been resolved. He had himself unwalled, and as a conclusion to his lengthy meditation on the *hwadu* "No!" wrote the following lines:

At the bottom of the ocean, a deer hatches an egg in a
    swallow's nest.
In the heart of a fire, a fish boils tea in a spider's web.
Who knows what is happening in this house?
White clouds float westward; the moon rises in the east.

After which revelation, Hyobong became a Zen Master, a respected teacher,
and was appointed spiritual head of the Chogye order—the principal order in
Korea. Thus, while cynics might not accept the validity of the *hwadu* system
nor the sense of the poem that resulted, it has to be accepted that the man
who so meditated, and the man who came up with this answer, was appointed
to a position equivalent to the head of a major Western church—a church
whose rituals must seem as strange to Zen Buddhists as their ways must seem
back West.)

Do Yaun, then, was off to contemplate his *hwadu* in the silence of the
meditation hall. It began at three; the monks bowing to the Buddha, then
taking their places for the first period of meditation, which began, as always,
with three strikes of the *moktak*. The period lasted for fifty minutes, ending
with a brisk ten-minute walk around the hall; this schedule continued until
nine or ten at night—fifty minutes' meditation, ten minutes' walk, for the
better part of eighteen hours. Do Yaun, however, had dispensation to look
after his guest, and was back at 9 A.M. "It is raining" he said, with a triumphant gleam in his eye. "You must stay another day!"

But I said I wouldn't—that I wanted to walk through the mountains in the
rain. "Excellent," he exclaimed. "I will walk with you. You do not mind? I
have no boots like you, but I know the back way across the mountains. We
will go together. Is this good?"

And so I bathed in the ice-cold water of the bathhouse, rubbing my skin
until it tingled deliciously. I took more soup and tofu and rice and water. The
other monks bade me their good-byes. Do Yaun gave me a small plastic-and-
bamboo umbrella to hold in case the rain fell more heavily, and he picked up
one himself. He had a pair of running shoes peeking out from under his vo-
luminous baggy trousers—his only concession to the walk ahead. I strapped on
my pack again, set my recorder and wound forward my camera, zipped everything that could be zipped to keep out the rain, stepped out and left the
guardian kings behind. A steep mountain range lay ahead and beyond that,
the province of North Cholla, the rice bowl of Korea.

CHAPTER

SIX

"*They believe there are but twelve Kingdoms or Countries in the Whole World, which once were all subject, and pay'd Tribute to the Emperor of* China; *but that they have all made themselves free since the* Tatar *conquered* China, *he not being able to subdue them. . . . Their writings give an account, that there are four score and four thousand several Countries; but most of them do not believe it, and they say, if that were so every little Island and Sand must pass for a Country; it being impossible, they say, for the Sun to light so many in a day. When we nam'd some Countries to them, they laugh'd at us, affirming, we only talk'd of some Town or Village; their Geographical Knowledge of the Coasts reaching no farther than* Siam, *by reason of the little Traffick they have with Strangers farther from them. . . .*"

—HENDRICK HAMEL,
1668

❖ ❖ ❖

THE PATH TO THE TOP OF THE NAEJANG MOUNTAIN ridge was narrow and muddy, and it was a bleak morning, gnawingly cold with a fine misty rain. But while I might have been miserable alone, Do Yaun was the perfect walking companion, and we chatted amiably as we wound our way through the thick, leafless, dripping forests. He had a phenomenal knowledge of the outside world and quizzed me endlessly about finer points of geography. "South Dakota—why is the capital called Pierre?" he would ask. Where did I think Columbus had first sighted land?

He was also very fit and nimble, so that even though he was wearing tennis shoes, he scrambled over the wet, moss-covered rocks like a mountain goat and never stumbled once. He somehow managed to keep his robes magically clean and free of the mountain mud, while I was splattered from end to end. When, after about four hours hard uphill going, we arrived at the summit of the knife-edge and the pair of us stood in the clouds looking down on the plains of Middle Korea bathed in the early afternoon sunlight, he looked just like a young god. I felt suddenly proud to have known him.

The downhill going was even tougher—fifty-degree slopes, wet earth and loose stones, and bamboo leaves that cut your hands to shreds if ever you were foolhardy enough to grab hold of one to stop you from sliding. (Bamboo, which grows in profusion in this part of Chollanam-do, is known to Koreans as *tae-namu*, or the Great Tree; while it is nowhere near as great to look at as the great ginkgos found near Seoul, nor as impressive as the huge Chinese elms and oaks, it is greatly revered here as in China. It has the advantages of strength, suppleness, and lightness, so it can be used to make scaffolding or baskets, chopsticks or tablemats, carved spoons or furniture. And its young shoots can be eaten. The oak and elm, ginkgo and cherry may be more spectacular, but they are hardly as useful, nor do they play as large a part in Korean life.)

As we reached under the winter snow line once more, so the flowers began to appear by the boles of the trees—the cosmos and the gentian, bushes of forsythia, and the first of the lilacs. The sun emerged suddenly from the clouds and beat down on our backs, warming the air in an instant and setting the earth steaming, the steam mingling with the perfume of all the wildflowers that rose in a heady bouquet. Do Yaun stopped and pointed to a mass of cherry blossom in the valley.

"That is so sad to see," he said. His voice was oddly thick with gloom.

I confessed I could see nothing sad in it at all; it looked astonishingly beautiful, and that was all.

"Ah yes, but soon it will be gone. Another few days, and the branches will be empty again. That is what is so sad, thinking of it going away."

I had read of Zen sadness at the idea of nature's transience. But it seemed pointless. After all, there would soon be leaves in place of the blossoms, and then other flowers would bloom, and then there would be the autumn colors— the books all say the slopes of Naejang-san looked as though they were on fire in early October. Was that not sufficient compensation?

"No, for all that says is that all beauty is transient. Everything passes by. Even this sadness!" and he laughed, and thus having cheered himself up, carried on slipping and sliding down the hill.

All of a sudden the slope flattened, and we emerged from a grove of maple trees and out onto a main road—a transition far more brutal than that between the seasons of a cherry tree. It was not a busy road—an occasional bus went by, a few tractors—but it brought the smell of civilization back again, and neither Do Yaun nor I was happy to see it. I could see the disappointment in his face; he had been sunny and cheerful up above, and now he looked nervous and uncomfortable. Up in the quiet hills, where he lived all his life, up with the mist and the crags and the distant sound of the temple bells, something of the more real Korea had been present. But it was a reality that had proved to be evanescent, and now the brash, new, prosperous busy Korea had asserted itself again.

An immense tourist hotel loomed suddenly from the mist, like a blockhouse in some Ruritanian frontier post. We climbed its steps and passed in through its electrically operated glass doors—no guardian gods here, nor any bodhi tree in the forecourt—and in place of silent monks there was a disconsolate-looking desk clerk and a pair of honeymooners wrestling with an umbrella that had blown inside out in the gales. I asked for the coffee shop, which was quite deserted. Do Yaun ordered a glass of Chinese tea, and I tried gamely to work my way through the worst apology for a hamburger I had had in all my days. I missed the rice and even the tofu soup, and when I told Do Yaun he laughed and suggested that I come back with him and become a disciple.

He turned back after lunch; he had to be in the monastery at the close of the canonical day, to take part in whatever was the Zen equivalent of compline. The last I saw of him was very much a Mallory and Irving sighting—the curtain of mist, which still swirled down from the jagged peaks, parted briefly, and I saw a tiny gray-robed figure moving briskly across a clearing in the woods. He had his straw hat on and seemed to be using his umbrella as an ice ax. Then he passed back into the trees, and the curtain of mist reformed, and a bus roared past me sounding his horn in what I thought was irritation, but turned out to be friendliness, because when I looked back everyone on board seemed to be waving and giving me the V-for-victory sign. I had to forget about Do Yaun for the time being.

The foothills smoothed themselves out, and the forests gave way to orchards and then to small fields filled with the curiously thatch-roofed rows that denoted ginseng plantations. It takes six or seven years for a ginseng root to grow to maturity, and during that time the soil that holds the precious plants must be protected from sun and frost and rain and wind, with straw strewn thickly on the ground, a timber frame built above it, and a thatched roof kept neat and rainproof above that. There had been little ginseng south of the mountains, where it was quite probably too warm or the soil was too thin or too acidic. But now, on the northern slopes of the foothills, just above the barley fields and the limitless acres of rice paddies, ginseng was grown in well-organized abundance to feed the ever-growing appetite for this most celebrated of nostrums and sexual tonics.

I came at last to Chonju, a town of very little distinction and even less beauty, where I stopped for the night. The hotel, for which no discernible reason had the Canadian flag flying above the front door, was a dreary place. The room boy, however, was an obliging sort and organized a washerwoman to scrub the accumulated dirt from my clothes and a pretty young girl to massage my back—there was a point somewhere near my right shoulder that burned, almost as though a welding torch was playing on it, after I had been carrying my pack for more than ten minutes.

The boy grinned as he ran off to get the masseuse. I knew why, of course. The girl he came back with, who looked like a young and perfectly respectable housewife, came into my room, shook my hand peremptorily, and started to take her clothes off with all the charm and allure of a coal miner who had just ended his shift. I told her—or rather, since she spoke not a word of English, I indicated to her, by pointing to her fast-accumulating pile of clothes and then to my back, and by making squeezing motions with my hand—that I wanted her to deal with my shoulder and (for reasons of fatigue rather than morality) nothing else, at least for the time being. She looked rather grumpy at this news, and assumed an expression of deep puzzlement: Most Koreans are inveterate call-girl fans, and there is a routine and a set of protocols to which this Miss Lee was accustomed. But she eventually agreed, got herself dressed again, and pummeled my back in a halfhearted way for ten minutes.

Then she began to make a fair show of real affection, and there was a moment of some temptation for me, but it passed as I considered the twin costs in *won* and in potential transmitted ailments, and I asked her to go. She gathered up her coat and sailed haughtily out of the room, probably to complain to the ever-eager room boy about having her time wasted. The room boy poked his head around the door five minutes later. "Massagee good, yes?" he asked. I grinned, he winked, and thus linked in conspiracy, he promised to meet me in the bar later that evening.

He brought three friends—a boy of nineteen (he being twenty) and two girls. I was the first *yangnom* they had met, and they were intrigued, and went through the routine of stroking the hair on my forearms. But their real purpose in coming, they explained, was to buy me dinner (I accepted) so long as I agreed to talk to them in English (I agreed). And so we all repaired to the nearest *bulgoki-jip* and feasted on barbecued spiced beef (though never lamb: Both the Koreans and the Japanese loathe the smell of lamb) and *kimchi* and rice and plenty of beer (which the girls drank with great gusto, and in consequence giggled a great deal), and I taught them idioms like "The game isn't worth the candle" and "Half a loaf is better than no bread" and the differences between "big" and "huge" and "catch" and "capture." They left me back on the hotel steps late at night, with addresses of my children and various friends back in Oxfordshire to whom they promised they would write and who, I promised in return, would write back to them (the promises, made after many bottles of O.B., were not ones for which any of us could vouch the next morning—and in any case, I could not be sure I had the addresses right).

The next day, which was bright and clear, I stepped out early. I had fifty kilometers to do, and I planned to keep going. Everyone had warned me that this would be the most tedious part of the entire journey, across endless tracts of flat, rice country, peopled by unfriendly farmers and the rural poor. And certainly as I strode away from Chonju, and the hills faded into the distance behind me, the countryside took on the aspect of northern France or Belgium, with haphazard and grubby little towns that looked like the setting for a Zola novel about grim folk enduring grim times.

Every few miles a large sign had been installed by the roadside—six lines of *hangul* script and the numbers 113, 112, written in red. I could just about make out the words, but there was no possibility of my understanding them, since the tiny dictionary I carried in my pocket only worked from English to Korean. After I had passed about five of the signs I started to get exasperated, and asked the owner of a shop where I had stopped to buy chocolate. He had replied "hello" when I greeted him with *"annyong-haseyo,"* giving me confidence to put the question. However, his English was virtually nonexistent, and the only words I could catch from his torrent of explanation were "north," "spy," and "telephone."

Getting nowhere (I was being especially obtuse, it now seems), he started to play charades. He put imaginary binoculars to his eyes (I pulled out mine, and he nodded his head vigorously). He began writing on an imaginary pad (I took mine from my pocket), and he took pictures with an imaginary camera (I pointed to the Leica slung around my neck). He nodded, and then his nodding slowed, and he looked at me with a strange expression on his face. And then I realized—the notices were warnings to the public to be on the alert in case of spies from North Korea, and to urge them to telephone 113 or 112 if any were seen or suspected. A spy, this Le Carré of the shopkeeping world seemed to think, carried binoculars, a notebook, and a camera—and I had all three! I edged from his shop, sliding the screen door slowly open, mustering as warm and friendly a smile as I could, slipping beyond the door and sliding it shut again. I wondered if he had his doubts. If he had telephoned, his message was lost in the bureaucracy, for I heard nothing more.

My destination was the town of Iri and at dusk, dog-weary and with badly aching feet, I reached the outskirts. (Miss Lee's ministrations, or something, had certainly improved my shoulder muscles.) I was rather surprised to find the place standing. And not just standing—Iri seemed a busy, prosperous little town, all lights and action, the shops crammed with people, the factories noisy with three shifts of production every day. It had not been that way eight years before, the night Iri blew up.

It was an icy midwinter night, and a munitions train was passing through town. Iri is an important railway junction, where the main line from Seoul divides into three, and this train, so it is said, was heading along the westbound spur line to the huge American air base at Kunsan thirty miles away. It was said to be loaded with bombs and ordnance for the storage dumps there, though the air force has never admitted as much. Whatever the precise nature of the contents, the train stopped in Iri to take on a fresh crew. It was about 2:00 A.M., and the guard took the opportunity to steal a few moments in one of the few *makkoli-jips* still open for a bottle or two of the milky rice wine and perhaps a piece of *ojingoa* brought all the way from the Falkland Islands and, if he was hungry enough, a delicious bean pancake known as *pindae-ttuk*. He forgot the tall candle he had left burning in his cabin.

An hour or so later the candle tipped over, setting afire a pile of hessian sacking. Within minutes the whole rear of the train was ablaze, and then, in one enormous, unforgettable blast of noise and white-hot destruction, the entire tonnage of high explosives went up, sending a huge shock wave rolling out from the goods yards by Iri station. A crater fifty feet across and twenty feet deep was all that remained of the railway station. Hundreds of surrounding houses were flattened—some say that a third of the town was either demolished or had to be. Officially, three hundred people died; today residents say the figure is closer to six hundred. There was an inquiry that blamed the guard; but no questions were ever raised in public about the nature of the load or about the wisdom of routing such massively destructive trains through so heavily populated an area. Questions like that are rarely raised, and even more rarely answered, in Korea.

Today, though, the guard is considered something of a hero—like the baker whose bread caught fire in London in 1666. Iri had been a cramped, sickly little town in the seventies; the rebuilt Iri, like most modern Korean towns, is an unlovely sight, but it has space and modern office buildings, houses, and schools. To that extent the guard performed a major civic duty, though at a somewhat exorbitant cost.

One of the new buildings was the Hotel Hannover, a gleaming, glass-and-chromium structure of stunning ugliness, in which I had been told to stay. I walked in through the restaurant, and a balding, bearded man in early middle age looked up from his beer. "Evening, boyo," he said, in an unmistakably Welsh accent. "You British?"

His name was Trevor Jones, and his stock-in-trade was the installation, all over the world, of biscuit-making machines. "Only half a dozen blokes like me in the world," he said. "Just been in the Gulf, doing ginger nuts. Here to do digestives."

Thus cued I mentioned that I had been sustained on much of my journey so far by packets of McVitie's Digestive Biscuits, well known in Britain and now apparently made in Korea under license. Mr. Jones pressed his thumbs to his chest. "That's what I said. Digestives. You're looking at the bloke as is responsible. I put in the machines four years ago, and now I'm back putting in some more! Bloody popular, they turned out to be."

I said I wasn't exactly sure I approved. I had been quite depressed by the sight of enormous piles of junk food in the village shops—marshmallows and Popsicles, Smarties and potato chips—where once there had been racks of vegetables and fruit and meat and bags of different kinds of rice. "Chosen the wrong target there, old boy," he said. "Digestives are very good for you. Full of roughage, you know. Keep you regular. Good for Koreans, good for everyone. Now, some of the stuff they make—well, I wouldn't eat it all myself. But if that's what they want, that's what they want. Sign of the times, I'm afraid. They get richer, they want what we have. And we're in the business of giving it to them—stands to reason."

I muttered darkly about dietary imperialism, but the remark was immediately lost because a new couple had come into the restaurant and greeted the biscuit man warmly. Then, "Jules Black," announced the man, thrusting his hand into mine. "San Francisco. My wife, Gita. Junk jewelry business is our line. Lots of outlets in the Bay area. You?"

He was a small, birdlike man, almost lost under the shoulders of the large check jacket he wore. His wife was huge—a bold blond woman with a Central European accent, with glasses dangling around her neck on a jeweled rope, and tight white trousers. "A writer?" she said. "Never met one before. Must be real interesting." The accent was Europe but the idiom was purest California. But they didn't find writing at all interesting, really, and turned back to Trevor. "Tell us about this machine of yours. Did I hear you right? Gita and I were talking about it in the room. You said it's two hundred yards long? One machine? How'n heck do you get it here?"

And so Trevor tried to explain the mechanics of biscuit making while Jules looked at his watch and Gita played with her bangles. It must have been the king of conversation repeated a thousand times a day between salesmen and dealers who fetch up in remote Ramada Inns and late-night airport cocktail lounges, neither party really listening, no one really interested—a sort of vaguely social Muzak turned on to keep away the unbearable silence. Maybe some of the facts would stick. "Remember that guy we met in Korea?" Jules might say at a jewelers' convention, prompted perhaps by the sight of a Ritz cracker under his canapé. "Biscuits like this come out of a machine as long as two football fields. That's what he said. Damn sure he did." And Gita would nod in confirmation, and the topic would promptly switch to something else. "See the game last night?"

The Blacks didn't like Korea. "The cities are damned dirty places, everyone's out to cheat you. Junk jewelry—well, that's what we call it; it's the less expensive stuff, you know—it's a very fast-moving business. Lots of competition, lots of cheating, lots of shady dealers. You have to be on your toes. But we found a guy here—or rather Trevor found him for us—who's real honest and nice. We've bought some stuff from him. Price pretty good too." Trevor winked at me.

We all went out to dinner in a local Chinese restaurant. "Can't take Korean food," said Jules. "So goddamn spicy, makes me nauseous. Know what I mean?" Mr. Kim from the Far East Gems Corporation—Trevor's friend, the man with whom the Blacks were now doing business—turned up with his wife. "How'd you know we was here?" asked Jules. "I just asked people in the street, Did you see some foreigners go past? It took about a minute to find where you were. You're probably the only whites in town."

Mr. Kim was a slick, snappily dressed, fast-talking man with an American accent and enormous bags under his eyes. His wife said little but smiled winsomely and said she understood all that was being said. "My English is very poor," she said. "She's shy, poor darling," said Gita. They talked stones—not diamonds or rubies or emeralds but their country cousins, amethysts and white zircons and blue topaz, and mysteriously named artifices like kunzite and xanthite that are apparently popular with the resort set.

They swapped stories of disasters. "Gal we know came out from San Diego," said Gita. "Husband had died, left her the business. She was going shopping for stock in Taiwan—Korea's big competition, isn't it, Mr. Kim? Anyways, we met her in Taipei in the hotel, saw her going off with some Chinese dude. Next morning she was very chipper. She had done this really good deal, she said. Paid him sixty thousand bucks in cash—all her money. He would deliver the stuff later that morning. Well, of course he never did. He just skipped town. She was in terrible shape. We did our best to comfort the sucker, but what can you do? There's one born every minute, isn't there, especially in this business?"

Trevor took me to the hotel bar after dinner. It was an astonishingly noisy place, full of drunken businessmen who were being lured onto the stage to sing to their colleagues, who all cheered and threw things about. We sat at the back, at a deserted counter manned by a pretty girl of about eighteen. "Anna," said Trevor with some pride. "My little darling," and he reached around her waist and kissed the girl on the cheek. Anna smiled sheepishly at me and shook my hand.

We tried to make conversation, Anna listening politely and pouring our beers, and replenishing the seaweed squares on the *anju* plate. I mentioned that I very much liked to eat the seaweed as I walked along, whereupon she reached under the bar and, making sure no one was looking, gave me half a dozen packets of the stuff and told me to put them in my pocket. At the going rate her gift was worth, I reckoned, about thirty dollars. "Bloody expensive, drinking in this country," said Trevor. "I can get through three hundred dollars in a night, easy. Hostesses are a bloody fortune. I get good pay installing these machines. But I end up my stay here in debt. Always the same. Have a good time, though, I'll say.

"So good, these Korean girls," he remarked later, after he had told Anna to meet him when she got off work at about 3:00 A.M. "She's a treasure. I'll be sorry to leave her. She really likes me. Virgins—they're the ones. Mind you, it takes a good few weeks of hard work and patience to persuade a virgin to come across. But it's good. Damned good." And afterwards? "Oh, well, Simon, ç'est la vie, I suppose." I said I thought Koreans set great store by virginity, and that a girl who had lost hers might well not be easily marriageable. "Pshaw," Trevor snorted. "Don't believe all you hear. 'Course they can get married. They may not get first pickings. But there's always someone around who's ready to take shop-soiled goods. No—if they knew they couldn't get married, there's no way they'd go with me in the first place, is there? Stands to reason."

He took me to the factory the next morning. Mr. Lee, Manager of the Tong Yang Confectionary Company's Orion Number Two plant, sat proudly in his vast office, surrounded by samples of his company's products—packets of brown lumps called Chocopies, Coconut Cookies, Animal Crackers, and Digestives. He offered tea—"and I hope you will have some fresh Digestible Biscuits."

"Digestives," corrected Trevor. "Ah yes, thank you, Mr. Jones, digestibles. Very good. Very crunchy. Very good for health."

The plant was clean and modern, and because of all the cooking, very hot. Trucks filled with flour—milled in Korea from Canadian red winter wheat, said Mr. Lee—were backed into the loading bays, as were tanker trucks, from which, via great silver tubes, life-giving liquid sugars and hydrogenated fats and oils were being sucked into the ever-hungry factory. Inside hundreds of young girls all in identical white uniforms, presided over the baking machines, which, with their lighted inspection windows, looked like skyscrapers that had toppled over sideways.

I thought the girls working as quality controllers on the Animal Crackers line had the most difficult job. As the rows of freshly baked beasts shot past them, so they had to pick out the deformities and the stillbirths—elephants *sans* trunks, neckless giraffes, pigs that had failed to inflate or had holes in their snouts. They were paid 120,000 *won* a month for their services—$35 for a forty-eight-hour week.

Mr. Lee was very much a company man, proud of Tong Yang and his association with it. "We are much more than digestible biscuits," he said. "Read what our chairman says." And he gave me a copy of the latest annual report, in which the extremely corpulent (and "sadly, rather unwell") chairman, Mr. Yang Koo Lee, explained the basis of his firm's fortunes.

"I am convinced that the real meaning of this enterprise's existence, as well as the entrepreneur's assigned mission," he wrote, "is to see to it that the happiness, prosperity and peace of the society wherein the enterprise inhabits bear fruit, by making the best use of its functions as creation and harmony, characteristics of the very organic body as enterprise.

"In this regard I am proud of having played a part in solving the immediate problems of eating and sleeping among those of the food, clothing and shelter, most basic desires of human beings, through the cement and food manufacturing industries which are the Tong Yang Group's basic business areas."

Mr. Lee's enterprise, the report summarized, makes Portland cement, clinker, gas stoves, tumble driers, Chocopies, road-paving machines, large ventilating fans, fried glutinous rice cakes, chocolate bars, cuttlefish-shaped peanut snacks, and Digestive Biscuits.

❖ ❖ ❖

The Far East Gems Corporation was, by contrast, a grubby, insalubrious place— a sweatshop of the old school, where three hundred cutters were crammed together in ill-lit, unventilated rooms, working nine hours a day slicing and polishing stones for Mr. Kim. The great man sat in his air-conditioned office, computers blinking, reading Telexes or taking telephone calls from dealers and buyers all over the world. "They come to us because we're the best," he declared as he put down the phone. "Sure, it's Antwerp for diamonds, and Israel too. But we're talking about rougher stuff than that. We don't touch diamonds. Germany, Hong Kong, and Bangkok, they're pretty good in this market—the Thais pay much lower wages than we do, so they're big competition. But we're just better at it—best cutters in the world. Don't know why. They've just got an eye for it here, I guess."

He employed large numbers of students from the local university. "They need the money, they've got good eyesight, they're quick. They're not about to complain about the conditions. They can make up to eighty bucks a week if they're good. And some of them are very good."

Before going into the cutting business Mr. Kim owned a small business making whale-muscle tennis racket strings for Kawasaki. He started cutting stones in 1979, with seven employees. At the end of his first year he had thirty employees and a turnover of $630,000. In 1986 there were three hundred workers, and he did $3.5 million worth of trade. "Profitable business—took my wife off to Hawaii on holiday last year. Couldn't do that on tennis racket strings, could I? Hey—your watch looks scratched. Let's give it a shine." And an aide, clearly accustomed to such little courtesies, removed the watch from my wrist with a prestidigitator's skill. It was returned two minutes later. "Plastic, not glass, I'm afraid," said the aide with a contemptuous glare. "Not possible to shine."

Trevor and his driver gave me a lift out of town on the Kunsan road next morning. "Never been to Kunsan base," said Trevor. "I have this strong feeling that when in Rome, do as the Romans do. And they'd stay away from the Yanks." They dropped me on a straight road that was lined with thousands of flowering cherry trees. Across the road from us the driver of an immense container truck had stopped and was standing up on his doorsill, cutting some blossom to take home. A line of cars had drawn up behind the truck, but no one honked at him, the drivers evidently supposing that what he was doing was well worth stopping for, and they were only sorry they didn't have the height to do the same.

It seemed a very, very long way to the Kunsan base. It was very hot and humid. The maps totally ignored the existence of the installation—not even the large-scale chart had an indication of runways or taxiways. Someone back in Mokpo had claimed to have known where it was, and had drawn a circle in pen marked on the northern tip of the Kunsan peninsula, and had marked it "Air-base." I always hid that map when talking to Koreans in authority, assuming that the more alert of them would rush off and dial 112 or 113. In any case, the self-styled geographer was wrong, for when I tried to walk to this projection I found the road running out into a mess of sand and shingle and the backyards of old factories and storage yards.

Another man directed me to the center of Kunsan City and walked with me for a mile until I protested, saying that there were surely too many houses for there to be a base nearby. "No, we go bus station," he said brightly, whereupon I struck my leg forcefully, told him I was walking, not taking the bus, and turned on my heel. "Wait," he called out. "Long way. Must go by bus. Too far."

I wished I had listened. The road, straight, narrow, streaming with murderous traffic, went onward and over onward. Plenty of American cars and dollar-only taxis went by; I was passed by the bus that came down every day from the big air base at Osan; a caravan of sleek silver buses bearing the insignia "8 TFW—Wolfpack" zoomed past—the base football team and their fans, coming home from a game. And each time I thought that the base must be just over that rise, or behind those trees. But it never was. I walked across the top of a pair of dams that held back an enormous lake; fishermen were stringing up their nets for the evening. I passed a village with an entrance arch that said "Welcome to Silver Town," and into which a few of the American cars were turning. But still the road kept on unrolling, and darkness was starting to fall, and my feet were getting sore.

Finally, a glimmer of lights in the distance, and a water tower—the surest sign, given the American penchant for the purest of waters, of an American installation. The tower had a revolving searchlight mounted on top, and the beam swept across the road before me. It was quite dark when I finally reached the gate—a copy of a temple gateway, with a greeting in both English and Korean, and in place of the guardian kings, four American sentries, two carrying automatic rifles, the other two with pistols.

I followed the sign marked Visitors, and found myself in a dingy hut, with one Korean and two American guards. I set down my pack and asked for the base information officer. The guard—a corporal—thought there wasn't one. Besides, it was too late, he'd have gone home. He was probably expecting me, I said; could he try him at home? The corporal, who clearly preferred the simple life, and waved other pass-holders through with no more than a perfunctory glance, sighed deeply and promptly announced his intention to go off duty. "Here, Mike, you look after this guy," he said to his colleague, and a much more cheerful airman, an Irishman named O'Keefe, took over the task.

He had his trials too. No one could be found. Offices were shut, desks unmanned. Finally, after about half an hour, the phone on his desk rang, and there was a muffled conversation. He handed the phone to me. "Good evening, sir," said a voice at the other end. "I'm sorry to have to say this, but we don't have any room for you here. You'll have to go back to Kunsan City. The base is absolutely full."

After an entire career that seemed at times to have been spent squeezing and cajoling and greasing and bribing my way into and onto things—planes, theaters, ferryboats—that claimed to be full, overbooked, closed, finished for the season or sunk, I was not to be put off that easily. Besides, it must be at least eight miles back to Kunsan, it was dark, I was completely shagged out, and there might not be a hotel to be found there either. So I asked the disembodied voice—Lieutenant Joe LaMarca, public affairs—if he had any idea I was coming. "We certainly did, sir. But we thought it would be next week. And anyway, I'm in the middle of softball practice. I really can't help. Why not call us tomorrow morning?"

He was just about to hang up and go back to his mound or his diamond or wherever, when I decided to play my only ace. I decided to lie. "But look, Lieutenant, I really don't want to disturb your game, and I'm in no hurry, really, so I can wait around here as long as you like, you take your time, but you know I wouldn't have come here—walking all the way, that is—if I hadn't been assured *personally* that there would be an accommodation waiting for me here."

"You were told there *would* be room for you?" said the lieutenant. "Who told you?" I spluttered something about U.S. Forces Headquarters in Yongsan—the camp in central Seoul where the commanding general has his office. He paused, then—in one of those magical moments, as when the reservations clerk finds your name on the computer or the final passenger fails to show up on time—he took the bait. "Well, you just better come in and wait. Go to Billeting. I can't promise anything. But get yourself over there. Hand me back to the sentry. I'll tell him to let you in."

There was still some more argument and what the Indian newspapers call "red-tapism," before I finally showed my passport to the sentry and was ushered aboard a shuttle bus. We passed down miles of identical streets—East Ninth Street, West Fifth Street, A Avenue, C Avenue—until the driver let me off outside Building 309, a bile-green shack that looked like a unit in a country motel in Mississippi but was, in fact, Billeting.

"C'mon in," drawled a female voice when I knocked, and when I opened the door it looked even more like a country motel in Mississippi. A tall black woman stood behind a check-in desk. She had a pencil in her mouth and a worried look on her face. Behind her, next to the charts showing which rooms were occupied and which were free, was a cooler filled with bottles of Michelob and Miller Lite; in front of the counter was an arrangement of plastic armchairs, a display case filled with tins of Spam and bottles of Coke, and an enormous Zenith television set that was showing very fuzzy pictures of a basketball match. The woman was called Staff Sergeant Nancy Morgan; she came from Covington, Virginia; she thought Korea was a "real neat place"; and she promised she would find me a room for the night. "Don't you worry about a thang," she drawled. "I kin fit you in someplace." And she was as good as her word and eventually found somewhere—Bingo! she said—and made me register and asked me to pay for the night in advance. "Four dollars a night—pretty reasonable, huh? Of course, it means you'll have to share."

My roommate was called Steve, he was a junior airman, he had a lot of pimples, and he drove a truck. He didn't talk a great deal, and whenever I went into the room he was parked inches away from the television screen, gazing with rapt attention at a picture that, because of some eccentric adjustment, had all its colors magnificently wrong, like a Fauvist painting. Whenever I went to the washroom one of the other inmates, a black man whom I never saw clothed, would bring in his radio, if radio be the word. It was a device about as big as a Volkswagen, and which he could barely lift. He would sit it across four of the handbasins and turn the volume controls to maximum before he went under the shower. Then everything in the room—quite probably every unbolted thing within five hundred yards—shook like jelly. The first time he unleashed the monster I thought the general alarm had sounded and the base was under nuclear attack.

Joe LaMarca turned up later, full of apologies, and bought me dinner. "You found a room, then?" he said, genially. He told me he was aching to go home. "Got another ninety-four days and some hours to go and then it's the Freedom Bird for me. Can't say I like the place, can't say I don't. I don't get off base very much. All I know is I'm going home to marry my Tracy, and stay stateside forever."

He showed me Tracy, of whom he had a large number of color photographs, all identical. She was a handsome, bright-eyed girl, a pharmacist in Plattsburgh, New York—"that's a SAC base, I'm sure you know. We got ourselves the FB One-elevens there, the ones we zapped that bastard Gadafy with." He had an uncomplicated view of the world. "Way I see it, Simon—we Americans are the strongest and the best. No doubt about it. And President Reagan's our commander in chief, and whatever he tells us to do—then, yes sir!—we're going to do it and do it proud." He kept repeating this firm conviction, interleaved with expressions of deep fondness for his Tracy, for all of the three days I stayed as his guest. We drove one afternoon along the seawall—coils of barbed wire, mines, arc lights, artillery (the guns in many cases manned by dummies, to fool would-be invaders into thinking security was better than it was), a full-time curfew. "North Koreans try and land here? Waste of time! We'd blow their asses clean back to China. No way they'd ever touch this mother. No indeedy!"

Kunsan is arguably the most important American base in Korea—the base that all the foot soldiers will be looking to for help if the North Koreans ever force their way across the frontier. It is the home of the reputedly tough and scrupulously trained fighting machine that likes to be known as the Wolf Pack but is in fact officially designated the 8th Tactical Fighter Wing. The wing's battle honors read like the invitation list for the cast party at the Pacific

Theater—New Guinea, Korea, the Philippines, Thailand, South Vietnam, North Vietnam, Laos, Cambodia, and now Korea again. Statistics are hurled at the visitor: Fliers from the 8th took part in nine campaigns in the Philippines, ten in Korea, flew forty sorties a day over North Vietnam, made 38.5 confirmed kills of MiG jets (though how one has 0.5 of a confirmed kill was a nicety left unexplained) during the Vietnam War. There are said to be few American units posted anywhere around the world with as much esprit de corps or as much confidence in their ability to deter again.

The Wolf Pack's task in the event of an invasion is simple enough: Once the North Korean tanks have rolled across the border and smashed through Seoul (which is regarded by the battle planners and war-games tacticians as a more-or-less indefensible capital, likely to fall within hours of an attack), then the fighter-bombers from Kunsan hack their way through the Communist supply lines and attack Pyongyang, bringing the attack to a full stop. Once this is done, the big bombers from Japan and California will come in and reduce the impertinent braggarts to a fine (and, if necessary, radioactive) powder.

David Kramer, the base commander, is quite obviously a man on the move, his appointment to Kunsan an indication of the importance of the place. I liked him as soon as I met him. (By contrast I thought that many others I met were most unimpressive: The fighter pilots I encountered were loud and unpleasant bullyboys, and many of the lesser functionaries were dull timeservers for whom air force life seemed to provide neither inspiration nor aspiration. But Kramer was different: He seemed low-key, highly intelligent, and sympathetically curious about the world he inhabited and that he had it in his gift to destroy.)

He came from Connecticut, he married a girl from Connecticut, he went to university in Maine. The upbringing left its own peculiarly New England mark on him, and when he stopped talking about the mission of Kunsan or the Soviet threat in the Pacific, he would talk knowledgeably and affectionately of Thoreau, of nighttime shopping expeditions to the L. L. Bean store, and of the call of the loons on the lakes of New Hampshire.

I felt—I suppose I have always felt—that I would have more faith in the judgment of the American man who had read his Thoreau, and knew of L. L. Bean, and what that institution meant in the great spectrum of American life, than in the regular Joe Sixpack from Toledo, who drove a Camaro, enjoyed the Happy Hour, and screamed blue murder at the ball game. Sadly—and perhaps fatally—the destiny of the globe seems increasingly to be left in the hands of soldiers and politicians of the latter group; the others—American men who have a sensitivity about them, if you like—are derided as effete, as bleeding hearts, as milquetoasts.

Some Britons—even the British military—still try to retain respect for the more sensitive in society: There was one sailor in the Falklands War, Hugh Tinker, who wrote eloquently about the futility of it all before falling victim to the war himself. But the times are changing for Britain too, and Lieutenant Tinker was widely criticized, even in death, for having betrayed the nation's fighting spirit. Others might suggest that it was to defend the right of spirits like his to exist that men fight proudly, rather than merely fight.

All of which seems a long way from the thoughts I had as I sat in Colonel Kramer's spartan office at Kunsan Air Base. My point, lest in digression it has been lost, is simply to remark—with relief—on how pleasant it was, and how unusual, to discover a man of real intelligence and sensitivity working at a senior post in the American, or indeed in any, air force, and to hope that others of Kramer's caliber are toiling there too, adding their seasoning of sense and sensibility to an otherwise dully dangerous war-making machine.

So he talked of his time in Nigeria (where he had been an attaché) and in England (where he had flown F-100s and presumably startled lots of country parsons off their bicycles), of his classes at the National War College, of work in Germany and his flying missions in Vietnam. (He was laughably overdecorated for various degrees of supposed heroism: a Distinguished Flying Cross with one oak-leaf cluster; a Meritorious Service Medal with one oak-leaf cluster; the Air Medal with nine oak-leaf clusters; a Joint Service Commendation Medal; an Air Force Commendation Medal; a Republic of Vietnam Cross of Gallantry, with palm.) He was fascinated by Korea (and had made sure his biographical notes were printed in Korean, in the event that any Koreans were fascinated by him), intellectually stimulated by his mission. "I suppose you could say I'm like the mayor of this town. I keep the town going so that the people in it can do the work they have to. I don't direct the war: I just ensure it can be fought."

His most difficult task was the security of the base itself. It was a long way from town, on the coast, and it had a good strong perimeter fence, guarded by heavily armed soldiers of the Korean Army, by American airmen, by the best of American technology and weaponry, and by vicious dogs. "But there are rice-farming villages right outside the wire. Who knows anything about the people we see in the fields out there. Are any of them North Korean agents? Who knows? People say they can tell North Korean accents—even the use of words has changed in the thirty years since this country was divided. There are certain words they just don't have in their vocabulary now. But the North Koreans aren't fools. They could probably infiltrate this region easily—probably already have. So we have to take extra precautions."

The Pentagon provides its own advice. All aircrew members arriving at Kunsan are given a letter headed "Human Intelligence Threat Briefing," which begins:

> Kunsan Air Base is considered vital to the survival of the Republic of Korea. Certain aspects of the intelligence collection effort by the North Koreans affect transient air crews.

Friendly conversation about your job with merchants or bar girls may not be innocent. When questions proceed much beyond the point of "Do you work at the base?" you go beyond innocent conversation. The appropriate response to these questions should be noncommittal or intended to direct the conversation in another direction. Many of these people understand far more English than they let on. Also, you cannot tell the difference between our ally, the South Korean, and our enemy up north.

If you think you were the target of collection activity, you probably were. If so, immediately notify the Air Force Office of Security Intelligence. Enjoy your visit, but remember to leave your job on base.

One of the homegrown precautions taken at Kunsan is a strictly enforced ban on any American serviceman living, sleeping, visiting, or even walking in a three-mile-wide *cordon sanitaire* around the three open sides of the base (the fourth side being the Yellow Sea, and jammed solid with mines and other high-explosive deterrents). Americans may drive—though only on "Route 26, the designated major curfew control area route"—and under certain circumstances "visit orphanages, churches, or schools." Otherwise, everything from the base wire to the three-mile line is off-limits, to avoid any American falling prey to subversive temptations.

❖   ❖   ❖

The archway-gate for Silver Town, which I had seen as I was walking in, turned out to be three miles exactly from the main gate. The town, which sat astride a small hill like an old Andalusian fortress-village, and had a population of maybe a thousand, had sprung up ten years before at this nearest legitimately on-limits point along Route 26. No one called it Silver Town—no one knew why it had been called that in the first place. Now everyone said simply A-Town. It was busy every night; but this was Friday night, and, moreover, it was the last night of the Team Spirit exercises. "Hookers' prices have doubled since these bastards came in," grumbled one captain. "So there's no alternative—got to do some serious drinking and go down and get ourselves some of the giggle-sisters."

So we climbed into a *kimchi*-cab ("When these guys crash they make themselves into human *kimchi*, they go so fucking fast"). "*Atashi*" said Joe. It was the only Korean word he knew—an overfamiliar way of saying "uncle"—and the drivers, indeed everyone to whom he said it, winced when he yelled it, but took his money anyway. "Hey! *Atashi!* A-Town. Disco. Pronto!" And we roared off in pursuit of the giggle-sisters. A sergeant, who was on his fifth tour in Korea, explained: "Call them that because even when you're screwing them, they giggle. Tell you what I call this place—'The Land of Sliding Doors and

140

Slit-Eyed Whores.' " Everyone in the car guffawed, including the driver, ex-cept that his eyes betrayed him and deep down he wasn't smiling at all.

As we drew up at the A-Town taxi stand the sergeant yelled out: "Pick your wheels, boys! One with the valve closest to six pays." I chose the left-hand rear wheel, and the tire valve sat precisely at six, had the wheel been a clock face. I paid up the four dollars, which might account for my dyspeptic frame of mind as we set off into the jungle of neon ahead.

Silver Town was a throbbing square of discos, bars, and cheap cafés, its narrow streets filled with a turgid river of American servicemen and the Ko-reans who chose, either cynically or by force of economic circumstance, to service their baser needs. Every bar was the same. There was a rickety stage on which, to the deafeningly unpleasant, cat-scratching din of a cheap sound system, sullen-looking women in dingily erotic costumes danced for five min-utes at a time. The flashier bars—the Paradise, the Hollywood, the Korea à Go-Go—employed a cast of perhaps six women, so the clients would have to watch the same girl perform every half hour; the cheaper places had only three girls, or two, so the sweat was still glistening on girl number one when she clambered onto the stage to dance again as girl number three. In the cheaper places the girls were slatterns indeed, and the turnover in the audience was rapid. "Christ, let's go down the road—these girls are dogs!" Air Force women were in the crowd of onlookers too, many of the more attractive ones attached, limpetlike, to the Team Spirit pilots. Disgruntled nonfliers would always com-plain about this phenomenon—that better-looking girls would join the Air Force for the sole purpose of finding a pilot for a husband and behaved like star-struck groupies whenever a new squadron came to town. A flight of FB-111 bombers had come in from Japan for the exercise the week before, si-phoning every pretty airwoman off the base. My companions that night—none of whom had ever been in a plane, let alone enjoyed the mystique of piloting one—grumbled endlessly about the unfairness of it all. They took out their *angst* on the Korean women up on the stage.

"Fuck me!" exclaimed a corporal, on seeing one particularly corpulent woman stagger through her routine. "She's so ugly she'd blow the buzzards off a fish wagon." He specialized in one-liners that were some way removed from Noel Coward. He wore a T-shirt that proclaimed: "I'm so horny even the crack of dawn isn't safe," that might have been a better joke had I not seen the same shirt just six months before in Olongapo, the Philippine equivalent of Silver Town, where the U.S. Navy men play when they have time off from Subic Bay. "Hey, Mack," the corporal said, turning to me. "Know how you fuck a fat woman like her? Roll her in flour and hunt for the wet spot!"

I smiled at the fat girl, and she came and sat next to me during her break. "You look bored," she said. I told her I was very bored indeed but that I felt obliged to stay with my hosts, who were all now drinking through straws from an enormous bowl of porridgelike punch (it was said to be a mixture of *makkoli*, vodka, whiskey, triple sec, brandy, beer, and crushed ice, and was guaranteed to lay you flat on the floor in fifteen minutes). She said she was bored, too; she knew she wasn't attractive enough for the pilots, "So I just get the maintenance men, and they can be very bad people, very cruel."

Her name was Miss Koh, she was twenty-three, she came from Seoul and had ambitions to be a dancer. "I feel ashamed of myself, really," she said. "You know how important it is for us to find a husband. Doing something like this ruins us. I don't know why we all do it. At first it's the money. But it gets boring soon, and because you've done it, there's not else things you can do. My mother thinks I am waitress. I am sure she really knows what I do. It is very shameful." She gave me her telephone number in Seoul, "because you say you like Korea," and promised that if I called her she would show me the city. She wrote her name in *hangul* in my Alwych. "I hope to see you again," she wrote. "Good luck." As she finished writing she got up from the table and said quietly: "I don't want you to see me here again. This makes me shamed. I want you help me proud my country. This is no good."

She pointed to her colleague who was even now drawing a chair leg between her thighs, to the raucous yells of a hundred airmen, including my hosts, who had by now drained the bowl of porridge and were demanding another. A security policeman had come into the bar on his rounds; He was an immense black man with strangely manic, staring eyes that gazed fiercely into the middle distance. "He'd crack your fucking skull like a walnut," said the sergeant and giggled.

We left an hour or so later. The lieutenant nearly got himself arrested for pissing on the back wheel of a taxi. He then insisted on insulting the driver all the way back to the base and stopped and made everyone piss on a cherry sapling that he said had been planted a few days before. (Early each April, Koreans go on a massive tree-planting binge, to help replace the forests that were stripped bare by the Japanese colonists during World War II.) The driver remained quiet, impassively dignified through it all, like a parent watching his wayward child pass through a trying stage of its adolescence. I felt very saddened by it all and very much the prude.

(A handbook given to all servicemen when they enter the country contains a preface that all are entreated to read: "As American guests of the Koreans we should strive to project the best national image possible. We are each judged as individual representatives of our country, and must act accordingly.")

The next morning I had my final breakfast on base with the liaison officer, a grease-smooth Korean called Mr. Kwong, who wore a double-breasted waistcoat under his suit. I was fascinated by the performance by which he kept producing cigarettes, one every five minutes, from deep within the waistcoat. Some form of kinetic magic was at work: He simply pressed the top of a pocket and the white tube slid automatically into his hand, no wires or magnets anywhere in view.

He had worked at Kunsan for twenty-five years. He was a schoolboy during the war and remembered vividly being in the city when the North Koreans overran it in August 1950. American infantrymen retook the city and occupied the base (their current title to it derives from its being one of the spoils of war) in late September. "The Communists had put all their political prisoners in the city jail. When they knew the Americans were going to recapture the place, they simply poured gasoline all around the prison buildings and set the whole place on fire. They were brutal people—strange to think they were Koreans."

(Or perhaps not so strange. Many people I met said that Koreans had an astonishing capacity for violence. Colonel Kramer had served in Vietnam with Korean paratroopers. "Know how they used to deal with any Vietcong they caught? They'd draw lots to choose one poor fellow who they'd then skin alive. They'd stake him outside to die. A body without is skin is a terrible thing to see. They'd show the other Vietcong prisoners what they'd done and then let some of them go. Their idea was they'd go back to their units with stories about how tough these Koreans were and scare them to death. They don't monkey around, these guys. Anything mean and nasty, they have the capacity to do it." The Japanese, it was always said, would use Koreans as guards and torturers in their concentration camps—in the same way that the Russians would employ Buryats from Mongolia and Siberia to perform the least pleasant tasks of battle or occupation. The Mongols, like the Koreans to whom they are related, have a reputation for being easy to brutalize. If you were a British or an American prisoner of war and you saw a Korean coming for you, you knew you were in trouble.)

Mr. Kwong was very much a Korean nationalist. He loathed the Japanese for what they had done during the colonial period (which included, ironically, building Kunsan Air Base in 1938), and he was determined his son should grow up with a loathing for them, too. "There is a program on our KBS television, a soap opera I guess you'd call it, about life under the Japanese. It is the only program I force my son to watch. It is too easy for young people to forget what those Japanese did to us. We can never trust them again. They seem friendly now, but deep down they are not. They have plans for us, just like they've always had. They are not good for the Korean people. I dislike them—in fact, deep down I have to say I really hate them for what they have done. They took away our language. They took away our names and made us take Japanese names. They took away our king. They stole our treasures. They ruined our land. No, I can never forgive them for what they did. You in the West seem to have forgiven them for what they did to you. Me, I can never forget what they did to Korea. I am determined my children will never allow it to be forgotten."

And yet, did I sense in him a growing unease about the American presence, too? It was difficult to know. On the surface Mr. Kwong was very much a base employee, almost an American himself, the owner, indeed, of a couple of bars that were much used by the airmen. "You've got to remember that three-quarters of the population of this country has never experienced a war. You can understand why there is a feeling of growing anti-Americanism, of growing antimilitarism. The young students—they don't know what the Communists did to us, they can't really see why the Americans are over here, and why we need so many troops in our own forces, and why they have to be called up and pressed into the services. I may not agree, but I can understand."

Just then two burly and unshaven airmen walked past. One wore a patch on his jacket that said "Munitions Storage—We tell you where to stick it!" The other had a T-shirt with the words: "Kill 'em All. Let God Sort the Bastards Out." Both were sporting newly stitched shoulder patches showing what appeared to be a small plane—the fuselage looking remarkably phallic— beneath the rubric "One Hundred Successful Missions to A-Town." Mr. Kwong shook his head with distaste.

"That's what I just can't take. Don't they ever learn? We need to be respected here, and they're not respecting us. They still treat us like we're some backward Third World country, and you know we're not. We're proud, we've got good reason to be. But this . . . " He gestured with despair. I said I hadn't found anything very offensive about the two passing airmen. "Maybe not, maybe I react too much," he said. "I have worked for twenty-five years trying to bring the two communities together. I organize them to go out to meet families. I try to persuade them to learn a bit of Korean, to eat some of the food, to understand why they're here. But they don't want to know. And it's the way some of them treat our women, and our men too. Some of them just have no respect for us. The way they see it, they're top of the pile, and everyone else is nothing. It makes me mad." He stubbed his cigarette out angrily, then performed his sleight-of-hand act, and another was instantly alight in his mouth and he was puffing on it furiously.

"Still, getting the communities together works in some ways. We have about three hundred marriages a year between Korean girls and American men. There are still a lot of girls who want to get out while they can, and an American passport's a good way to do it. But in other ways it's not so easy to get girls down here. We're getting to be a much richer country, you know. Girls won't come and dance and do all the other things they have to as hostesses in places like A-Town. They don't have to. They can get other jobs now. You take a look—the average age of the dancers down there is going up. The girls aren't very pretty. And there's still this stigma of getting involved with a foreigner. Korea is racially very pure, still, more so than Japan. There's a feeling that we shouldn't dilute our stock if we don't have to. I tell you, I've got a difficult job down here; it gets more difficult, too. I earn my money, that's for sure."

I ended up rather liking Mr. Kwong, despite his outward similarity to a snake-oil salesman. It was all an act, designed to impress his masters on the base. I think he knew it cut little ice with me, and so he dropped the pretense and became just an intelligent, acutely sensitive Korean. It is said that Koreans have an unusually developed *nunchi*—a deep sensitivity to the moods and attitudes of those around them—a very finely tuned set of psychological antennae. Mr. Kwong had more *nunchi* than most, which is probably what has made him so adroit a liaison officer for the last quarter of a century, able to arbitrate between the conflicting cultures of the air base and the people on the two sides of the cyclone fencing. But the cultural divide was widening, without a doubt: His job was becoming more difficult, and he was shrewd enough to realize it.

❖   ❖   ❖

I left the base later that day. One of the air force captains came to Kunsan City with me, and we took the ferry together across the Kum River (which had been such a Maginot Line during the early stages of the war, defended by the American Army, but crossed with depressing ease by the southward-racing North Koreans) to a grimy little town called Changhang. The captain had been stationed at Kunsan for the better part of a year, but he had never been on the rustbucket of a ferryboat, and he looked uneasily about him at the smoky little lounge, crowded with its very ordinary Korean passengers. "God, the smell of *kimchi*. I'll never get used to it. Lot of our men come over here to the train station. They can get the train clear up to Seoul," he said. "But I never did. Guess it's a lot easier to stay on base. Everything you need there, so long as you get to A-Town once every few days." He was still hung over from the night before, and grinned sardonically. We had left him in the Hollywood Bar with a girl twice his size, and he looked bruised and rather sheepish at what must have been the inevitable outcome of the encounter.

We stepped off the ferry on the Chungchongnam-do side. True to form, it had started to spit with rain. The air force captain had been planning to walk around town, but then said he thought he would feel a little easier going right back on the ferry to Kunsan. I shook his hand and thanked him for all he had done. He took my picture and then stepped back onto the boat, timidity, I thought, having got the better of him.

I watched the ferry draw away into the gray mist, and his face disappeared gradually into the blur of the crowd on the rails. My last contact with America thus faded, I turned and confronted Korea once again. My expedition to Kunsan had brought me some way off to the west of the track of those long-dead Dutchmen, and I had some stiff walking to do to get back onto their trail.

CHAPTER
SEVEN

"*The Houses of the* Coresians *of* Quality *are stately, but those of the common sort very mean; nor are they allowed to build as they please. No man can cover his House with Tiles, unless he have leave so to do; for which reason, most of them are thatch'd with Straw or Reeds. They are parted from one another by a Wall, or else by a row of Stakes, or Pallisades. They are built with wooden Posts or Pillars, with the Interval betwixt them fill'd up with Stone up to the first Story, the rest of the Structure is all Wood daub'd without, and cover'd on the inside with White Paper glew'd on. The Floors are all vaulted, and in Winter they make a Fire underneath, so that they are always as warm as a Stove. The Floor is cover'd with Oil'd paper. Their Houses are small, but one Story high, and a Garret over it, Where they lay up their Provisions. . . .*"

—HENDRICK HAMEL,
1668

❖ ❖ ❖

THERE WERE HILLS AHEAD. THE MAP SHOWED THAT to the north lay an immense region of tightly packed contours and triangulation points, small, fast-flowing streams, and twisting roads. The horizon was ragged and blue where the mountains rose from the coastal plain. None of the hills was very high—a twelve-hundred-foot hill here, another at fifteen hundred, another at two thousand. The Kum River, over which I had just been uncomfortably transported, meandered its way lazily along the range's eastern flank: The Dutch sailors had been ferried across it on their way up to the court, and I would have to cross it twice as I headed back onto their track.

About an hour out of Changhang—a grubby, mean little port that smelled of smoke and rancid fish—I climbed a small, pine-covered knoll for no more sensible reason than to switch on my little radio to see if I was beyond the range of the American transmitters at Kunsan, and thus define the local limit of the base's cultural influence. (I was almost out of range, twenty miles north as an F-16 flies: Through the hissing and crackling of the overworked ether I could just make out a litany of college football scores and an announcement for an aerobics class that night in the base gymnasium.)

From up here among the pines I could see more clearly to the north the hills of Chungchongnam-do. To the south I could see the estuary of the Kum, and to the west, the battleship-gray mass of the sea. Between the wide waters and where I stood, the land was flat, and whenever the sun came out it glittered briefly on hundreds and hundreds of rice fields, like tiny mica mirrors.

149

But there were no such glints of light to the north of me. The fields were larger, and there were cattle and the beginnings of another season's tall field crops. It was beyond a doubt that I had left Korea's rice country behind for good. I was getting within the penumbra of the now not-so-distant capital city, and the sights and the people, their standing and their attitudes, all were beginning to change.

I found a yogwan on the north side of a small and rather pretty market town called Sochon. It was a far cry from the kind of hostelry that greeted Isabella Bird, when she made the first of her celebrated Victorian journeys to Korea. "The regular inn of the towns and large villages," she wrote,

> consists chiefly of a filthy courtyard full of holes and heaps, entered from the road by a tumbledown gateway. A gaunt black pig or two tethered by the ears, big yellow dogs routing in the garbage, and fowls, boys, bulls, ponies, mapu, hangers-on, and travellers' loads make up the busy scene.
>
> Low lattice doors filled in with torn and dirty paper give access to a room the mud floor of which is concealed by reed mats, usually dilapidated, sprinkled with wooden blocks which serve as pillows. Farming gear and hat boxes often find a place on the low, heavy crossbeams. Into this room are crowded mapu, travellers and servants, the low residuum of Korean travel. . . .

The "low residuum" of Korean travel is rather more kindly treated today. The yogwan is not the most basic of local inns—there is an institution called the yoinsuk where the rougher trade takes its nocturnal ease, but even the meanest yoinsuks are tolerably clean and welcoming. The yogwan, though, particularly if you are careful to ask for one that is cho-un (good) as I would do when feeling reasonably flush, is as comfortable and pleasant a place to spend an inexpensive night as any I have known anywhere. Indeed, it can fairly be said that the tradition of the Korean yogwan is the true tradition of the wayside inn, forgotten almost everywhere else, where a local family will take in the weary traveler almost as much by way of civic duty as for commercial gain.

The inn I found in Sochon was typical of the marque. I found it in the usual way—from some distance I could see the tall brick chimney, and closer to it I could see the red-and-white stylized sign for a steaming bath (a sign I always confused with a Viking ship; and I agonized for weeks over what possible links there could be between Erik the Red and the early Koryo kings). Both chimney and sign indicated the presence of a public bath, a mogyoktang, and more often than not, I had discovered, a yogwan came alongside a mogyoktang so that bathers could rent a room by the hour or so, the better to cool off and to relax.

The inn was a modern brick building of perhaps three floors, with what passed for a reception desk upstairs. Two old ladies—the venerable owner and her almost equally venerable daughter, it later transpired—were lying on the floor beside their tiny telephone switchboard. They were playing *hwatu*, the ancient game of "flower cards" (known in Japan as *hanafuda*), and I was loath to interrupt them. *Hwatu* is a pretty game to see being played, with rules like rummy: The cards themselves are tiny, gaily colored squares with pictures representing the various months—a pine tree for January, a plum tree for February, cherry for March, and so on. The players—who often stake considerable amounts of *won* on the turn of a card—become amusingly excited; and when I approached the stairway of the *yogwan* I could hear the old ladies' cries long before I found them.

But they broke off quite happily and took me off to see a variety of their rooms. This particular *yogwan* had only *ondol* rooms—some of the more modern inns have Western-style quarters, with beds and carpets, in the event of a wandering foreigner happening by—and the ladies seemed keen that, subject to this one limitation, I should have just the room I wanted. The first was pleasant enough, except that there were two men already lying on its floor, fast asleep. The second was about an inch deep in water, but I was shown it nonetheless, perhaps in case I was interested in floating myself to sleep. But the third room was perfect: The clock (all Korean rooms have massive clocks with enormous pendulums) had all of its hands lying in a heap at the bottom of the glass, but the rest of the facilities appeared to be working normally. I agreed to take it, paid up my 8,000 *won*—about $9—and took possession.

The bathhouse next door closed at eight, and although there was a perfectly good shower beside my room, it seemed a waste not to try Sochon's public facilities. There was a moment of confusion when I handed over my dollar and proceeded through the ladies' entrance (the only difference in the two silhouetted heads being that one had slightly longer hair), but I was eventually upstairs in the proper side: I tucked my clothes into a locker, snapped the keychain around my ankle, and walked somewhat self-consciously—the postage-stamp-size, all-purpose towel held rather ridiculously around my middle—into the bathing arena.

A *mogyoktang* and its more modest relation, the *taejungtang*, or "masses' bath," are monuments to egalitarian cleanliness, reducing all who enter to the basic entities of bone and muscle, freed from all pretensions of riches or power. In a place like Sochon there can in any case be few enough who are rich, and I daresay all those in the bathhouse that evening were farmers and shopkeepers and clerks and their sons, with their wives and girlfriends and daughters behind the partitions next door. The traditional reason for the huge numbers of bathhouses in Korea is that until very recently few houses had baths, or indeed water supplies, of their own: A person's *mogyok* had to be taken in privately gathered and fire-warmed water, especially during the bitter Korean winters when the rivers would be frozen solid. Now, though, most houses have water, and a bath can be had at home with ease and economy. But the old ways die hard, and if Koreans no longer have to visit their bathhouses for reasons of frugality and space, they do so now in pursuit of that most Confucian of ideals, the civilized pleasure of the purest kind.

The main bathing room was immense, with a tough red tile floor and white-tiled walls, and mirrors, mirrors everywhere. It was a positive plumbers' heaven: There were shower heads, taps, faucets, douches, spouts, plunges, fountains, sinks, basins, footbaths, bidets, sitzes, lavers, tanks, cisterns, buckets, baths, and other unnamed devices of steel and enameled iron and vitreous china placed at convenient points everywhere. Thousands of gallons of hot water seemed to be running from everything—pure steaming oceansful of the stuff streamed, gushed, trickled, cascaded, sprayed, splashed, sluiced, sloshed, surged, foamed, bubbled up, poured down, raced across, and welled from under until everything and every surface, be it horizontal or vertical or sloping, curved or plane, smooth or rough, hirsute or bald, pink or yellow, was wet through and wonderfully warmed, with every pore wide open, every square inch of flesh glistening and gleaming and becoming brighter and more polished by the second, by virtue of its mere proximity to all these limitless acre-feet of cleansing water.

Once my eyes had become accustomed to the comfortable blanket of steam, I began to see the other figures who had come from their homes to wallow in all this warmth and wetness. There were perhaps eight men and two young boys. Each of them appeared to be obsessively fascinated, Narcissus-like, with making his body as clean and perfectly presentable as possible. One young man was scrubbing his back with a long loofah; another pared his toenails; two shampooed their hair; one rubbed vigorously at his legs with a chunk of pumice; the others—including the boys, whose hands were grubby, from an afternoon of taekwon-do practice, no doubt—were standing under showers either hot or cold, covered with foam that came from the various liquid potions and the pink or green or yellow bars of perfumed soap that the management thoughtfully provided.

I was struck by how spare and rangy and fit the men all looked—there was no spare flesh, there were no thickened waists, no blotches or bulges of fat. They were all perfectly formed, Adonis-like figures—smaller than the average European or American maybe, but they looked a lot neater and more efficient. A sensible diet, long working hours, compulsory military service—probably all of these had conspired to whip their bodies into such enviably good shape; and the bathing probably helped too, by undoing all the evils of the drink that the Korean men habitually and conspicuously consume.

The walking had had its own effect on me, mind you. I was getting leaner, and I had a good farmer's tan on my arms and face. So I didn't feel too intimidated by the presence of these more ideally fashioned men as I began to scrub and soap and rub myself clean. My presence did cause a ripple of interest, however: Korean men's bodies are almost wholly hairless, and the introduction into this naked world of a creature who even while clothed was thought of as a gorilla did trigger some consternation and alarm, though mercifully it evolved into nothing more than friendly curiosity. From the trajectories of some of the gazes I once suspected their interest to be uncomfortably priapic, but that seemed more my problem than anyone else's, and after ten minutes or so the crowd's attention wandered—the harder they stared at me, the harder I stared back, and that seemed to do the trick.

After the cleansing I climbed into the massive hot bath—my first encounter with a *mogyoktang* some months before had taught me the etiquette: I shall not easily forget the withering glares when I jumped straight into the common bath and began lathering myself there—and soaked for a while. Next, the sauna—far, far hotter than anything I had known back home, it seemed heated with volcanic and sulfurous gases, and breathing was almost impossible. I staggered out after two minutes, my lungs cripplingly scalded, and leaped into an ice-cold plunge pool, then back into the hot bath, then under a cold shower, was tempted back into the sauna, and so on for two hours at least, until I was pink and glowing with good health and felt intensely reluctant to leave this womblike home and go back to the hard floor of the *yogwan* next door.

In fact, sensible to such needs, the management had provided a halfway house, an airlock in which the customers could slowly prod themselves back toward the real world. There was a long sitting-out room, a withdrawing room furnished with reclining chairs and a television, on which a mildly erotic film was unrolling, and from which pretty girls blindly blew kisses at the rows of sleepy, half-broiled bodies ranged around the room. I ordered a can of a much-advertised restorative drink with the unlikely name of McColl—it was ice-cold, but it tasted of a mixture of corn oil and methylated spirits and smelled of mercaptan, and if it did me any good it had a funny way of showing it, because I was very nearly sick on the spot. But maybe the actual effect was the intended one: I got up and left, collected my clothes and dressed, and then went out for a solitary dinner, curled up on my *yo* on the *ondol* floor, and slept like a top until dawn.

The old ladies woke me with breakfast at seven. I am still not convinced that the best way to start the day is with *kimchi* and rice. Day lilies, aralia shoots, royal fern bracken, bluebells, wild asters, broad bellflowers, mugworts, and sow thistles—all of which are used in dishes to spice up the average Korean day—I could just about imagine being placed before me at seven, with the morning's *Korea Times* and a cup of *oksusucha*. But when the inn's Mesdames Park placed their tureen of year-old cabbage and turnip soused in sour vinegar and brine, and with garlic and red chilies stirred in for good measure (which is what *kimchi* essentially is, though anything, not only cabbage and turnip, can be *kimchi*'d, in the same way that anything can be curried in Hindustan)—

when they placed that sorry-looking mess in front of me that morning, my stomach gave an unpleasant little nudge to the back of my throat, and I suddenly longed for a five-minute egg or a bowl of Weetabix and cold milk. It was the only incident of what I could actually call homesickness, and it vanished in a trice.

Henry Savage Landor had never cared much for the *yogwans* of a century ago: "The Corean inn—and there are but few even of those—are patronized only by the scum of the worst people of the lowest class, and whenever there is a robbery, a fight or a murder, you can be certain that it has taken place in one of those dens of vice . . . it is within those walls that sinners of all sorts find refuge, and can keep well out of sight of the searching police." My own experiences, here in Sochon, and in every other country inn I have spent nights in, have led me to a quite contrary view. I was quite sorry to leave this place; the old couple turned out, with their cleaning ladies, to wave me off on the next leg, and they solemnly gave me their set of *hwatu* cards, with which they saw I had been fascinated, as a remembrance.

Spring was rising fast up the peninsula now, and this morning was hot again, and all the blossoms were out. For some reason my rucksack was a great deal heavier—the Americans had loaded me down with lots of booklets on improbable topics like *How to Adopt a Korean Child*, and I had picked up the odd sample of rock or piece of interesting wood. Anyway, the going seemed tougher than for a long time, and I had to stop at the tops of most of the hills and catch my breath.

I called in at one small café where two girls were working preparing lunch. I was the only customer, and I ordered a cup of cold coffee and a plate of biscuits, and the order was taken with what seemed to be sullen bad grace. It turned out to be shyness. Within five minutes the larger of the two girls—she was very comfortably chubby, in fact—was pawing at my arms and then, like her less respectable sister in Naju, suddenly thrust her hand right down the front of my shirt and squealed with misplaced delight. I found this all a great joke and thrust my own hand down her dress, discovering much the same as I had in the Room-Salon, only more. She wasn't in the least bit offended, and in fact her friend rushed into the back room to get her camera for a picture of the happy scene. Both girls then asked me to stay for lunch (I had to say no, sadly) and then refused to accept a single *won* for the coffee. They came out into the sunshine and helped me on with my pack, and were waving me good-bye from beside their little café when I was half a mile up the next hill.

Korean women, I am bound to think, present a most bewildering and complicated mixture of emotions and attitudes. One woman can at the same moment be delightfully shy and yet alarmingly forward, liberated and yet coquettishly deferential, sexually ignorant and yet wantonly promiscuous, aggressive and argumentative and yet strangely sulky and passive. So very different from the Japanese—so friendly, so curious, so studiously attentive. The baser side of me would often think that for stimulation and curiosity value there could probably be no greater woman than the Korean, but life could at the same time perhaps be pretty hellish, I have no doubt.

Some miles along the road I encountered another woman. This lady, however, was of a great age, and she was waiting for the bus to Puyo. She was a little stooped and a little wizened, and she was standing at a bus shelter with a young man who waved to me as I passed and greeted me in English. The afternoon was very warm and I was glad to stop, and for the next fifteen minutes or so, until the country bus arrived to bear the couple away, I talked to them—or rather the old lady, who had a razor-sharp mind and a puckish sense of humor, talked to me. I had gathered that she had lived in this same village for the last fifty years, and I had asked her whether any battles had been fought here during the Korean War, or, as Koreans call it, the Civil War.

She stepped back, puffed up her chest and steadied her legs, and started to talk as though she were delivering a seminar by Clausewitz out of John Keegan. Yes, she said, she had seen a considerable amount of action. A battle royal had been fought in this valley and on these surrounding slopes. The Reds, she said, warming to the theme, were gathered on that hill, there, you see it? with their artillery behind those trees, there. They had dug trenches where you see those pigpens, and had set up a battery of mortars over there. Now the United Nations—most of them Americans, though she had heard that some Britishers were with them too—came through here with their tanks one afternoon and set them down behind that bluff to the west . . . and so the lady went on, delivering (via the good offices of the boy, who acted as translator) a blow-by-blow account of the battle for her village, as though it had taken place just yesterday. In one field, she said, a hundred men had been killed, and she had been shocked to find, when the tide of war moved on, that the grass had been left rust red. She was talking when the bus swept into view, and she was still offering her interpretations of the various stratagems as the boy and the bus driver helped her up the steps, and the bus took her away to the town where she planned to visit her son-in-law and take him some vegetables for his dinner.

❖   ❖   ❖

It took me the better part of the day to reach the Puyo bridge and cross the wide, slow-flowing Kum River once again. A mile before the crossing I had been intrigued by the sight of a large and very secure-looking installation set down behind high walls beside the main road. It looked like some kind of military headquarters, or perhaps a secret laboratory or research plant, except that there was a sign outside the main gates and below the guard tower with the word *insam* in huge letters and the picture of a gnarled root beside it. Could this, I wondered, be what many disciples would regard as Korea's single most strategic possession—the main factory for the processing and packaging of that most precious Korean product, prime quality red ginseng? I resolved to inquire the moment I had found a room and could safely use the old Paekche capital of Puyo as my base.

There were any number of friendly little inns in the red-light quarter of town—which was easily identified by the scores of signs for barber shops and *saunatangs*—but the taxi driver who picked me up at the bridge insisted on taking me to what was laughingly called the Puyo Youth Hostel. This gaunt institution had clearly enjoyed a more ambitious history: Some Korean investor must have once thought that tourists would flood in to inspect the Paekche relics and had constructed an immense, Soviet-style hotel in which the masses could stay. But few did; such visitors as had made it to Puyo town had based themselves father north in Kongju or over in Taejon to the east, and the hotel remained empty for most of the year. Then someone had the bright idea of relaunching it as a youth hostel, affiliating it to the international movement, and encouraging parties of youngsters on educational tours to stop by. It was an odd idea—a youth hostel with suites and a ballroom and cavernous restaurants—and it didn't seem to have worked: I was the only guest and a pretty discontented one at that, since the management forced me to pay top rates, of about forty dollars a night. I railed inwardly at my folly and at the taxi driver's insistence, but he clearly thought that such a palace was the only worthy home for a visiting foreigner and would have been ashamed to have offered me anything less.

Puyo town itself is, like most Korean towns, outwardly not a pretty place; it is just an agglomeration of very forgettable little brick boxes in which commerce of one kind or another is carried on. But beneath the surface it is more charming, to no small extent because of the part it once played in the country's beguilingly complicated history. Puyo is to Korea as Ayutthaya is to Thailand or Angkor to Cambodia or Kyoto to Japan—an old royal capital, revered for past achievement; it is nowhere near as memorable as Kyoto or Ayutthaya—far from it—but neither is it a town to be ignored.

Korea has spent the better part of its four thousand years being invaded, crushed, subjugated, colonized, or in other ways trampled on: All its neighbors have made good use of the little peninsula—the Chinese, the Russians, the Mongols, the Manchus, and the Japanese have all seized and invaded and wrecked according to their wants and moods. (The cynical though not wholly unreasonable view, on which I shall expand later, is that today's Americans are following in the same ignoble tradition.) But through this all the Korean people have remained culturally inviolate, and in no small part because of their fierce attachment to their colorful and complicated history.

It begins, like so many Eastern histories, with a legend—though woe betide you if you publicly declare your skepticism: I have a friend who was thumped on the jaw during a rowdy party in Seoul, for scoffing at the story of Tangun, the man who is supposed to have founded it all. Tangun himself is certainly no less believable a character than Adam or Noah, though the popularly accepted account of his own origins does strain credulity just a little. He is said to have been descended from Hwanung, who governed the universe in 4000 B.C. Hwanung happened to overhear the prayers of a male tiger and a female bear who wanted to become humans, and decided he would do them the necessary favor: He gave them twenty pieces of garlic and a chunk of wormwood and instructed them to live on this evil diet for a hundred days, without benefit of light. So the pair retired to a cave and glumly chomped away, the tiger giving up after a fortnight. Lady bear stayed on and was duly rewarded by being turned into a female human being. Her first wish being to have issue, she did what was apparently natural in those days and prayed for one beneath a sandalwood tree. A child whom she named Tangun was duly born on October 3, 2333 B.C. (the date is still celebrated as National Foundation Day, showing how keen is the attachment to the legend), and promptly ruled Korea for the following 1,211 years.

More prosaic work by archeologists and anthropologists suggests that the Korean peoples were in fact descended from Manchurian and Mongolian nomads, tempered by influences from Siberia and even Scandinavia, and that they have been on the peninsula since paleolithic times. The oldest known true Korean settlement has been dated at 4270 B.C.; the oldest city proper was at a place called Lolang, close to the site of today's North Korean capital of Pyongyang, but its nature is indicative of the frustration and tragedy that were to lie ahead, because it wasn't Korean at all but Chinese—a commandery of the Han Dynasty that lasted for four hundred years.

It says much for the early robustness of the Koreans that they eventually forced the Chinese out: All the commanderies were closed in very short order, and only Lolang held out before it, too, was dismissed by the now-settled nomad Koreans. These first settlers came to be called the Koguryo, and by the fifth century they had managed—by virtue of constant warring with the aggressive Chinese—to maintain dominion over a vast tract of territory in the northern half of the peninsula, as far north, in fact, as the Amur River of Siberia and the Laio and the Sungari of China.

At about the same time two other informal alliances of nomads—also on the run from, and pushed south by, the Chinese—staked claims to land and power in Korea. To the east—farthest from China, and thus less influenced by her and more waywardly independent—were the Shilla people; to the west, ranging across a huge tract of territory running down to the Yellow Sea and stretching from the Han River in the north to the Cheju Strait coast in the south, was the kingdom called Paekche, which had its first capital near Seoul and then retreated to Kongju and finally to the town in which I had found myself, Puyo.

At its most basic, history's judgment on these three kingdoms is thus: The kings of Koguryo (who operated from Pyongyang) were warlike; those of Shilla (whose capital was Kyongju in the southeast) were skillful and ambitious (and eventually triumphant in dominating the monarchs of the other two); and the rulers of Paekche were cultured and religious. Paekche, indeed, may have been a military starveling, but her influence far outweighed her standing as a relatively minor Korean power.

It was Paekche, for instance, which introduced Buddhism to Japan. Paekchean architects built temples and statues in Japan, the great Horyu-ji temple at Nara being one such. (Koreans delight in the knowledge that the word *nara* means "country" in Korean—proof positive of their early dominion over the Japanese.) Paekchean and Koguryon tutors taught in Japan. Paekchean embroiderers worked in the Japanese court. Koreans, who have suffered much at the hands of the Japanese, are fond of telling themselves of such early triumphs. A new book about which I read while I was walking across the old kingdom went so far as to claim that Paekcheans actually conquered Japan in the fourth century—that the Empress Jingu was a Korean who invaded Japan and not (as other less nationalistic histories have it) a Japanese who invaded Korea. Of such airy debates are theses made, and the chatter in certain kinds of bars enlivened.

But only the history books make much of such achievement. You don't come away from Puyo feeling that you were at the epicenter of a glorious movement. You don't leave as you might leave Durham or Cadiz or Heidelberg, feeling that from here something was spread that changed the face of the world.

Virtually nothing of the pride today's Puyo people might deserve to feel is, in fact, even notionally evident there. Quite the opposite. The side of history of Puyo that today's people cherish is—like the side of history cherished throughout much of Korea—the tragedy rather than the triumph. I have heard it said time and again that Koreans revel in their sadness, wallow in their misfortunes, and make much—too much, critics say—of their having been invaded and subjected so many times. Feeling sorry for oneself seems a peculiarly Korean trait, and the impression I received most powerfully from my stay in Puyo is that on a historical level, at least, a Puyoan wouldn't be a Puyoan and a Korean wouldn't be a Korean without being able to feel happily miserable about himself, his heritage, and his history. Tell a Puyoan he's exported Buddhism to Japan, and he will look blankly at you; tell him that the Shilla kings and the T'ang Chinese conspired together to defeat him, and he'll perk up, with an almost Pavlovian response to gloom.

Nowhere is this better reflected than in Puyo's most memorably dispiriting memorial, a place called the Rock of Falling Flowers. (Another Puyo monument known as the Paekche Pagoda can also compete for the honors: When Puyo was captured by the Chinese in A.D. 660, the victorious general had a calligrapher carve a brief history of his triumph onto the side of the pagoda.

The characters have come to be regarded as forming a classic of elegant Chinese literature, but the Puyo people immediately thought of it as a blot on their corporate escutcheon and, as soon as the Chinese had gone away, promptly buried the entire pagoda. However, an American dug the pagoda up again in 1890, and now it stands in a park in the center of town, National Treasure Number 9, and a humiliation of which the Puyo people are now—given my theory about reveling and wallowing in misery—truly proud.)

I went to the Rock of Falling Flowers on a warm late-Sunday afternoon, having spent a tedious hour looking at interminable rows of celadon pots at the Puyo branch of the National Museum, a modern structure of great ugliness built beside my hotel.

To reach it I paid my 900 *won* to enter a park that crowns the summit of Puso-san, the hill around which Puyo is built, and which causes the Kum River to make a brief sideways lunge on its way south. Like the Thames as it passes through Oxford, the Kum changes its name as it passes through Puyo and around the base of Puso-san: It is known here not as the Isis but as Paengma-gang, or White Horse River, because the conquering Chinese general was forced to go fishing for a dragon that was known to lurk in the deeps, and to use the head of a white horse as bait. (The powerfully shamanistic symbol of the horse's head did the trick: Said dragon was hooked, whereupon General Su dispatched him with a blow of his sword and marched his troops across the stream to conquer the remainder of Paekche territory.)

The park's maze of footpaths was crowded with ordinary Koreans enjoying the sun, the warm smell of pine needles, and the slightly sultry breeze that blew up from the river. There were quartets of old men in their pale silk *hangbok*, baggy, ankle-length trousers called *paji*, and *chogori* shirts, all fastened with strings and ribbons; there were women in their more vividly colored *chima chogori*; young girls in their best Western dresses; soldiers in uniforms, and student-cadets in their curious jungly camouflage—Korea on a holiday afternoon is like the *paseo* on an evening in Barcelona, everyone kitted up to the nines to show off to the neighbors.

At the hill's summit are the various Paekche relics—exquisite little pavilions and shrines and temples that were used by the great kings for the ceremonials that accompanied their kinghood. *Yongil-lu*, the Pavilion for Greeting the Sun, is as lovely as any and stands facing east on the site where the monarchs would traditionally watch the morning sun rising over their lands; *Songwol-tae*, or Seeing the Moon Go Home Tower, faces west, for precisely the opposite reason. Most of the pavilions are open to the elements, have two floors, and are made of massive oak timbers the bosses of which have been carved and painted into extraordinary figures; the mansard roofs are tiled and have elaborately carved and chased antefixes; there are finial plates and a gablet and false rafters—the whole of each pavilion painted and lacquered in deep reds, sky

blues, yellow, gold, black: A Korean pavilion is at once fantastical and se-
rene—great fun to see, not at all serious, and yet despite its apparent frivolity,
possessed of a profound beauty and inner meaning.

I passed the summit of the mountain, which then rather abruptly fell away
to the river, glittering in the early evening sun. To my right was a well—
the Chinese characters called it the Kum River Great Water Supply Raise
Water Place; below me and also slightly to the right down a flight of granite
steps was a much smaller Raise Water Place, a tiny spring that trickled from
the mountainside by a temple called *Koran-sa*. It takes its name from a medicinal herb, the *koran-cho*, which grows beside the water; the herb was used by
the old Paekche kings as a guarantee that a particular pitcher of water did
come from this particular, very pure spring—a sprig of *koran-cho* was placed in
each vessel, a sixth-century version of the Good Housekeeping Seal of Approval.

And then I came to the Rock of Falling Flowers, the saddest memorial in
town, and for that reason above all, the most popular. It is a bluff, a hundred
feet or so below the Seeing the Moon Go Home Tower, and is reached by
steps cut into the mountainside. Old ladies had set up stalls under pine trees
beside the path and were selling balloons and tins of orange juice and wooden
snakes. At the top of the bluff is a small pavilion, and knots of people—many
carrying balloons, tins of orange juice, and wooden snakes—were having their
pictures taken or were gazing down the sheer rock face into the fast-moving
waters of the White Horse River two hundred feet below. A fence prevented
them from falling.

Whether or not a fence existed in A.D. 660 is not known. The last of the
Paekche kings chose the mountaintop as the site of his last stand, trying in
vain to beat off a joint attack that had been mounted against him by the
armies of Shilla and T'ang China, the latter led by the dragon-catching general, Su Ting-fang. The king's courtiers were around him as Su's forces steadily
advanced from the eastern hills. But when it became clear that his position
was hopeless, and he and all his followers were likely to become prisoners of
the Chinese, his women made a collective decision to commit suicide. They
leaped in the hundreds from the top of the bluff and died on the sharp rocks
or in the waters below.

It is said that three thousand of the Paekche women died—more than the
Jews who killed themselves at Masada, more than the Japanese soldiers who
threw themselves off the cliffs of Saipan. And it is when you see the prettily
dressed Korean women of today that the image becomes so aptly macabre: it
is easy to imagine their colorful dresses billowing up as the figures tumbled
through space: From a distance a waterfall of rainbow-colored petals would be
falling down the cliff face—hence the Rock of Falling Flowers, *Nakhwa-am*.

I had my doubts. I spent a few moments at the top of the bluff, watching
the young boys lean dangerously out into space, pretending to push their girl-

friends the way the Paekche women had gone thirteen hundred years before. And then I went down more stone stairs to the ferry station beside *Koran-sa* and bought myself a beer and sat in the prow of a skiff that swept its way slowly, with the stream, back to town. I lingered briefly at the base of the *Nakhwa-am* and wondered if the legend could be true. I thought the bodies would bounce or be caught up in the many ash and willow trees that sprouted from fissures in the face. Few enough would make it all the way to the river, and fewer still would be dead. But their dresses probably would billow and flare, and there would be flashes of color as the women twisted and tumbled through the air. Three thousand of them? But still, who cared? It was a good and adequately sad little tale, just the sort of thing the descendants of Paekche would like.

❖   ❖   ❖

There was by now one other man in the youth hostel, a small and rather taciturn man named Mr. Sung. Ten years before he had lived in Baltimore, and took a job working on the General Motors assembly line in nearby Dundalk. Dundalk, it turned out, was a place with which I had a more than nodding acquaintance, since over the years I had lived in the United States I had taken various cars and motorbikes to Dundalk port for passage to Liverpool. Mr. Sung had come to Puyo with little enough idea that he would find someone at his breakfast table who could name the streets and bars of Dundalk, Maryland, and perhaps because of this he quickly became a friend and guide-companion, though not so intimate as to permit the use of his first names, which were Kwang Ok.

He persuaded the hostel owner to reduce the price of the room. He found me the most erotically pleasing *saunatang* in town. He took me to the best *bulgoki-jip* in Puyo, and we feasted more than once on beef and oysters and cucumber *kimchi* and quails' eggs and pickled garlic—the robust fare of the Korean countryside, so magnificently different from the insipidly elegant toy food eaten in Japan. Mr. Sung loathed Japan with a passion. "I wouldn't eat *sushi* if it was the only food left on earth," he once declared.

He also introduced me to a girl. I was never quite certain of his relationship with Miss Ko, a pretty artist who rented a small shop near the entrance to the National Museum and did a modest trade in calligraphers' brushes, ink pads, pieces of lacquer-covered driftwood, and pots of polished basalt. Miss Ko displayed a skittishly filial affection for Mr. Sung, which suggested that he might have been a distant uncle; he behaved as though he were intensely proud of Miss Ko, almost as though he were trying to advertise the remarkable charms of Korean womanhood to this idiot stranger who had blown into town.

And Miss Ko Seouk-young was, by any standards, a remarkable young woman. She was extremely attractive and dressed very eccentrically, with a large straw hat plumped on her head. She drove a large car very fast and daringly. She painted with great skill, and her sculptures and framed sketches were all around her shop, but she did not want to sell any of them. She ate and drank with great gusto, her favorite tipple being a foul concoction that she called a *soju* cocktail, which included *soju*, 7-Up, and slices of cucumber. "If ever I go to your country, I give it to barman to make," she threatened.

I liked her, which was either what Mr. Sung had wanted or else he didn't object; he was so impassive about it I never knew if I was poaching and he was being polite. But he appeared quite content when, one sunny afternoon, Miss Ko suggested that she take me up to Chonggak-sa, a small nunnery in the hills south of Puyo. She drove very well along a perilous mountain trail I would be reluctant to tackle, and an hour after starting we drew up below a vast mass of cherry blossom, at one of the most exquisite temples in all Korea.

Only four nuns lived there, gray-robed and shaven-headed in the T'ang Chinese style. On this afternoon eight women from a nearby village had walked up for a visit, and the temple's tiny living room was filled with the recumbent forms of the ladies taking their siestas. A few sat quietly, hulling strawberries or peeling apples for afternoon tea. They all scattered when we arrived and sat around by the walls, watching with fascination the nuns' courtesies toward me.

I was asked to remove my shoes and sit cross-legged on the floor. A small black lacquer table was set before me, with tiny rice cakes, slices of orange and apple, fresh strawberries (which Koreans grow under plastic sheets, endless tubes of which extend over all the fields in these parts), and a fist-size pottery cup filled with a fragrant pine liqueur that tasted like an unusually strong retsina. The abbess introduced herself as Lee Seunim—Lee Soon Woo in the days, ten years ago, before she made the decision to take the Buddhist equivalent of holy orders.

She was tall and well built and graceful to a fault. Her hair was shaved down to a fine stubble—every full moon the women shaved again, she said, and it would be a full moon next night, so she had to travel down to the valley to buy razor blades. It would provide a welcome interlude—her life and that of her three colleagues could be austere, especially in the winter when the temple might be cut off for weeks, as it had been until very recently, by the ice and blowing snow. Even now the women were chopping the wood for the next winter's fires—this past winter had exhausted their stock, and there was no man about to help with the heavy work of replenishing it.

The routines of temple life at Chonggak-sa were much the same as those at Paekyang-sa or in any other Chogye temple, and involved long hours of study and meditation, hard work, simple food, and little by way of entertainment. The women, who like Miss Lee were all in their mid-thirties, were intelligent and well informed about the condition of the modern world. They were all philosophy graduates from various universities across the country, and their evenings, I imagined, were spent in constructive contemplation of mankind's follies.

Their temple was something like a common room at a small but excellent country college, perched high up among the cherry blossoms, with the tinkling sound of the wind chimes at the Buddha hall a few yards above us and the murmur of a stream a few yards below. The old temple dog snored gently in the sun. I could hear two of the nuns talking softly as they chopped the chunks of wood for the next cold season. The ladies from the valley muttered among themselves. And then, among all this heaven-sent peace, came the bang.

It was a loud double thud, like a sudden clap of thunder, that sounded from somewhere up in the sky, stopping us all in mid-conversation. The dog woke with a start and raised its head with an expression of canine perplexity. The sound of chopping wood halted. The birds stopped singing. Only the wind chimes and the stream were oblivious to the interruption. And then, after a self-conscious pause, everything resumed, and the dog stretched itself and lay down once more, and work and talk began again. "Pay no attention," said Miss Lee, glancing at her watch. "It's only the Blackbird."

An American surveillance plane had just raced across the mountain chain. It was made by Lockheed—how very alien that name seemed up here!—and it was ten miles high above us, hurtling along at twenty miles a minute. The thunderclaps had been its supersonic bangs as it hurtled northward to the borderline, where the pilot's duties called for him to point his radars at the northern armies and make sure they were staying put for another peaceful day.

"You have to get used to it up here," the young abbess said, rather wistfully. "If we were in Seoul, we wouldn't give it a thought. Down here, where it is so peaceful, it sounds much worse. It reminds us of things that have nothing to do with Buddhism—and not much to do with Korea, either. I used to find it a very sad sound. Every afternoon at three we heard it. It was very confusing during meditation—it set you thinking about things that had nothing to do with the *hwadu* we had been set. But now it seems part of the natural order. It has a certain Zen quality about it, too. It is a reminder of the frailty of our state, and of our existence. Just like the cherry blossoms; you know that although we appreciate their loveliness we mourn their existence because we know of their coming extinction. Well, the explosion we hear every afternoon is the same, in a way; we hear it, and it reminds us that all is not as perfect or as stable and secure as it looks. It is easy to become lulled into feeling that all is right with the world—just look at the view! Listen to the sounds! Smell the air! But then—bang!—and you remember the imperfection of it all. So this is how I have made use of the American jet. I doubt if the pilot thinks of it the same way."

It was tricky getting into the ginseng factory. Mr. Sung knew the manager and telephoned him to ask for access, but he had been told the processes were confidential, and visitors were not too welcome. I made some telephone calls to Seoul, however, to the institution known as Office of Monopoly (no definite article is ever used in its title) that regulates all matters relating to red ginseng. An official said they would retire to consider the matter, then telephoned the Youth Hostel: A Mr. Ha—"Ah! my friend!" cried Mr. Sung—would receive me at four. No cameras, please.

Although I have half-facetiously suggested that the most apt symbol for modern Korea would be the tiger-striped security barrier—you see them everywhere, potent reminders of the heavy hand of state—there can be no argument about the most readily recognizable icon on the peninsula. You see it under bell jars in ancient pharmacies. You see it on the labels of sweets and cigarettes, on hair restorers and after-shaves, on chewing gums and face creams. Huge posters carry its image. If Korea were run by Californians I daresay somewhere there would be a statue. The ginseng root is a curiously anthropomorphic thing, anyway—a thick, pinkish root with a fat body, two elephantine "legs," a couple of thinner "arms," and an assortment of lesser limbs—a "head" with hairs and on some specimens a navel, a penis, and knees. Sometimes it stands erect; other specimens are bent at the midriff and seem to sit back, contentedly dispensing their magicks. The Chinese character for "gin" is "man," though to confuse matters the word *ginseng* is not actually used in Korea: The Korean word for what the Chinese call *jensheng* and for what the English-speaking world calls "ginseng" is actually *insam*—hence if you ask for a cup of ginseng tea in Korea the phrase is *insam-cha chuseyo, putokkhamnida,* and if you asked for ginseng you would get very blank looks indeed.

Semantics aside, ginseng *is* Korea: Thanks to the efforts of the monopoly that musters and markets it, the world now firmly associates Korea with ginseng and ginseng with Korea. Not many people beyond the Orient know exactly what it is; there is the vaguely terrifying (but not wholly wrong) assumption that is has something to do with the curious activities of the Reverend Sun Myung Moon (a figure of quasi-religious bizarrerie, well known in the West, who is either despised or unknown in Korea). Few people can be precisely certain if ginseng will do them good or harm, if it is an aphrodisiac, a life-extension drug, a sleeping draught, a Menace to Society, or some cunning fungus through whose use the sinister East will subtly extend its dominance over a bewildered and drug-fuddled West. But whatever, it is *the* symbol of Korea, without a doubt, and it is all made, processed, and packed in Puyo, behind the high white walls and guard towers of Number 200, Naeri Street.

It was once all made in Kaesong and exported in huge quantities to a China that had been fascinated with *yin-yang* restoratives (in which field ginseng claims preeminence) since the third millennium B.C. The Koryo kings were forced to pay levies to the Yuan Dynasty's Mongol emperors: gold and silver;

cloth and grain; falcons, eunuchs, young women—and ginseng, always ginseng. Ginseng was stiff with *yang* energy: No Chinese, no Mongol, could possibly function well without it. The principal factory for its mass production was established in Kaesong in 1908, a branch office of the Ginseng Division of the Royal Ministry of Finance.

But Kaesong was swallowed up by North Korea in 1953, and the factory was moved south to Puyo. Kaesong still makes some ginseng and exports it under the historically accurate name of *Koryo* ginseng (since Kaesong was the Koryo capital). A little is made in China, and both the Russians and the Americans grow the plant and toy with processing it. The biggest exporter in the world, by far, is Korea, and all the export-quality red ginseng comes from the factory at Puyo.

There are two kinds of Korean ginseng. There is *paeksam*, or white ginseng, which is grown for four years, then washed, sorted, graded, and sold. This type of ginseng is regarded as inferior enough for private enterprises to make and market, and such magisterial characters as Puyo's Mr. Ha have no interest in it at all. Red ginseng, or *hongsam*, on the other hand, is the real McCoy of the *insam* world. It is exactly the same ginseng, except it has been matured in the earth for two years longer than that selected as white ginseng, and it has been steamed and dried. This curing process, then, and the two years' maturation in the field, is all that separates two ginsengs that are treated as differently as gold from pyrite. Red ginseng—stronger, more concentratedly beneficial—is the subject of the hugely powerful Office of Monopoly, and on that subject, Mr. Ha waxed lyrical indeed.

He was a fat man with bulging black circles under his eyes—not the best advertisement, perhaps, for so efficacious an elixir. He sat in his office with four colleagues, and they nodded and smiled broadly as servants trooped in with a steaming silver pot. "You are very welcome," said Mr. Ha. "You will take some red ginseng extract, please?" And a servant poured a deep red liquid into an egg-shaped china cup that had handpainted flowers on its side. Mr. Ha stood and made a short and rather formal speech: "Red ginseng is good for your life, Mister Simon. It will purify you. It will help your body to make more blood. It will clean your liver. It will cleanse your hangover. It will make you live much longer. Gentlemen, drink!"

And we all stood and sipped the scalding liquid. It is not easy to describe the taste. Sweetish rubber, perhaps. Glue? The faintest hint of drying paint. A freshly baked Victoria sponge cake, cooked in a pine wood on a warm spring afternoon. Ginger and balsam dipped in molasses. All these tastes and smells came to mind as I drank the vaguely medicinal liquid. Not at all unpleasant but rather odd, as though someone had slipped a mickey into a glass of decent claret, and I suspected it but drank it all the same.

"You will feel its effects very soon," said Mr. Ha and then showed me his motto. It was arranged under the glass of his tabletop: "I believe that the able industrial leader who creates wealth and employment is more worthy of historical notice than any politician or soldier. . . ." "So you see, we create wealth and employment, and by making something that is beneficial to everyone. Can we do any better than that?" He beamed. The other men at the table beamed and bowed. One of them released a most enormous belch, and Mr. Ha beamed even more. And then an escort arrived to take me around the factory.

It turned out that the Korean War had left a problematic legacy for the ginseng makers. The original Korean factory had been at Kaesong, as I have explained. It was strategically placed inside a fifty-mile-wide circle where the better six-year ginseng was traditionally cultivated. Then came the war, and Kaesong fell into Communist hands. Most of the fifty-mile circle, however, remained in the South—mercifully, for the Korean export trade. The new factory that the Southern authorities then built in Puyo was right in the middle of a fifty-mile-wide circle where four-year ginseng was grown. The inconvenience was considerable: Everything grown around Puyo was destined to become white ginseng and was sent up to Seoul to be processed by private enterprise factories; everything grown around Seoul (and particularly on a beautiful island called Kanghwa-do, an hour west of the capital) had to be trundled south to Puyo to be made into red ginseng. The mistake appears to have been to plant the red ginseng plant in the middle of a white-ginseng-growing area; when I asked my guide why this had been done he looked at his feet and shuffled them uncomfortably. I think someone had made an almighty mistake.

Trucks bring boxes of the precious anthropomorphic roots of *Panax ginseng* down to Puyo every day. For the six years before this transport the roots had matured in their shaded mulches of chestnut leaves. The red raspberrylike fruits, which had appeared every summer after the plant was three years old, had grown and withered, grown and withered. The leaves, protected from the damaging sun, had sprung up and then had faded and died six times, each time leaving another callus that, welded together in the crucial six-year maturation, became the head that is so important to the root's status in ginseng society. No head, no deal, basically; a hydra-headed beast, or one that looks like a cross between E.T. and the Mekon, is much favored and pried from the ground with reverential care, packed all about with straw, and dispatched to Puyo for the attention of Mr. Ha and his hundred pretty Puyo girls.

The girls wash each root as though it were a child, lovingly toweling between its little legs and under its wizened arms and patting its head dry and smooth. Then baskets carry the creamy roots into the steamers, where the cream becomes a deep and angry red, the smooth roots craze and buckle like frying bacon, and the whole factory fills with the aroma of rubber and ginger, molasses and sponge cake. And from this moment onward the roots, ugly in their dismemberment, are weighed, sorted, graded, and dealt with according to the commercial pressures of the moment.

The grades are given names that are appropriate to the standing of the root in botanical society. The least good (although all are superior to the various grades of white ginseng) is known as Tail ginseng, the next is Cut ginseng. Then there is Good Grade, then Earth Grade. And finally, in red-and-gold packets that will cost its devotees small fortunes in folding money, Heaven Grade. The girls—who, when I was there, seemed to spend an inordinate amount of time fighting playfully with each other—fed the sorted roots into the maws of silvery machines, and from the various orifices of these engines came the substances that Korea then exports to the waiting non-Communist world—9,200 metric tons of the stuff each year—to be sent off to Hong Kong, Singapore, San Francisco, Seattle, London, Athens, Santiago, and Mexico City (the places where Korea has set up Ginseng Centers), and to the sixty countries where the root is eaten, drunk, or otherwise ingested.

Puyo's managers offer it as unadorned root, sold in flat tins decorated with paintings of pretty girls in *hangbok*. They sell it as extract (which is what Mr. Ha gave me); there is powdered ginseng tea; there is spray-dried powder, and there is ordinary powder; there are tablets, capsules, and pills; there are fine-cut pieces, and there are polygonal slices—all to be taken with honey if needed, or with pieces of the dried *Zizyphus* fruit we know as a jujube, and all guaranteed to make the taker feel a great deal better. The trucks that bring the earth-covered roots down in the morning leave in the afternoon with the red-and-gold packets of polygons and slices and pills and capsules. The great ships that leave Pusan and Inchon each day, filled with Hyundai cars and Samsung televisions and Daewoo refrigerators, also hold, in every available corner, small and very valuable boxes from the factory over in Puyo town.

The chemistry of ginseng is bewildering, and books on the topic (which Mr. Ha pressed into my hands at every available moment) combine folksiness with utter incomprehensibility. I nearly gave up at the paragraph that started, "Therefore, let us turn our attention to terpenoid," and then did abandon the struggle at another that started with the declaration that "ginseng saponin is a glycoside structured with dammarene from triterpenoid." The words that made greater sense were those that claimed ginseng had an "anticancer effect," was "anti-aging," was analgesic, antibiotic, inhibited overfermentation in the gut, was antidiabetic, and had been declared by chemists at a doubtless grand institution called Kinki University to be full of magnesium and therefore very good for one's general health.

Professor Oura of Toyoma University in Japan cut out the livers of rats and fed them ginseng, whereupon good-size parts of their livers grew back. A Dr. Lee of the Ginseng and Tobacco Research Institute found that tar left in smokers' livers was cleansed away by ginseng. Dr. Kim of Wonkwang University injected lead into mice, gave them ginseng, and most of the lead vanished. Professor Huh of Youngnam University made his rats into chronic alcoholics, gave them ginseng, and they went corporately on the wagon. Professor Joo of Yonsei University fed rabbits with a forage that contained lots of cholesterol, gave them ginseng, and the cholesterol levels in their blood dropped away to nothing. A Bulgarian doctor found that ginseng lowered stress. A Professor Hong found it made hens lay more eggs. An English researcher named Fulder gave ginseng to nurses on night shift and found that they perked up—the list goes on and on, credible or not I cannot tell. The claims made for the improving qualities of ginseng are perhaps more catholic and numerous than for any other substance known.

My own impression is that ginseng *does* do good. Mr. Ha had told me that the effects of his infusion would be noticeable within minutes—and noticeable they most certainly were. I became unaccountably full of energy. I had all the cheerful enthusiasm of an early drunk, and yet all my faculties were quite normal and I was in full control. I have in consequence taken ginseng pretty regularly ever since. I will not know for many years if it prolongs my life; I have few enough serious ailments to know whether it is chipping away at their effects; I cannot look at my arteries to see if the cholesterol is being corroded nor into my liver to see if dying cells are being regenerated. If it is, as claimed, an elixir that promotes spermatogenesis, then I am happy to know but have no access to proof. All I do know is this: When I take ginseng, I end up feeling pretty good. (Not that I feel bad if I don't take it—there is no suggestion that ginseng is in any way addictive.) People tell me I look fitter than for some time. And I like the taste. Maybe it *is* all some mighty Korean confidence trick; maybe ginseng extracts have no more than a placebo effect, and one that works wonders on the suggestible psyches of people like me. I am well aware I might be being taken for an almighty ride and that Mr. Ha and his brother tricksters at Korea's Office of Monopoly may well be laughing behind their hands at how all the *yangnom* fall for all this guff about saponins and terpenoids and help jolly along Korea's millions of dollars in profits each year. Maybe, but somehow, knowing full well for how long the Chinese have accepted the medicinal value of the root, I doubt it. Puyo town provided a revelation for me, and one that will take me some long while to forget.

❖   ❖   ❖

Mae-young, my friend who had climbed with me on Halla-san, had telephoned while I was away. She had been in Vancouver and had planned to come back to Korea for a few days. If I promised not to walk so fast as I apparently had on Cheju-do, could she come on down? Two days later she was in Puyo, eager to hear of my various adventures. It was good to see her again—her good cheer of our days on Cheju was still in full spate, and she made great friends with the artist Miss Ko and came with me up to Chonggak-sa to see the mountain nuns and to learn a little of how her own Buddhism had gone awry during her years of work and Westernization. "Very stimulating," she said, as we climbed down the hillside after listening to the young abbess for more than an hour. "I envy them their life." Did the nun, I wondered, not in fact envy her? Did she not wish that she could travel away from a remote mountain, albeit a very beautiful one, to places like Vancouver and Hong Kong? "No, she has no desire. She knows about the world. She thinks her duty is to make her own small part of it as good as possible and not concern herself with visiting the rest. There is too little time to be wasted traveling far from home." I felt that both of us had been taken down a peg or two.

Once Mae-young had gone again, I walked northeast for thirty miles and eventually came to the Kum River again where the Dutch had crossed it, at the other old Paekche capital of Kongju. This was a livelier town than Puyo, a bustling little place, with an assortment of fine Victorian churches and colleges, an excellent *yogwan* where I stayed for two contented nights, and any number of little cafés and bars. I went to see the remarkable tomb of the twenty-fifth Paekche king Muryong—a tomb that was only discovered in 1971 and that had been quite undisturbed since the monarch was buried and his tomb sealed in A.D. 523. Thousands of pieces of jewelry and pottery brought from the tomb were said to be displayed at the Kongju museum, but I felt suddenly and unaccountably weary of all this history and embarked for the countryside again. I was going through a period of feeling happier walking than stopping, and as I set out and clanged my way across the great iron bridge that spans the Kum-gang, I confess I felt more in my element again.

The countryside ahead was rich and prosperous and hilly, and the village houses were colored gaily in chartreuse and violet, tangerine and royal blue. From the tops of the schools and barns flew the three-leaved green-and-white flag. This was a part of Korea where the nationwide self-help movement known as *Saemaul Undong* was particularly strong.

Saemaul Undong, or the New Community Movement, is the reason there are so few thatched roofs in Korea and why so few old men wear horsehair hats and why one sees so few young girls playing on the traditional swings and seesaws that all villages sported only a decade or so ago. *Saemaul Undong* is the reason why Korean villages are, by and large, clean and well-furnished places with electricity supplies and big schools and warehouses and grain elevators and clean wells and perhaps piped water and sanitation and multicolored tiles on the roofs of the houses, new and old. *Saemaul Undong* is the driving force behind all those cement trucks rushing along the country lanes, behind the telephone linemen who are installing new lines on Sunday afternoons, behind the endless rows of polyethylene-covered greenhouses that are built each season to warm the strawberries or the asparagus or the okra and other city food from which the farmers now make so much of their money.

Saemaul Undong is the line of modern tractors, the chugging "rice rockets," the new bridges and spillways and culverts and irrigation channels. *Saemaul Undong*, run from a massive office you see on the road to Seoul Airport and, with its flags and songs and legions of eager acolytes, is at once a mightily efficient grass-roots political organization and a self-perpetuating memorial to its creator, President Park Chung-hee.

It was begun in 1971 after President Park and his colleagues realized, as the government now says, that the gap between the circumstances of Korea's farmers and its urban citizenry had become unacceptably wide. The movement, based heavily on propaganda, was launched "to cultivate positive attitudes in the rural masses, to assist them in gaining confidence in their future, and to train them for more active self-reliance and cooperation." It began modestly enough—the government provided the material for village houses to be repaired, experts provided advice, and the farmers did the work themselves. It was extended into cooperative efforts on a larger scale—irrigation channels and roads and bridges were built by entire villages, and everyone began to learn about organization and cooperation. And then group farming projects started—collectively owned factories and marketing facilities—the principles of the kibbutz had spread to Korea.

On one level it appears to have worked magnificently: Rural life in Korea seems to have improved beyond all imagination, and the gap between the urban and rural masses has narrowed (although that between urban rich and rural poor has widened hugely). Romantics can argue that some of the essence of Korea has been lost in the process of its modernization—and I, having seen the relict beauty of those few villages in remote corners of the country where permission has been granted to keep out the *Saemaul Undong* organizers—count myself among the romantics. Something very tangible has been gained, no doubt; something evanescent, something mysterious and spiritual has been lost. But most important of all, the *Saemaul Undong* has enabled a strong and powerful central government to extend its tentacles deep into the fabric of the country's rural society, and when, one afternoon on my way north from Kongju, I saw a group of policemen with guns moving out along the levees toward a remote hamlet on the distant skyline, I wondered if the *Saemaul* movement was all that much of a benefit.

There were ten men, all of them heavily armed with rifles and submachine guns; they had parked their police cruisers on the roadway and were moving out on foot. The flags of the New Community Movement fluttered from the houses through which they passed. What were they looking for? Whom did they seek? What wayward foe of the government would find himself in custody tonight? When would his family learn of his fate? With what specific crime would he be charged?

Of course it was entirely possible that the man they wanted was a heavily armed bank robber, a dangerously criminal clone of Bonnie or Clyde. But I doubted it. Bank robbers, armed criminals, drug smugglers, syndicate bosses—these were not the stuff of Korean criminality. Far more likely that the state was moving against one who had once moved against the state, and likely, too, that the green-and-white flags that more usually marked economic good fortune and self-reliant triumphs were this time indicating the presence of a telltale, of a village spy, of a neighborhood watch gone bad, and that a movement perhaps conceived with good intent had ended up as part of the apparatus of a state that is all-powerful, all-suspicious, and not at all benign.

I shuddered as I watched the men fan out and walked on northward. I walked on toward the city and away from the flags and the uniquely Korean social experiment they were said to represent.

CHAPTER

EIGHT

"*The Nobility, and all Free-men in general, take great care of the Education of their Children, and put them very young to learn to read and write, to which that Nation is much addicted. They use no manner of rigour on their method of teaching, but manage all by fair means, giving their Scholar an Idea of Learning, and of the Worth of their Ancestors, and telling them how honourable those are who by this means have rais'd themselves to great Fortunes, which breeds Emulation, and makes them students. It is wonderful to see how they improve by these means, and how they expound their Writings they give them to read, wherein all their Learning consists. Besides this private Study, there is in every Town a House where the Nobility, according to antient Custom of which they are very tenacious, take care to assemble the Youth, to make them read the History of the Country. . . .*"

—HENDRICK HAMEL,
1668

❖   ❖   ❖

THERE CAN BE FEW AMERICANS WHO WOULD VOL-
untarily give up their citizenship and exchange it instead for citizenship of the
Republic of Korea. Few enough people anywhere, indeed, would wish to re-
nounce the national allegiance of their birth and assume the nationality of
another place—save, of course, those who wish to become citizens of the new
nations that, like the United States or Canada or Australia, have been built
almost entirely from immigrants, and save those who have chosen to flee from
repressive societies and regimes to enjoy a life of liberty in some more progressive nation far from home.

But to go from the free, wealthy, and developed West to the less free, less
wealthy, and less developed East, and to go forever, with all the old rights
renounced and with all the new customs adopted—this kind of move is an
eccentric and unusual one, undertaken only after great thought and often by
unusual and fascinating people. I have a dear friend, an Englishman who chose
twenty years ago to become a citizen of India and endure poverty and discrim-
ination and restriction: He now lives contentedly in Bombay, never regretting
his decision, refusing to show any envy or sadness when, on arriving for a
holiday in London, he is made to stand in the aliens' line at the airport and
is asked brusquely how long he plans to stay in the land of his birth and
whether he has enough money to support himself. I have met a handful of
Britons and Canadians and Americans who have been officially assimilated
into China for many years and have endured revolutions and turbulences they

175

can never have foreseen. There are runaway spies who now live in strange luxury in Moscow and East Berlin. A few romantics still follow Gauguin's path into the blue Pacific, and go as seriously "troppo" as to acquire a new passport along with the "sleeping dictionary" with which they provided themselves on arrival. And there are, of course, many millions of long-term rootless residents dotted around the globe—the great cheerless crowd of "expats"—who exercise their fading memories on frozen and time-warped images of home and order their amahs and bearers about with age-induced ferocity and incivility. All these we know.

But those who reject the West purposely, to satisfy a spiritual and intellectual yearning to become part of the East are rare birds indeed. Over the years, as I have wandered around forlorn corners of the globe, I have enjoyed seeking such people out and have listened with fascination as they explained their reasons for having taken the fateful step.

Lafcadio Hearn, the Irish-Greek romantic whose *Writings from Japan* is one of the classics of what one might call truly disinterested travel literature, summed it all up. Hearn wrote scores of elegant essays from the East that now seem to be what so much other writing is accidentally or carelessly not—almost wholly free from the taint of his own patriotism. Hearn managed this simply because he had no patriotism and owed no allegiance to any nation but only to himself. He summed up what my new Bombay-wallah friend and perhaps what those Britons who have buried themselves deep inside the fabric of China were all searching for—the reason for their having come and settled in for life. He used the Japanese word *kokoro*—"the heart of things": Lafcadio Hearn searched for *kokoro*, and his writings testify to his having found it, to a greater degree than most.

My friend in India is searching for the *kokoro* of Maharashtra, and Carl Ferris Miller, whom I met one Sunday afternoon in a tiny seaside town called Chollipo, is an old man evidently searching for the *kokoro* of his beloved Korea.

Ferris Miller, as he is generally known, and who was born in Wilkes-Barre, Pennsylvania some seventy-odd years ago, became a Korean citizen in 1977. Like most of those "old contemptibles" who chose to settle here, he came in 1945 with the American navy. He came officially to help reconstruct the country after the years of Japanese occupation; he came less officially to help gather intelligence (he had majored in chemistry at university, which may or may not have helped); he came unofficially to dabble his toes in the muddied waters of the battered and bruised postwar society. And he fell in love with the place, instantly.

It was, he says now, a real and hopeless love, and it began when he was on the troop train that brought him, ship-weary and innocent, from the southeastern port of Pusan to the northwestern ditto of Inchon. (His train would have passed through the city of Chonan, which lent a pleasant symmetry to my hearing of his story, since, as I shall shortly explain, it was at Chonan railway station that I first set out to meet him.) He stayed with the navy for six years, and then escaped to Japan when the Communist forces invaded. Once the UN forces had secured for themselves the city of Pusan, Ferris Miller was brought back and went north with the advancing forces when they recaptured Seoul. Then he caught hepatitis and was flown back to Japan—a prudent enough move, since Seoul was recaptured by the Reds once more, so he would in any case have had to move again. Finally, in 1953, he returned to Seoul yet again, and took up a residence that he was determined should endure. He stayed with the army for a while, then joined the Bank of Korea, and then retired to play on the vibrantly *sportif* Seoul stock exchange. He has lived in Korea ever since. He never married, but he adopted a son, with whom (and with whose wife and children) he now lives, enjoying a life of blameless con-tentment.

He will not easily forget renouncing his American citizenship. "I went along to the embassy and explained. They didn't try to talk me out of it. They were very decent about it. I handed over my passport, and I signed a form, and that was that. Someone shook my hand and wished me well, and I walked out of the office. I was back in a week with my Korean passport, applying for a visa to visit the States. I wanted to go back home to Pennsylvania. I knew I'd have to go through all the hassles. It didn't bother me. I'm not at all senti-mental about giving up American citizenship. I had to. I had to take Korea and let Korea take me. It was an affair of the heart. There is no other expla-nation."

He had bought a small piece of land on the coast near Chollipo back in the mid-sixties. He needed somewhere to swim, and the Yellow Sea coast is the best by far in northeast Asia. Since the peninsula tilts gently down toward the west, the beaches are long and have only a very shallow slope; and the tides in what the Koreans call the So-Hae—the West Sea—are the second biggest in the world (after the Bay of Fundy). The combination of long white sand beaches and enormous tides make the Korean west coast a most amusing place for a swim—and so Ferris Miller had a tiny country cottage built there and visited it most weekends.

And then he started to get interested in flowers and conservation. Koreans, in spite of their professed Confucian closeness to nature and their fondness for animals and plants, have not taken a particularly constructive attitude toward the preservation of their wildlife. True, some creatures—the Manchurian crane and Tristram's woodpecker among them—are classified as Living National Treasures. In recent years bans on shooting birds everywhere except in the pheasant- and snipe-hunting areas of Cheju-do have helped bolster the num-bers of orioles and hoopoes, wood warblers and kingfishers. The noble ani-mals—the tigers and bears for which the peninsula was once famous—have all but gone; and such is the Korean appetite for any meat that moves that, except for the odd weasel or mouse, Korean forest floors are like vast empty ballrooms, dark and quite silent.

The forests themselves have suffered, too: The Japanese took most of the usable wood to help their war effort, and so at the beginning of each April there is a concerted attempt to persuade everyone in Korea to plant a tree or two, to help the woods regenerate themselves. Pollarded poplars march in battalions along the country roads; there are ginkgo trees and maples that flame magnificently in October; there are London plane trees, seemingly culled straight from Notting Hill and Kensington, on many city streets; there are persimmon trees and ailanthus and sumac, bamboos, pawlonias, and fine stands of old bamboo. But these are exceptions and are not often found beyond the national parks and the temple grounds. Out in the countryside proper there are millions of dull acres of pines and firs—good lumber perhaps, but not good trees. The variety suffered under the Japanese, and there has been little enough imaginative concern to reseed the country with any trees other than those of immediate commercial use.

Korea has many wildflowers, though—there are fields full of gentian and azalea, forsythia (which was said to be President Park's favorite) and cosmos, lavender and lilac and daphne—and the rose of Sharon, which, although not a rose (it is a type of hibiscus) is Korea's national emblem. The beastly Japanese did their best to destroy it and replace it with their own chrysanthemum, but the rose of Sharon (as in Steinbeck) is a doughty plant and clung to rock and bank, and like Korea itself (for the symbolism is not lost) grows in ever greater profusion.

But Korea commits little effort or money to preserving its plants and animals, and the needs of the economy far outweigh the less strident demands of ecology. Which is why Ferris Miller, who noticed how well the wildflowers grew on the clifftops above his seaside cottage, decided to teach himself about plant life and devote a sizable period of his later life to preserving the very best that western Korea could grow.

He bought up more and more land and fenced it off from prying trespassers. He imported—from the distant fields or from far countries—the first of what was to become the biggest Asian collection of magnolia trees. He started to plant the first of the hundred of ilexes—the hollies—for which, along with the magnolias, the Chollipo Arboretum has become world famous. He imported and ferried in a number of traditional Korean cottages—thatched roofs were all right at Chollipo, no truck there with the modernizing zeal of *Saemaul Undong*—and had them rebuilt among the woods and sculpted landscapes of his paradise. He planted daffodils and crocuses, maples and oaks, plants with wonderful aromas, trees with extraordinarily exotic flowers and fruits—and the result has become a botanic and an aesthetic legend.

I had heard of Ferris Miller on every journey I made to Korea—of this kindly, eccentric old man; this financial wizard who had marshaled the proceeds from his wizardry to improve the stock of Korea's countryside; of this rather scholarly, rather private man who had devoted his life to this austerely difficult, but unforgettably beautiful and graceful little country thousands of miles from his home. I had long wanted to meet him, and now, having made an arrangement to join a mutual friend at the railway station at Chonan one Friday evening, all seemed set for me to do so.

I had walked all day from Kongju: A young German friend who had accompanied me for the trek dropped out after twenty miles, complaining of sore feet and general exhaustion. The hills between the two towns were severe indeed; and once I reached the village of Hyangjong-ri and the railway line from Pusan swept into view, and my little country road was joined by the great artery of Route 1 (which I last tramped along down south at Kwangju, where it was a very much smaller road), all the noise and nuisance of the approaches to Seoul began to assert themselves. So I didn't blame my friend for catching the bus instead: The miles to Chonan were grim, unpleasing miles, and it was comforting to know that for the diversion west to the coast we would go by car.

George Robinson, a young Englishman who ran a stockbroking office in Seoul and had come to know Ferris Miller both through that and through the very energetic Korea branch of the Royal Asiatic Society (of which Miller was current chairman), had arranged to meet me at the station—he having come south on the express from Seoul at the end of his week's work. He had brought another chum along from Tokyo; and my one-day walking partner, a writer from Germany, made up the foursome. We took a taxi to where we planned to stay the night, an enormous holiday resort at a spa town called Dogo (and where I had dined once on a disgusting monster known as a King Dogo Burger—which, bearing in mind the Korean fondness for munching their way through roast dogs and dog soup, could well, I thought, have been fashioned from somebody's long-dead Rover). Our stay was brief but wild: We engaged the services of two hostesses from the hotel's dance floor, who chatted amiably enough in halting English until we left at midnight. At three in the morning, when I was sleeping peacefully, there came a furious hammering at the door of my room. Both girls were there: They had come to minister jointly to my particular needs, and there was no need to pay any more since the paltry sum we had paid for their company on the dance floor would more than compensate them for their services until dawn. They looked eager and excited, and I wished (as I daresay the reader might wish, too) I had said yes. But in fact I decided there and then—and it was an extremely difficult choice, for the girls had been utterly charming—on a course of behavior that was both prudent and medically responsible. I kissed each girl politely on the cheek, said a regretful *annyong-hee kaesayeo*, shut the door, and retired for a fitful sleep. I was derided for extreme foolishness at breakfast the next day.

We rented a car—a process that was rather simpler than I have known before. The Dogo hotel alerted a man in Onyang, a nearby town that, like Dogo, is famous for its thermal springs. The Onyang man turned up with his car half an hour later. He accepted a cash handout of 50,000 *won*—about $60 at the current exchange rate—handed over the keys, and told us to telephone him when we had finished with his car. There had been no paperwork. No insurance. No formalities of contract or agreement, no fiduciary bond or hand-shake. Nothing, in fact, other than the kind of mutual—and perhaps mutually foolish—trust that evaporated elsewhere (except perhaps for some corners of rural Ireland) a long while ago. We drove off to the west, each one of us just then loving Korea for that small and simple act of informal kindness. "We like Korea because it retains something that has vanished everywhere else in the world"—that was how a visitor from Osaka once explained his fondness for the place, and with that small act by the Onyang car owner, I could see again precisely what he had meant.

The countryside became lower and more meanly furnished as we headed west. Our destination was on the coastline of what looked like a hammerhead extending out to sea beyond the prevailing sweep of the west coast—two bays pinched at the shaft of the hammer—and where Mallipo and Chollipo lay was on the flat topside of the hammer, a coast of cliffs and tiny islands and long white beaches of pure sand. It looked exactly like Oregon: The islands were topped with fir trees, there were rain clouds on the horizon, the tidal currents traced steely patterns on the sea surface, and small fishing boats murmured distantly.

We took lunch in a small café on the Mallipo beach—the raw eel was vaguely disgusting, so I asked the owner to find me eggs, butter, and milk, and I cooked sea salmon omelets for the four of us, and we ate fresh bread and drank cold beer in the afternoon sun. Then another group of friends—a soldier from Scotland, his Korean wife and baby, and a young woman who was over on holiday from Battersea—arrived, and we drank more beer, and then set off for Ferris Miller's place, five miles farther down the coastal track.

His cottage, set on a rise beside the hamlet, was itself surrounded by wild-flowers and curiously exotic bushes, all labeled. Ferris himself proved a mag-nificent figure—tall and dressed wholly in *hangbok* from his ornately embroidered silk *chogori* and his baggy *paji*, all connected by silk strings and loops and small amber buttons known as *hopak-dan chu*, to his neat *komusin* slippers, boatlike shoes with dainty upturned toes. His "family" were with him and everyone spoke Korean—he seemed wholly assimilated into the country in which he had lived for the last four decades. We should wander around the arboretum, he said, for as long as the light and the weather held.

And so, for the remaining hours of the sun, we were beyond his fences and among his trees. Our new visitors set down a gingham picnic cloth under a magnolia tree and beside a huge bed of daffodils, and we all lay dreamily around in attitudes of Confucian idleness, drinking cool Burgundy and eating strawberries, listening to the pounding of the waves below and of the sighing of the breezes through the magnolias above, inhaling the scents of the jasmines and the sea, and feeling blessed at having entered heaven through the front door. And then our friends went back to Seoul, and Ferris came down and talked his way around three hundred varieties of magnolia and four hundred types of holly and about conifers and lobelias and the orchids he was just then trying to raise on a bank beside the potting shed.

He had just been over to England with the Magnolia Society and had toured eight country houses to see which *Magnoliaceae* they had and which cuttings he might supply for them. The society, now based in Louisiana, regarded Ferris Miller as having one of the finest stocks in the world, and he was the star of the Cornish visit: The following year the society planned to visit him, and he would show off the results of his fifteen years of labors. He rarely let strangers in beyond the fences; he did not care for people, he said, only for plants and animals. He would spend all his money, and as much of his remaining time as possible, tending to this little oasis of beauty and charm, and pass it on to his adopted son, and hope that it would remain no matter how busily Korea continued with her headlong rush in pursuit of economic miracles.

We spent the night in an old Korean house at the top of a cliff. We watched the sunset from the terrace and saw the night fall on an island that Ferris had bought the year before, and on which he had built a cottage only to be ordered to have it taken away lest North Korean boatmen rest there on their way to infiltrate the South—you are never far from the memory of war, even in a place as beautiful and peaceful as this. We ate in a local shop—the owner cooked us rice and soup and fish, and we had apples and strawberries afterward, and drank *makkoli* and beer, and from a bottle of Glenlivet that my Scottish soldier friend had left for us. And then we climbed up to our clifftop and slept on our *ondol* floors, more content than it is possible to imagine with a Korea preserved in all its old magnificence, by the sea and away from the crowds.

We rose at dawn and drove sadly back east. We took coffee at Dogo by noon and rang the Onyang man and gave him back his car, not much the worse for wear. The hostess girls from two nights before emerged from somewhere and insisted that a villager took our photographs—they had never seen foreigners before and wanted their boyfriends to see our gorillalike arms clamped amiably around their shoulders, and we were naturally happy to oblige. And then my friends took off for Seoul by train, and I set off walking north again along the road to Pyongtaek, and the final run to the capital, now less than two days' march away. I turned my atlas to its last page and the province of Kyonggi-do, tightened the grip on my walking stick, hitched my fardel to my back, and strode out for the last few miles.

❖　❖　❖

This was American territory—a fact that became readily apparent when I was just a few miles south of Pyongtaek. I had been walking quite fast through deserted woodlands. I was, quite frankly, bored. The countryside was less interesting than it had been: I was hemmed in by tall trees, and the road, for some reason, had degenerated into a dirt track that was thick with mud after the rains of the night before. Construction machinery churned past me, belching out diesel smoke and splashing mud in every direction. It was hot and sticky, and I felt liverish and wished at that moment I had clambered up onto the Seoul train as my friends had suggested. "It's only an hour or so," they had beckoned. "No one'll know."

Thus I trekked on, hour after hour. I passed some signs of recent soldierly occupation—"Headquarters, I Corps" read a wooden sign ten yards into the woods, and I could see barbed wire fences and Quonset huts and wooden lean-tos and shadowy figures that moved along distant forest paths. They must have been relics of the spring exercises, for otherwise the woods were quiet, and the rutted roads were empty of the tanks and mobile howitzers that had been there days before. It could have been the woods at Versailles or the Thuringian—or great Gromboolian—plain: It looked not one whit Korean.

I came across a stretch where men were asphalting the road, and my boots were mired in thick, sweet-smelling blackness that it took a good mile to shake from between the cleats. The road snaked over a hill, and just as I was coming to its summit, two American children came flying on their bicycles from the other side. "Hey, Mister—whatcha doing here?" They were straight from Norman Rockwell via Sears Roebuck, and suddenly the road might have been in Chevy Chase or Bel Air, no longer a Thuringian lane. There was a rational explanation, of course: There was an enormous infantry base here, one of the few where families are welcome from stateside, and the children were venturing briefly beyond the cyclone fence to see something of the country where they lived.

They may well have found it a likable place. The man I encountered no more than an hour later most certainly did not. He was American too, and he was driving a juggernaut of an old Chevrolet into the outskirts of Pyongtaek when he spotted me. He stopped to offer me a lift and then unlocked a sluice gate somewhere in his brain and unleashed a waterfall of vitriol. "Goddamn place, this Ko-rea," he began. (He was a construction foreman from Kentucky.) "I jes' hate it. Goddamn dirt everywhere. Goddamn people eating their goddamn garlic and *kimchi* stuff all the time. I see'd people pissing in the streets. I see'd all kindsa stuff here you wouldn't credit. Man, I hate the place." I told him I had seen some remarkable things and met some extraordinary men and women in the past weeks. "Oh sure, the people is okay. You gotta admire them, I admit that. No, it's not the Ko-rean people I can't stomach, it's their goddamn country. The people, they work real hard, they get on and do things. Why, some of my workers are better than the guys back home.

"But no sir, I ain't gonna be taking no good memories of this place back to Tampa. Wife and kids gone down there. Got me a real nice condo, and I'm fixing to go into the aircon business in Florida. Make some real money, not like the shit contracts you get from the air force. My wife? Oh, sure, she'd been back there for 'bout a year now. Some of the gals here are pretty nice, so I haven't been too lonesome." He chuckled evilly. "No, like I say, it's not the people I can't stand, it's the goddamn dirty country they live in. People's fine, real fine folks. Won't miss 'em, though. Not back in old Tampa."

I spent the night in a hotel he suggested in Songtan. I should have known better. It was a grimy establishment a few hundred yards from the main gate of the Osan Air Base, which is in itself the main gate for GIs coming into Korea, and the plasterboard between the rooms creaked in disharmonious rhythms to the sound of commercial exertions. My room showed the spoils of its previous occupant, a pilot (said the room boy) who had checked in at three and checked out at six.

His flight plan was crumpled up in the wastepaper basket. It showed that he had flown his C141-B in from Hickam Air Base in Hawaii, and that before that he had been at Travis Air Base in California. He had carried forty thousand pounds of crew and cargo. He had flown across the Pacific through a dozen or so of those oddly named airway marker-points, Bebop and Bandy and Bambo and Gritl and the rest of them, before making Koko Head and Barbers Point and the top of his long gentle slide down to base. And he had presumably taxied his giant plane into the holding area, had "locked and sealed the aircraft and left the key, combination and seal number with the Airlift Coordination Center," as required by Osan's laws, and then headed straight for this grim warehouse and 180 minutes of dubious and not inexpensive pleasure.

He had also been given a handout that suggested itself to be of the utmost importance. Officers of the United States Customs, it said, were presently giving their almost undivided attention to the importation from Korea of bogus versions of Cabbage Patch Dolls, Members Only T-shirts, Lacoste socks, Vuitton suitcases, Gucci shoes, and jackets by Polo. Cabbage Patch Dolls in particular would be regarded by the ever-vigilant officers with the greatest degree of suspicion, lest they be Korean-made counterfeits. Therefore be ye warnèd, pilots of America, that only one such beast would be permitted home per flier, and none could be sent stateside by post. This document had bitten the dust as well as the flight plan.

I spent an unmemorable night in Songtan and woke to a furious and ice-cold rainstorm. The whole day was a struggle: The wind blasted in from the east, the rain lashed down on me, and I was drenched and shivering and in some danger of developing a classic case of exposure, which would have made a dreary end to the venture. The road widened into another emergency airstrip, and the gale whistled mercilessly across it. It was like being at sea somewhere in a cold high latitude—doubling the Horn in August, maybe, or the Bering Strait in March. The towns that came and went were deserted, the wreckage of trees and collapsed fences blocking some smaller streets: The gale was almost typhoon strength, the last efforts of the Chinese winter hurling themselves against the hills of Korea.

At the top of one hill stood a monument and a café at its base, and—as much in search of a scalding cup of coffee as in seeing any history—I crossed the road and climbed its rain-slick steps. It turned out to be the site of the first major battle of the civil war—the site, fifty-odd miles south of the 38th Parallel that in 1950 formed the boundary between the two Koreas, where the southern forces turned and started to fight back. The monument said little, but what it said minced no words:

"As the vicious troops of the North Korean Army crossed the 38th Parallel, U.S. troops were ready to fight to preserve freedom, determined to punish the aggressors.

"Lieutenant-Colonel Smith's Special Task Force stood on Jukmi Pass supported by 17 Regiment, Republic of Korea Army—the first of the United Nations–Korean Joint Operations commenced.

"Blood formed a stream after over six hours of fierce struggle—firing line stretched as far as the Makdong River.

"While forlorn souls sleep on this hill, how can we forget our friendship with Allied nations created in blood?"

A police patrolman who had stopped by for a break bought me a cup of coffee. "Walking?" he said. "You mad." I felt it but, not wanting to abandon the adventure, launched myself back into the stinging rain and marched on. The Dutchmen had been on horses, and they had journeyed during June; in probable consequence of this relative luxury they recorded no complaints about their journey. I cursed them silently.

Three hours later and I was sheltering miserably under an overpass near the proud city of Suwon: The name, which means "water field," seemed singularly appropriate as the rain hurled itself down, and the bat-blind cars, their lights flickering through the thick gray mist of the downpour, ground slowly and painfully along the road. Suwon's city walls rose before me—massive structures that had been built by King Chongjo at the end of the eighteenth century. The king had built the walls and a magnificent fortress—lately reconstructed, and just visible through the rain—in memory of his father, Crown Prince Changhon. The prince had been the cause of a curious court battle between two Yi Dynasty court factions known as the Party of Expediency (*Sipa*) and the Party of Principle (*Pyokpa*). Their battle had developed in the mid-1770s over whether or not each approved of the prematurely senile buffoon who was then Korea's king, Yongjo, and the extraordinary manner in which he treated his son, the crown prince.

Basically the king accused Changhon of some trifling misdemeanor and had him locked up inside a rice box until he died—in the same year as the American War of Independence, with which not quite *all* the world was then obsessed. The Party of Expediency thought the young man had been given a raw deal; the Party of Principle applauded the kingly act; the two sides fought bitterly. When the king himself died, and his grandson Chongjo assumed the Yis' mantle royal, the prince was given a posthumous retrial and found innocent.

Chongjo then decided to build the Suwon fortress in his father's honor, and further to consummate the fondness of his memory by moving the Korean capital down from Seoul, thirty miles away. And so up went the walls and the parapets, the embrasures and the cannon platforms and the command bunkers, and a meditative moonwatching pavilion known as the *Panghwasuryu-jong*, within which the Confucian elders could ruminate on the wisdom of their scholar king. But the capital never was moved south, and when Chongjo died in 1800 his dream city, Korea's Taj Mahal, was only half finished. It took another reign to complete, and it cannot have been very well built, for after two centuries of ice and rain and summer heat and the depradations of the Civil War, it was reduced to a crumbling shell. The government rebuilt it in 1975, spending more than 3 billion *won* and four years on doing so. And now it stands, foursquare and quite magnificent, and it loomed grandly through the storm, a memorial to an ill-judged prince, a dour and fateful place, and like so much of Korea enwreathed in sadness and tragedy.

I took a car—the weather was simply too terrible to consider pressing on by foot—into the center of the next town, a dormitory suburb called Anyang. This was clearly home to some of Seoul's more chic set, since there was a Cartier shop and another selling genuine Gucci shoes. The small hotel the driver found, however, was a reasonably low establishment with mean, old-fashioned rooms and explosive-sounding plumbing. I was too cold to care, and I lay in a blood-heat bath for an hour, feeling very sorry for myself. I then slept until dark and awoke to find that all my joints had seized—or rusted—and the simple act of getting off the bed had become an agony. Life's return was painfully gradual.

Dinner was no great success either. I will take some time to forget the error I made in choosing to sit at a table beside the restaurant's fish tank, unaware that this night had been chosen for the tank's spring cleaning. I was halfway through a bowl of turgid and half-cold soup made from what tasted like rat when I glanced to my left, expecting to see some exotically colored guppies and gudgeons and saw instead two large and very horrid-looking human feet. I dropped my spoon with a resounding clang and nearly spat the soup right across the room, at an elderly gent who seemed to be the only other client in the room.

The feet walked across the tank's sea bottom, the guppies fleeing in open-mouthed terror. Then the pedal progress stopped, and an enormous net broke the silver undersurface of the water and groped down for the guppies, who panicked and fled behind the yellowish leg-pillars. But they were ruthlessly rounded up, and the legs, which turned out to belong to one of the hotel waiters who had been lifted into the tank to give it a scrubdown, vanished and reappeared on the carpet. I slept fitfully that night, and dreamed.

But the next morning was fresh and bright. The storm had passed out into the Sea of Japan (or the East Sea, as the Japan-loathing Koreans know it), and such blossom as had been spared by the gales was trembling against a background of a pale, new-washed blue sky. The boundary lions—or more properly the *haetae*, which are mythical, lionlike guardian beasts that eat fire—of the City of Seoul appeared on Route 1 after I had been walking for no more than half an hour: The journey—or at least, that part of it which coincided with the expedition of the Dutchmen—was almost at an end.

Seoul! One of the world's biggest cities, and yet one of the world's least known. A city invariably mispronounced (it is homophonic with what it doubles as—the soul of Korea) and a place that is not amenable, unlike all other Korean cities, to having its name (which means capital) written in Chinese characters. A city that has been marched through and devastated by no fewer than four invading armies in this century alone. A city whose population had grown by 80 percent in the last ten years—fewer than half a million struggled in the wreckage that remained after the Civil War, and today 10 million people jostle and scurry and beaver away in the fantastic jungle that has created itself—in an immense, uncontrolled, unlovely, unforgettable mitosis—in the past dozen years.

It appears to have been set down in the middle of a range of mountains, and it is a city of great visual drama. Immense peaks of granite and schist—some rounded, some razor sharp, all scarred with pale streaks where vegetation has been unable to gain a foothold—soar from amidst the concrete. The peaks look vast, but they are in fact just hills—the tallest, at 2,627 feet, is no taller than Helvellyn—and they are no longer as wild as once, when leopards and tigers wandered down from them and ate people who were taking their ease on the city streets.

Isabella Bird thought the city looked magnificent:

> Arid and forbidding those mountains look at times, their ridges broken up into black crags and pinnacles, ofttimes arising from among distorted pines, but there are evenings of purple glory when every forbidding peak gleams like an amethyst with a pink translucency, and the shadows are cobalt and the sky is green and gold. Fair are the surroundings too in early spring, when a delicate green mist veils the hills, and their sides are flushed with the heliotrope azalea, and flame of plum, and blush of cherry, and tremulousness of peach blossom appear in unexpected quarters.

But that was from afar. She had a rather different opinion once she had entered the city walls:

> I shrink from describing intramural Seoul. I thought it the foulest city on earth until I saw Peking, and its smells the most odious, until I encountered those of Shao-shing. For a great city and a capital its meanness is indescribable. Etiquette forbids the erection of two-storied houses, consequently an estimated quarter of a million people are living on "the ground," chiefly in labyrinthine alleys, many of them not wide enough for two loaded bulls to pass, indeed barely wide enough for one man to pass a loaded bull, and further narrowed by a series of vile holes or green, slimy ditches which receive the solid and liquid refuse of the house, their foul and fetid margins being the favourite resort of half-naked children, begrimed with dirt, and big, mangy, blear-eyed dogs, which wallow in the slime or blink in the sun. . . .

A hundred years on, the stamp of invasion and the crump of artillery shells, the fires and the floods and the grand ambition of the new Koreans have utterly altered the city of Seoul. It is a city that is old, not ancient: it was founded in 1392, and before that Kaesong was the capital—and yet hides its antiquity behind high walls or so perfectly preserves and displays it that you feel it must be *ersatz* or plucked from a museum. The old is there, all right, but not as in Oxford, or Florence, or Istanbul. There are no ancient walls or leafy lanes of tottering houses, no tiny temples dating from Koguryo times or from the days of Unified Shilla, which nestle among the newer blocks of flats or beside the railway station. No, all Seoul looks fairly modern, like Tokyo now, or like Shanghai in another ten years' time, or like Tulsa—the oldest buildings are the strongest creations of a century ago, and the truly ancient ones are hidden away, unused, on display for payment in folding money.

Walking the road from Anyang northward, once I had slipped between the *haetaes'* suspicious glowering, was rather like being in a film running in reverse—a film on the Rapid Development of a Modern City, with the newer shops and houses as the introduction, the less and less modern, the more and more faded structures making up the body of the story. The road into the city was lined with hundreds upon hundreds of shops, selling all the paraphernalia of an advanced society. In a flash the simple country life had gone, and in its place not merely congestion and pollution and rush but comfort and luxury and all the familiar icons of mercantilism and materialism. Cameras, stereo sets, silk dresses, fast food, antiques, ornate embellishments for the car, lamps, wristwatches, climbing gear, porcelain, books. Once in a while there would be the kind of shop that had evidently been around for ages—a grocery or a man who sold calligraphy brushes and *tojang*, the name seals, with their pots of sticky red ink, or the snake dealer or the deer-horn seller or the ginseng shop.

It was all a pleasant bustle—not overnoisy (for Koreans, at least when sober, speak quietly), not overcrowded (not in the way Hong Kong's Wanchai always is and the smaller streets of the Ginza can well be), not tempered with a bullying or a threatening feeling, for the Buddhist and Confucian spirit tends to preserve a degree—diminishing, my friends all say—of gentility and courtesy. I had been to Seoul many times, but this particular foray, through a southern suburb that looked as anonymous as any suburb anywhere in the world, was comfortable in its civilized ordinariness—old ladies out shopping for cabbage, chige-men carrying heavy deliveries on their backs, schoolboys hurrying back from lunch, young blades eyeing the young girls, salesmen in blue suits on their rounds of the shops, workmen digging holes in the road, inspectors checking on the times of the arriving buses, mothers with children tightly strapped to their backs, and every few moments a young woman in her bright chima chogori or an old man in a tall black horsehair hat and a gray suit, neatly pressed. John Betjeman, I thought, would have liked this road—Shihungdae-ro, it was called—and so would Auden. Here was the mysterious Orient rendered benignly prosaic, getting on with its life without any fuss.

Then a siren began to blow, and everything started to move very fast. Cars screeched to a halt, their drivers slewing in to the side of the road. Passersby dashed into the nearest available doorway. People snoozing on the street benches woke up and dashed inside, looking sleepily ill-tempered. I was hustled into a shop that made and sold tennis shoes, and a dozen other men and women came in with me. I stood around, wrinkling my nose in the glue-sodden air, wishing I could venture out into the comparatively fresh outside again. But there were policemen by the door, and a cruiser was rumbling slowly down the road, observers inside it peering at the empty streets.

I had fifteen minutes to wait. I knew that well. Once a month, shortly after lunch, the Seoul government stages a civil defense drill; the sirens blow, the police fan out, and everyone must take to shelter. The roads must be clear, too—no traffic other than police cars and emergency trucks, is allowed to run. Anyone caught driving or walking on the streets is fined stiffly. Korea intends to have as many of its civilians as possible left living should the Communists invade again: Too many were killed in June 1950, when the Northerners tried it for the first time. So the Southerners practice ways of improving their fate.

The seconds ticked past interminably. My civilly defended colleagues smiled nervously at me, and a mother looked embarrassed as her child, spotting me, fled behind her skirts. There was a girl wearing a T-shirt bearing one of those meaningless, half-formed sentences that have become almost an art form across in Japan. Hers said: "Westwood. We will be just like standing over. 1955." She smiled and told me she was a student at Seoul National University.

"Civil defense is the government's way of keeping the people nervous," she declared, assuming, probably correctly, that she and I were the only English-speakers among the shop's captive clientele.

"But what if the North attacks?" I said. "Better to survive, isn't it?"

"They won't attack. They don't have to. They're more clever than that. Our only enemies here are the Americans."

I said I thought she was being a little unfair. Didn't she remember the sacrifices the Americans had made for Korea during the Civil War? "It was a civil war. They should have kept out."

But the all-clear sirens began to wail just then, and she waved cheerfully and took off for class. The others in the shop had vanished too, leaving me standing among the avalanches of Reeboks and Adidas and Nikes, and the manager was coming to ask if I wanted to buy . . .

An hour later, after I had passed the undamaged magnificence of the Oriental Brewery Company—brewers of O.B. beer, the better of the two local brands of *maekju*—I was at the river Han. My first sighting of what, for me, was supposedly a landmark of some moment, was of a less than impressive trickle, the southern nullah that separates Yoido Island from the shore. But Yoido itself is an impressive sight, though of a rather bloodless kind, and in no way redolent of Korea: It is all office blocks and government headquarters— IBM on one side of the road, the Korean Broadcasting System on the other— and the eastern tip of the island is dominated by the enormous gold-tinted skyscraper of the Daehan Insurance Company—at the time of writing the tallest office block in Northeast Asia but soon to be outdone by the new Bank of China building in Hong Kong. (And already out-sky-scraped by the Raffles Towers in Singapore—some comfort being taken in Korea by the fact that it was built by their very own Ssanyong Construction Company.)

But perhaps Yoido is best known for its mighty plaza, a lone and level plain of hard asphalt and stone a good mile long and half a mile wide—the kind of place that all totalitarian states (and many others besides) seem to have at their disposal for laying on the most impressive demonstrations of national unity and power. This is where Armed Forces Day is celebrated each October; it is where the pope offered mass and where the Korean masses came out to vent their anger at the shooting down of their airliner over Sakhalin in 1983. Today I was almost alone and felt mightily insignificant as I traced my way along the patterns of white lines that showed where the tank commanders should place their tracks or where the armies of schoolchildren should set their slippered feet and begin their routines of patriotic dance.

At the far end of the plaza was the main stream—the Han River, mightiest in all Korea, a rival to the Yalu and the Kum and the Imjin. It was an impressive river, a real city river, with tall buildings on each side and a feisty flow against the buttresses far below me. But the impression that the Han

189

might give, of power and strength and great utility, is a false one. Politics have made the Han a sad sort of stream, a river that is pointless at one end and now supposedly very dangerous at the other.

The dangerous end is a long way upstream, where the North Koreans (from whose territory the river's northern branch flows) have lately said they plan to build a dam. The inference taken by the ever-suspicious Southerners is that the dam would then become a highly potent weapon in the hands of the manic Northerners. At a word from Kim Il Sung or one of his deranged generals (this, I hasten to say, is how the Southerners see things, and they are almost alone in so doing), their dam could be blown up, a wall of water would course down the north fork of the Han, smashing through towns like Hwachon and Chunchon, demolishing the small dams that have already been built there by the South Koreans, and running straight to the capital, inundating and destroying factories, railway lines, houses. It would be a masterstroke, a military *coup de main*, an attack that could not be repulsed and that could, moreover, be classified by the attackers as a terrible accident. We've destroyed your capital? How perfectly frightful. Do let us lend you ours.

Perhaps the danger is overstated: The South Koreans do have perfervid imaginations when they consider their brothers north of the line (though perhaps not surprisingly: North Korean attacks—like the infamous bomb in Rangoon that wiped out half the Southern cabinet—have tended to be furious and bizarre), and it may well be that Pyongyang just wants the extra electricity. In any case the South Koreans are talking about building a big new dam themselves to catch the northern waters, should they ever come on down.

The other end of the Han is perhaps not so dangerous, but, like the seaward end of the Colorado River (which is bone dry), is somewhat lacking in point. This has nothing to do with topography, however. A quick look at a good map will display the worthlessness of the river. (A good map only: Most South Korean maps of this region are quite hopeless because they refuse to admit the existence of a division between North and South Korea. Technically, of course, they are right—the division is merely an armistice line, not a border or a frontier, and neither side regards it as anything other than a temporary holding point, the equivalent of a start line in battle. This can cause the innocent traveler some problems: The map most tourists use shows, for example, the province of Kyonggi-do extending quite uninterruptedly from Pyongtaek in the South to Kaesong in the North. True, there are not too many roads shown around Kaesong, and if you look carefully it is possible to see that all the northbound railways and roads end rather suddenly and without explanation. But Route 1 continues all the way, and one might suppose that it is possible to take the car for a picnic up at the old Koryo capital. The car would be utterly destroyed, and all its occupants, before they had managed to get within ten miles of Kaesong, for the city lies well within North Korea, despite unwillingness of the South's official cartographers to recognize the fact.)

Anyway, armed with a good map, it is possible to see the reason for the pointlessness of the Han. A boat heading downstream from Seoul can proceed with blithe unconcern for about twenty miles. After that patrol ships will stop it, minefields will blow it out of the water, machine guns will rake it from stem to stern. The seaward end of the Han may enjoy flowing water and tides, but there is a thin red line across the river mouth that shows where the southern border of the Demilitarized Zone runs through. The Demarcation Line runs in midstream, where the Han meets the Imjin, and on the far bank are the northern border of the DMZ and the guardposts of the People's Democratic Republic. Any Southern boat foolish enough to wander into such waters would be sunk or evaporated within seconds. The effect of this reality—the thin red line the better maps show crossing the mouth of the Han—is to stop the river to navigation as effectively as a cork or as the kind of chain barrage the Chinese once put across the Pearl River near Canton, or the Orangemen across the Foyle at Londonderry.

Seoul in other words, can receive no oceangoing ships no ships at all, in fact. The only craft you see on the capital's broad reaches are lighters carrying hay or sleek motorcruisers carrying tourists along the most pointless—headless, tailless—of rivers in Asia. The cargoes come and go via Inchon, twenty miles to the west.

It was June 26, 1654, when Hendrick Hamel and his crew crossed the river "as wide as the Maese is at Dordrecht" after "lying many Days at several Places," and they proceeded straight to see the king:

> . . . we humbly beseech'd his Majesty, that since we had lost our Ship in the Storm, he would be pleas'd to send us over to Japan, that with the assistance of the Dutch there, we might one Day return to our Country to enjoy the Company of our Wives, Children and Friends. The King told us it was not the Custom of Corea to suffer strangers to depart the Kindgom; that we must resolve to end our Days in his Dominions, and he would provide us with all Necessaries. Then he order'd us to do such thing before him as were best skill'd in, as Singing, Dancing and Leaping after our manner. . . .

But I decided—there being no current king before whom I might Leap after my particular manner—to have a haircut instead.

❖ ❖ ❖

A Seoul haircut, it has to be stressed, is a very different animal from its namesake out in the ruder world: It is more a Korean institution than a mere trim, and it has little enough to do with hair. Any man who feels tired or a little jaded, who requires his spirits lifted or his psyche toned to perfection, visits a barbershop. In any case I, long before this moment, had promised myself that as a reward for getting the three hundred-odd miles from Cheju to the Han River I would enjoy a few moments before the altar of hedonism before pressing on for the final miles up to the borderline. So, once I had entered the city proper—the city walls were knocked down fifty years ago, but five of the nine great gates are still there, and I counted myself as being in Seoul city once Namdae-mun, the huge south gate (National Treasure Number 1) was safely behind me—I scanned the streets for the rotating red-white-and-blue electronic "poles" that indicate the existence of a barbershop.

There were scores from which to choose, even though I had deliberately kept away from Itaewon, the American forces' lubricious playground, where the prices would be higher and the delicacy of the operation lessened by its frequency. The *ibalso,* for the Korean man, is a port of refuge, an oasis for Confucian pleasure-seeking, a place to forget the trials and travails of this unnervingly fast-changing country. The Korean barbershop is perhaps the best example of the subtle infiltration of true pleasure into a society that appears on the surface to be strict and unyielding in its approach to Work and Duty and the Love of State. The Japanese, we all know, blow off steam, but they do so in an exaggerated, slightly repellent, and often atavistic way, a way that is a fascinating and spectacular phenomenon, incredible to many Westerners, the subject of many recent books. But the Korean, when he attempts to win release from the tensions of his life, often does so in what has always seemed to me to be a more truly civilized manner: He reminds me of the old Confucian gentleman who, pipe in hand and book at elbow, ruminates idly on the contentment that is possible in life without the frenetic pursuit of pleasure, Nippon-style.

Thus the *ibalso,* and the one I had chosen was a type specimen of the breed. The room was divided into three curtained enclosures, inside each one of which was a barber's chair, a basin, and an assortment of unfamiliar machines. I was greeted by a young man in a blue jacket, and from benches behind him four young women, all in identical short white dresses, stood to appraise their customer. I undid my pack, took off my angler's jacket, and replaced my New Balance boots with slippers that were very nearly as comfortable—perhaps more so. There was the usual giggling—palms placed beguilingly over mouths—before I was ushered to the chair, and the young man proceeded to snip away at what little hair remained on my sunburned head. He worked silently for no more than ten minutes and then stood aside to let me see in the mirror that he had taken enough away (and not too much: That might mean it could be a full fortnight before I *needed* to return); then he vanished behind the curtain, the better to let the real business of the *ibalso* begin.

The girls came into the cubicle and closed the curtains securely behind them. The chair tipped back until I was horizontal. One girl—how pretty they were, prim and virginal, and deliberately chosen for this reason—took the slippers from my feet, drew off my socks, and lifted my legs up onto a cushion she had placed at the edge of the basin. At the same time her colleague had drawn up a stool beside me and had sat down and placed my hand in her lap.

The third girl—who introduced herself in English as "Sue, your razor maid"—started to apply cool shaving foam to my face and stropped a pair of tiny-bladed razors. The last girl fiddled with the tall, cranelike device that I had earlier failed to recognize. It now emitted puffs of steam, and the girl directed its broad nozzle close to my right cheek, and a jet of hot damp breath riffled pleasantly against my skin.

All three then began to work in concert. The foot girl started to wash my toes one by one with warm water; the manicurist, burying my hand in her lap, started to wet and trim the nails; and Sue started to nick, hair by individual hair, the stubble from my skin. Her friend directed the jet, Sue applied the foam, and—snip! scrape! snip!—away went another few blades of hair. She began with my cheek, moved on to my forehead, went with infinite care and patience down to my neck; inch by inch, every single follicle was probed, and any lurking hair was cut off at the stem with an edge of perfect sharpness.

Meanwhile the foot girl had dried my toes and was now, my heel between her soft thighs, trimming the nails. From time to time she tutted; when she found one nail in a particularly battered condition, I tried to explain that I had walked, and she seemed to understand but could not comprehend why I had not, in that case, visited a barbershop every night of my journey and had a girl such as her attend to my needs so that I never reached this stage. "Naughty man," she cooed.

All this cutting and polishing and repairing—hair, nails, tiny long-forgotten pieces of skin—went on for about forty minutes, during which time the girls either talked softly to one another or said things to me—I had not the foggiest idea what—and then giggled. It was all very pleasant. Sue's friend had by now smeared some aromatic compound all over my face, and it had dried hard, so that it felt as though I had on a rubber face mask. It was difficult to smile, and one of the girls tickled me to make me laugh, deliberately to cause whatever was on my face to crack, which it did, with a small, explosive click.

Then Sue leaned over and whispered in my ear, *"An-ma?"* and I nodded. Massage time. One girl to each leg, one girl to each arm, they kneaded and pummeled and stretched me, at one moment causing intensely pleasurable pain with finger-pressure massage, at another levering back my joints to the very limits of orthopedic endurance. As I lay there, one girl—she had now introduced herself as being called Kyung-ah—sat beside me and asked me to drape my arm around her back while she did something to my rib cage. She giggled as my arm encircled her. "Tighter!" she said, and squealed with delight as I rubbed her waist. One of the other girls then clambered completely on top of me and began to probe the deeper recesses of my stomach muscles and my chest, while I gazed happily down the front of her dress, and she saw me and arranged herself so that even more was visible. "Seventh heaven, yes?" she asked, and smiled. I loved her.

And all this went on for an hour, until one of the girls broke off and decided she had forgotten my face; she ripped off the opalescent mask and began to pluck at my cheeks with her tiny fingers, like a violinist, *pizzicato*. She inserted a tiny bamboo whisk into my ears and twirled it until its amplified scratches sounded like a hammer on a drum. She kneaded my nose and squeezed my neck. And all the while her companions were applying their skills to ankles, ribs, wrists, back—until that small, exquisite finale when my fingers were clicked back until the joints sang out, and I felt the catlike sensation of fingernails running along my palms and the delicate breath of the girl blowing on them to tell me that her duties were now officially over. A cup of tea appeared. The girls disappeared. I dozed pleasantly until there was a slight cough from behind, and it was suggested I might like to hand over just 8,000 *won*, $10. I had been in the chair—which was now tipped discouragingly vertical again—for two hours. It was quite dark outside, and I felt that I had been in heaven.

❖   ❖   ❖

I had dinner that night with friends—the most English of food, served with impeccable calm by an elderly Shanghainese who had lived in Korea since 1949 and now stayed in the small Chinese community that clusters around the Taiwanese Embassy. The Chinese, indeed, are the only real minority living in Korea; this is a society of almost total ethnic purity, with none of the racial minorities of Japan, no Gypsies, no untouchables and outcasts other than the poor foreigners—those who are known collectively as *sangnom* and are to be treated politely but without any need to waste any Korean emotional energy. The *sangnom* are unpersons, and few enough Koreans fall into this category. The Chinese would, for even if they are born here, they are not Koreans, and the Koreans do not mix with them, nor do they mix with the sons and daughters of Choson.

The ethnic integrity of Korean society can at times be a frightening phenomenon and is one of the reasons for the power and energy of the miraculous economic performance the nation has displayed in the last twenty years. The whole country, on certain topics, thinks perfectly alike; the whole country, when urged in certain directions, can be an unstoppable giant, everyone working in concert, no disagreement, all with the same degree of comprehension and sympathy.

❖   ❖   ❖

The thirty-five Dutch sailors had little enough to say about the Royal Palace; they were embarrassed, it seems, by the attention they were receiving from a citizenry who fully believed them to look like exotic sea monsters, kraken, or blond-haired serpents. Hendrick Hamel noted that the local people thought that when these strangers drank, they had to tuck their noses behind their ears, and such huge crowds gathered outside their house that the militia had to issue a regulation that forbade such gatherings.

The king before whom they were paraded was Hyojong, a man who knew well what imprisonment was all about since he had spent eight years while crown prince as a hostage in the hands of the Ch'ing Manchus in China. The meeting almost certainly took place in the throne room of the Changdok Palace—the Palace of Illustrious Virtue. It is an impressively lovely building, still in excellent condition today and, indeed, housing the remaining members of Korea's royal family. Hyojong was the seventeenth king of the Yi Dynasty: There were to be only nine monarchs more before that unforgettably wretched day in August 1910 when the twenty-seventh king, Sunjong, issued a proclamation yielding up his throne and his country to the Japanese. They had annexed his country; it fell upon his shoulders to bring to an end a dynasty that had ruled Korea, for good and ill, since 1392.

Sunjong died on June 10, 1926, in the Changdok Palace (there were angry demonstrations at his funeral: "Long live Korean independence! Twenty million countrymen—drive out the enemy! The price of liberty is blood! Long live Korean independence!"). His relations and descendants and ancient court retainers live on, and in some style, in a palace annex called Naksonjae, the Mansion of Joy and Goodness. Once in a while the man who would now be Korea's twenty-ninth king—Yi Ku, now known as Mr. Kyu Lee, a nephew of the deposed Sunjong—returns from the United States to take part in the annual May rituals honoring the royal dead. He wears the extraordinarily elaborate robes of Confucian majesty, including a hat that looks like an Australian mortarboard, with colored beads hanging in long rows where the corks would otherwise be. Mr. Lee is an architect; he lives in California and married a girl called Julia Mullock. He was not in the country when I called at Changdok, and deep expressions of regret were uttered by elderly chamberlains. He prefers the West Coast climate, it is said, to the rigors of the Korean winter. He looked a pleasant sort of king, a bespectacled man with a benign expression, and the pictures of his performances at the Confucian ritual show him looking, understandably, more than a little wistful at how matters had turned out—the Japanese who had forced his uncle out had been replaced, all right, but the country had been split asunder, and now malign dictatorships ruled on both sides of an artificial divide. The dynasty of which he is still the notional head had taken the ancient Korean name Choson—the name given by the son of the she-bear, Tangun. Choson, as the advertisers tell us, quite ludicrously, means "morning freshness and calm"—the idea that the country Mr. Lee might head is still the Land of Morning Calm being absurd in the extreme and one that he would doubtless find deeply ironic and sad. The Land of the Rising Sun had helped put an end to the idea that the Land of the Morning Calm could ever be calm again.

I had wanted to see the modern equivalent of the palace, the so-called Blue House where the president lives and has his offices. But you are not allowed within a mile of the place, and once when I was walking with a friend on a hill north of the city, soldiers stopped us and made us look another way, for fear we might see the house in the distance and take a picture of it. I once went with a photographer to the roof of the Seoul Hilton to have pictures taken of the city skyline: The guide instructed us strictly not to point the lenses to the northwest, where the presidency was hidden. So we turned the other way and found that the far corner of the roof housed an antiaircraft gun, covered in camouflage netting, ready and waiting for an attack from the Communists—surely the only Hilton, we thought, that had an ack-ack gun above the restaurant. (It turned out that it was in fact a model, made of wood and manned by a dummy.)

❖ ❖ ❖

Yet in a way the new kings of Korea are not the generals who run the place— and they may not be running things for much longer, given the apparently reforming zeal of President Chun's nominated successor, Roh Tae Woo. The real kings, though their palaces are much smaller than before, are the men who run the great *chaebols*, the huge industrial empires that so exemplify the miracle state of the new Korea. I had called on one of the greatest of these men the last time I had passed through Seoul; he was called Kim Woo Choong, and he ran the Daewoo Corporation from an office next door to the Hilton Hotel.

He owned the Hilton, actually. And he had recently bought, "to dress up the lobby a little," a Henry Moore reclining figure, in bronze. It had cost him the best part of a half a million dollars. He had hired an American public relations company, Hill and Knowlton, to dress up his company's public image. He had hired a former official of Mr. Reagan's White House to try to lower his firm's tax liability in the United States. He was worth tens of millions of dollars, and controlled an empire that made cars and refrigerators and shirts and microprocessors, steel bars and container ships and bridges—an empire whose companies laid pipelines and built new towns, baked bread and sweets, ran supermarkets, and ran the best hotel in Seoul and the best French restaurant to boot.

Kim is a small, modest, punctilious man, with glasses and gray hair, and rather more of a sense of fun than is customary among Oriental businessmen. One afternoon I watched someone take his photograph in his hotel lobby—he is very famous within Korea, an almost deified figure—and he offered to sit on the plinth beside his Henry Moore because he thought it might make a more memorable image. But he was far too short and had to jump up backward, failing several times before he finally triumphed and sat grinning with his arm

196

through the figure's central void, waiting for his fan to take the picture. He had not, it seemed, lost too much of the common touch.

Daewoo—the name means "Great Universe"—was no more than a small engineering company twenty years ago. Kim Woo Choong had seven employees back in 1968, and a total capital of $10,000. Now he employs more than a hundred thousand men and women, and his empire is worth billions. Brilliant organization, Confucian dedication, an innate sense of duty, carefully applied company paternalism, and an unforgiving regime of discipline—all this, coupled with low wages and precious little interference from union organizations—all helped to bring Kim and his colleagues at Hyundai and Gold Star and Samsung and the other *chaebols*, who started, as he had, from nothing in those ruined days following the war, the immense power and industrial might they enjoy today.

The Japanese industrial giants are often much older and more venerable institutions or were founded by men with great fortunes or by the members of ancient aristocracies—Sony, for instance, was created by a man whose family firm had made a fortune out of *sake* more than a century ago. But the Korean firms, like Daewoo, are generally the creations of self-made men, of poor men, of farmers and engineers and soldiers who saw an opportunity in the wake of war, seized it, held on to it, and triumphed with hard work against what must have seemed like impossible odds. Korean miracle-making is invariably the product of the very same virtues that have made the survival of Korea something of a miracle. The fact that *hangul* remains intact, that a very real Korean identity still exists, that nearly all traces of all those defeats and those subjugations have all been shrugged off once again—once it is possible to accept that Koreans are capable of such miracles as these, then it is possible to accept the industrial miracles that have happened in Korea since the end of their war.

Of course, one can reasonably say that there is a distaff side of the Korean character—a side that brings cruelty and ruthlessness and moodiness and melancholia and uncontrollable outbursts of temper—but that same character also brings the better traits of stoicism, grim determination, the ability to weather almost anything, to meet almost any challenge, and to come back for more—and the ability to make the impossible possible, time and time again. Kim Woo Choong, tireless and single minded, seems a personification of the Korean character, an exemplar of the success, personal and national, that has radiated from the little country in the last thirty years.

"Education is the key," he had said to me over a cup of ginseng tea in the foyer of his hotel. "The people in this country take an enormous pride in seeing that their children are educated well. A worker at one of our factories will do almost anything—he'll endure anything, work as hard as he can—just to ensure that his children get the best possible schooling.

"Look at the villages all over Korea, and see which is the biggest and most imposing building in every one. It'll nearly always be the school building. We worship teachers here; we worship schools. We pay our teachers well. They are respected figures in our community. Are they still in the West? I have heard not, not as much as before. Look at the universities in Seoul—there are dozens of them. People crawl over each other to get to attend classes. They really *want* to learn. They want to be trained. There is this intense desire to better themselves, and to do it with their brains if they can. If anything can be specifically thought of as responsible for our country's success then it's that—the intense desire to learn, to become properly educated at the best schools that can be afforded. No matter what the cost, no matter the hardship, that's the prime duty of a parent, to get his children educated. That's the key.''

Kim is not a flamboyant figure, though he does dress well and maintains a renowned art gallery in a suburb of the capital. He is seen to mix with friends who play golf at the Han Yang Country Club north of Seoul, where a year's membership can cost 35 million *won*—$40,000. And this was apparently enough—this illustration of what was said to be the growing gap between the wealth of employers and that of employees in Korea—for Daewoo to be plagued by serious strikes during the summer of 1987 and for riots to break out (during which one demonstrator at the Koje Island shipyard was killed, hit by shrapnel from a police tear-gas grenade). Kim stood up to the strikers for a week, then gave in gracefully, offering more money, compensation for the dead man's family, and better conditions. As a consequence of a wave of strikes organized at the same time as the one against Daewoo, the unions have considerably more power and influence in the Korea of the late 1980s than they did at the beginning of the decade. Whether this means that the astonishing rate of economic success can be maintained remains to be seen.

❖   ❖   ❖

I managed to get myself hopelessly lost on the way back from the palace— Seoul has the appearance of modernity but in fact is divided into a mass of tiny villages that, like palaces themselves (or Moorish bazaars), huddle behind the walls of their own outer houses and inside are like vast mazes. Old women staggering about with *kimchi* dishes, the *yontan* man delivering the coal, the milkman delivering, the children playing *paduk*—the Korean version of the ancient Japanese game *go*—on tiny boards; all seemed wrapped up in a rabbit warren of streets and staircases that ended in blind alleys miles from where I had wanted to go. A child finally led me out into the street again, and I found the entrance to the subway and took a train out to Kupabal Station on the far northwestern side of the city.

Route 1 was here again—the road to Panmunjom that had once been the road to Peking. Indeed, old maps show the road—now jammed with buses and high-speed cars and underlain by subway trains—to have passed through a defile called Pekin Pass. Henry Savage Landor liked the drama of the place. It is, he wrote:

> . . . the road by which the envoys of the Chinese Emperor, following an ancient custom, travel overland with a view to claiming the tribute payable by the King of Corea. As a matter of fact, this custom of paying tribute had almost fallen into disuse and China had not, I believe, enforced her right of suzerainty over the Corean peninsula until 1890, when the envoys of the Celestial Emperor once again proceeded on their wearisome and long journey from Pekin to the capital of Cho-sen. It was here at Pekin Pass, then, that according to custom, they were received with great honour by the Coreans, and led into Seoul.

My subway train had undershot the pass by about a hundred feet, and I left the city without ceremony, passing between the northern *haetaes* with no more than a glance. The blossom trees were full and huge, the day was clear and bright, and the road ahead—which in theory passed to China, to Mongolia, to Manchuria—was arrow straight. But there was no chance that I could use it to pass to China or even very much farther into Korea. I would manage, in fact, to walk precisely thirty-five miles more along it until I passed the barbed wire and the electric fences, and between the artillery pieces and the tank compounds, and until I reached a row of markers and a battered bridge that took the enfeebled extension of this roadway across a muddy little stream. The bridge, I had been told, was called the Bridge of No Return, and if I made the calamitous error of walking across it, I would be lost forevermore. So, they said, thirty-five miles more, and not a single pace beyond.

CHAPTER

NINE

"For Martial Affairs, the King keeps abundance of Soldiers in his Capital City, who have no other Employment than to keep guard about his Person, and to attend to him when he goes abroad.

"Their Horse wear Currasses, Headpieces, and Swords, as also Bows and Arrows, and Whips like ours, only that theirs have small iron points. The Foot as well they wear a Corselet, a Headpiece, a Sword and Musket, or Half-Pike. The Officers carry nothing but Bows and Arrows. The Soldiers are oblig'd to provide fifty Charges of Powder and Ball, at their own cost.

"Corea being almost encompass'd on all sides by the Sea, Every Town is to maintain a Ship ready rigg'd, and provided with all Necessities. . . . They carry some small pieces of Cannon, and abundance of artificial Fireworks. . . ."

—HENDRICK HAMEL,
1668

❖   ❖   ❖

FROM A DISTANCE IT LOOKED LIKE AN ENORMOUS bridge—an unappealing structure of gray concrete blocks that stood astride Route 1, with a sentry box beside it. From within the box came the glint of a steel helmet and the barrel of an automatic rifle. Even from afar, though, the structure looked rather odd—it seemed somehow out of place, a bit suspect, even phony.

For a start it clearly was not a particularly useful sort of bridge, since it didn't appear to be carrying anything across the road. There was no railway line leading up to it; there was no track to allow cattle or people to pass above the endlessly roaring torrent of traffic; the bridge appeared to support no lesser highway, no water pipeline, no trunk cable for the national grid. Of course, it might once have supported a right-of-way that had fallen into disuse, but it didn't look a very old bridge, and besides, Korea isn't a country where things fall into disuse. If the people stop using something, they tend to tear it down and build something else in its place. There are virtually no ruins in Korea— no modern ones, anyway. So whatever this mysterious object was, it performed a function of some sort.

I walked closer. To the left and right of the structure, reaching away to the distant horizons, were long lines of immense concrete cubes. They were like building bricks that had been set down across the landscape by some giant child on a day when he was bored. The bricks—which must have been eight feet tall and have weighed fifty tons apiece—were arranged in three staggered

203

rows, such that those in the middle line covered the gaps between the bricks in the two others. On the outer, northern (and thus North Korea–facing) side of the line there was a deep ditch with precipitous sides—rather like the Vallum, the defensive moat built by the Romans on the Pictish side of Hadrian's Wall. The parallel was inviting and, as it happened, appropriate.

It would be quite impossible for any vehicle yet designed by man to pass across this formidable line of defense—for this, indeed, was precisely what it was. In much the same way as the old Seoul city walls had been designed to keep the Mongols at bay—though the walls proved a costly failure—so this new, and not very much more technologically advanced, city wall had been designed to keep the Communists at bay. American intelligence reports have it that there are 3,500 tanks north of the Demilitarized Zone—"most of them indigenously produced copies of the relatively modern Soviet T-62, supplemented by numerous M-1973 Armored Personnel Carriers mounting the 73mm smooth bore gun." The ditch and the concrete blocks, it is fondly hoped, will halt them all in their tracks.

And the "bridge" too, is all part of the same defense mechanism. As I walked beneath it—the sentry saluted me smartly, though only after he had eyed me with the most intense curiosity, for I was the only walker on the road—I could see exactly what it was. Just beneath the huge mass of cement and iron that was poised over the road were a number of long tubes drilled into the structure's vertical supports. A cable emerged from the end of each tube, and the cables—twenty or so of them—were gathered together and passed into a duct that took them below ground. There was no doubt as to their purpose: They would, on command from some central bunker, transmit the signal that would detonate high-explosive charges lodged inside each of the tubes—tubes placed in such a way that their detonation would shatter the bridge supports and bring the whole mass of ferrocement and iron crashing down onto Route 1. The explosions would totally block the road and would with luck prevent the southward passage of all those T-62 tank squadrons and the M-1973 Armored Personnel Carriers that were waiting, even now, for a chance to swoop down on Seoul.

I passed through four more such bridges during the next hours. A couple of them had special hinged steel doors that could slam shut at a moment's notice, also blocking the road but allowing it to be reopened quickly should the Northerners turn tail after a firefight. And there was a bridge over a river, too, that was similarly equipped for self-destruction. Stout ropes were looped through holes in the roadway and, if I craned over the railing sufficiently far, I could see that suspended from them like hams in a delicatessen were high-explosive charges—mines that would blow the bridge to smithereens and deny the Northern tanks another opportunity of clanking southward.

Everything en route—every bluff, every defile, every bridge, every crossing— is designed with the defense of Seoul in mind. This is because current thinking about Northern strategy has it that the Communist forces—should they ever decide to invade, as they did in 1950—would mount a sudden and massive blitzkrieg, storming over the DMZ when least expected and when the Southern guard is down—Christmas Day, perhaps—and try to capture the capital, or at least the capital's supply lines. The advance, which might take a week, would then halt, and the Communists would neogotiate a political settlement based on the now vastly changed military situation.

Since 1973 the most effective counter to this particular threat has been to place American forces, in very considerable numbers, in the area through which the North Koreans would have to advance—the area through which I was now walking. This would have a duel effect: First, it would bring the North Koreans into direct conflict with what the Pentagon regards as some of the best-trained and best-equipped fighting men it is possible to find—and the Communists might then lose the battle; and second, it would pit the North Koreans against the unique political disadvantage of doing battle with Washington. It is one thing, the argument goes, for the North Koreans to fight their Southern brothers, even if the Southern brothers are linked by treaty with a United States that is more than willing to help defend them; it is quite another for North Korea to take on the United States from the very start. Pyongyang, it is thought, would not wish to take the risk of a direct conflict with the United States—hence the decision to place American troops well forward, almost as pickets, tempting the Northerners into striking a blow, is also a carefully constructed way of warning them not to play with the kind of fire that battle with Washington would inevitably bring down on them. (It is said that the latest battle plan, should the presence of the American troops fail to deter a North Korean attack, requires the Southern forces to mount a major counterattack, crossing the DMZ and pouring deep into the North Korean heartland. Since a huge proportion of the Southern troops are well to the north of Seoul, the presence of dynamited bridges and collapsed river crossings would not present too much of a problem in logistics, since the barriers would all be well behind them.)

The countryside around me had all the delicacy of an old watercolor—the blue sky lapped vaguely against the blue hills, a distant tracery of lime green poplars framed a rice paddy that glinted softly in the evening sun, the tractors purred distantly, there was a sweetish smell of woodsmoke in the air. But the place-names, the signboards, the half-hidden camps—all of these had the feel of war about them, a reminiscence of misery and glory and brief episodes of heroism. The sinuous strip of asphalt ahead of me was after all a classic Korean invasion route, a road that had been tramped or rumbled or fought along by Chinese and Mongols, and by the First and Second Corps of the North Korean Army just three decades before. Over the low ranges to my right—where road signs pointed to quiet market towns that had been terrible battlefields not so long ago—there were, I knew, two more valleys, near parallel, that made up

the notorious Uijongbu Corridor, along which hundreds of tanks and infantrymen had swept on that bleakly wet summer Sunday in 1950 when, as one
author put it, "the South Korean soldiers mistook the rumble of enemy artillery for the sound of thunder."

So all the names round here—Munsan, Komchon, Tongduchon, Pyokche—
are to many Koreans (and to not a few Americans) redolent of gunsmoke and
defeat, and then victory and defeat again, and final stalemate. (Uijongbu means
"the City of Ever Righteousness," which some may find ironic.) "Down these
roads came the North Korean 3rd and 4th Divisions," wrote Robert Leckie—
one of the Civil War's most recent historians—in *The Korean War*. "The 4th
was on the west road [close to where I was now stepping out], the 3rd was on
the east, and both were behind the bulk of the tanks of the 105th Armored
Brigade. There was no stopping these armored columns, for there was nothing
with which to stop them. The American 37mm antitank guns were hardly
better than pistols against the T-34s. . . ."

Today the preparations for war are more impressive, and they look more impressive
too. No one, this time, is going to be caught napping. Up on the hills, above the
canopies of the pine woods, radar dishes that point ever northward rock and turn
rhythmically. Convoys of American Army trucks grumble along the road. Korean
foot soldiers, their rifles tipped with bayonets, clamber over stiles on their way to
patrol the fields. And every few miles there is a camp—usually American, with a
prosaic name like Camp Smith or Camp Edwards—behind barbed wire entangle-
ments and lines of arc lights. The sentry posts, the Quonset huts, the pay offices, the
water towers, and all the other paraphernalia of a foreign base are familiar enough;
they look less than threatening, being merely the conventional aspect of the new
American colonialism, if you like, that you see in Turkey or the Philippines or in
East Anglia. But then, at the far end of each camp, is the vehicle park—and that
invariably looks very threatening indeed. Up here, so very close to the Zone, the
parks are jammed solid with camouflage-painted, net-shrouded battle tanks and howitzers and armored personnel carriers, jeeps, scout vehicles, machine gun platforms,
field ambulances, ammunition trucks, mine scourers, bridge layers, mobile mortars—
a concentration of battlefield equipment for a great field army, ready and waiting in
its lair to fan out and deal death to the enemy or, in the case of the ambulances, to
deal with the death and the dying of its own.

I seemed always to feel a tingle and a chill of apprehension creeping along my
spine as I walked past these camps; and the camp fences were very long, and so my
walks under the great grooved barrels of the howitzers and the siege cannons took
time—too much time for comfort. I think I felt much as I remember feeling when I
saw my first IRA man holding his smoking rifle in a Belfast slum street years ago. To
read about such people, or even to see them on film, manages to be not at all chilling.
Print or celluloid, however graphic, can be a neutralizing medium. But to see a gun
in the hands of an angry man—or to see, as on this day, hundreds of mighty weapons
in the hands of ever-watchful and ever-fearful guards—that was a frightening thing.

I was glad each time to walk away free of the wire fences, to get away from the malevolent presence of the guns, and back to the color-washed quietude of the Korean pastoral.

I made the dirty little village of Kumchon by twilight and found a *yogwan* where a matronly concierge gave me a room with a Western-style bed. She had hung up a poster of a naked girl, who peered coquettishly down at me, and the matron stood in the doorway pointing at the girl and then at me, and looked inquiringly. I muttered something about having a bath and began to ease off my socks, and she retired to her room muttering, and I could hear her switch on the television. I sat in the little bath—Korean baths, when you find such things, are engineered for tiny people who sit bolt upright, and they are not kind to those of us longer creatures who like to languish in the foam— and I felt a little depressed: There were only twenty miles to go now, and I was coming to the end of a journey that I wished could go on forever. Why couldn't I carry on across the borderline? Why could I not, as I had originally wanted, walk to Pyongyang, or indeed right up to the banks of the Yalu River? Wretched politicians! I cursed, and lathered myself furiously.

But an hour later, cleansed and refreshed and my feet powdered and dried, and wearing the last fresh shirt I could find in the bottom of my bag, the gloom had lifted. I called a friend in Seoul, a pretty interpreter called Choon-sil whom I had tried to find while I had been walking through the city, but without any luck. This time she answered the phone and seemed instantly excited. "I have been so very sad," she said, without further explanation. "And now I am a little drunken. But you not mind? I come to see you? In Kumchon—that's only half an hour in the taxi." I was pleased, of course, though a mite offended by the casual way she had reminded me that a distance I had taken a day to walk took less than thirty minutes in a cab. But, then, all Korea would only take eight hours by car: I could be back in Mokpo by dawn, if I started now.

Choon-sil was very "drunken," as she would say, when she arrived. She had come home from work at six and had started on the beer—four cans, and another in the taxi on the way. She insisted on taking me to a café she knew well from her student days, and she swayed slightly as she walked.

We sat in the candlelit gloom of this little cavelike bar late into the night. The tables were worn sections of an old oak, the rings picked out by a decade of student ballpoints. The chairs were deal, the floor was warm stone. Each table seemed to be enveloped by low rough walls, and all manner of intimacies were encouraged in the fuggy coziness of the place. We ordered *pindae-ttuk*, a big, steaming-hot bean-flour pancake, and endless bottles of beer. Rosa—her parents, devout Christians, had suggested the name to her when she was fifteen—was indeed very sad. She suffered the classic dilemma of so many intelligent Korean women—for intelligent she very much was, with a mind like a razor, a splendid facility for language, a wide assortment of clever, and foreign, friends. She was thirty-two, her teenage prettiness perhaps fading a little. Her parents had wanted her married, and she had duly gone to the matchmakers and seen what was on offer. But she had always made it clear that she would never warm to the idea of performing the kind of uxorial duties expected by a Korean husband. So she had turned all suitors down and opted for an independent life, teaching English, interpreting, doing research work for foreign visitors. She was much loved and admired, but she knew, as the years slid by, that she had a diminishing chance of marrying or bearing a child.

A few months before she had met and fallen in love with a married man—the only kind of man, she had to acknowledge, who might yet marry her. And by what she regarded as great good fortune he was also, she felt, the sort of man who would regard her as a spiritual and intellectual equal: She would not have to follow meekly in this wake, as is the lot of most Korean wives. But her pleasant fantasies were not to be: A week or so before we met he had returned to his wife, and she was cast down into the deepest of glooms. "My only chance is with a *yangnom*," she said, forcing a smile. She was probably right. Marriage to a foreigner—however alien to her principles it might be to marry beyond her country-caste—would give her the freedom to travel (she had never been out of Korea, nor ever would, she supposed) and a married life that promised her some form of equality.

She stayed the night—she was far too drunk to go all the way back to Seoul, and besides, an American sentry at one of the pseudobridges had warned that the road was curfewed after midnight, and here it was, 12:45 A.M. So we weaved our way through a cold, spitting spring night, to the flickering lights of the Arirang *yogwan*. The matron was still awake, idly watching the television, and she poked her head around the door as we were removing our shoes. (There were a dozen pairs, and all, as is common in Korea, had their backs broken down—a consequence of a system of politesse that requires the shoes to be taken off and put back on maybe twenty times a day. Cobblers, and shoe shops, make good money in Korea.)

The concierge whispered a few words to Choon-sil, who promptly collapsed in a fit of drunken giggles, and I had to hush her and take her to the room and quiet her down. When she had caught her breath she explained: The old woman had remarked on how sad it would be for this nice room—Western bed, naked girl on the wall, deep bath, and so on—to be wasted on a man alone. So good, she said to Choon-sil, that someone was going to share. "Except," Choon-sil said, her voice slurred both with weariness and an excess of *maekju*, "that I go to sleep, right away." And she did just that, and she snored boldly for hours. When I woke at seven she had already gone, and there was a note in English, saying how sorry she was for her distemper, and how she wished me good fortune with my final few miles. She had to be in her office in Yoido at eight: given the rush hour she had to wake at six, and the concierge had duly obliged.

I was up and on the road by nine. It was a brilliant Friday morning. The roadside grass was still damp from overnight rain, but the sky was now cloudless and clear, and a cool and quite stiff wind was blowing down from the north. Kumchon sits a half mile off the road, and I had to walk along a crowded spur road—a market was in full swing, and there were dogs and chickens and piles of vegetables on sale from a hundred tiny stalls—and cross the railway line—well fortified, with machine-gun emplacements beside it and another collapsing bridge—before I was back on the highway. I had been walking for ten minutes along Route 1 when I suddenly became aware that passing motorists were waving at me much more cheerily than ever they had done before. I realized what had happened. I must have been on television.

The day before, when I had crossed the Han River, a small television team had been waiting for me. MBS, one of the two Korean networks, had heard that an Englishman was making a journey along the path taken by the sailors from the *Sparrowhawk* and had sent a crew out to find me. I had had some kind of warning the day I left Kunsan base, when one of the American airmen had reported hearing from a Korean news agency, who had been asking how to find me. He told them I had already left. The MBS people had missed me at Chonan and missed me again at Anyang; they therefore laid an ambush on the south side of the Mapo Bridge, and I walked straight into it.

The interview was short and much as I had feared. Koreans are properly proud of their country, or they are in public, at least, even if a lack of confidence, and self-pity, and deep and inconsolable melancholy sometimes seem to be the national malaise—and while they find foreign attention flattering, they regard themselves as eminently deserving of it. So there is—I had been warned—a touch of condescension about their response to anyone who takes an interest in them—much as there is in Japan. And so the interviewer asked me to speak in Korean, not to laud my efforts with the language but rather to show how badly a foreigner speaks so complicated a language. Then again, I was asked to sing a Korean song—to demonstrate how difficult it was for anyone other than a son of Choson to tackle the mournful rhythms of the local music. No one in the interview had wanted me to lose face; it wasn't as crude as that. But I was expected to offer a display that would reassure the viewers of their unassailable superiority in all things I might attempt—and I, having been told exactly what to do, wasn't going to disappoint them. The television people knew what they wanted, and I think they knew that I knew what they wanted—so everything was conducted in good spirits, and the results, I thought, were probably usable. They apparently were. It turned out the network had used seven minutes of the interview on the MBS breakfast program that morning—yes, Korea has breakfast-time television—and all the drivers who hooted and waved (and the few who stopped to shake my hand) had evidently watched as they took their morning *kimchi* and their soup and rice and cold barley tea. I had to realize that I had become, over these past three hundred miles, a small celebrity.

The plan for the final few miles had had to be agreed on in Seoul with the commander of the UN garrison. To walk right up to the frontier, to the strange border-that-is-not-a-border that is formally known as the Military Demarcation Line, requires special permission. Military escorts are needed. Sentries need to be forewarned. One of the North Korean duty officers is told, out of politeness, and to head off any possibility of trouble that might stem from so unexpected an arrival in the sensitive area. And so that everything is expected—and because soldiers run the final miles—a timetable has to be agreed on. I had thus promised to be at the southern end of Freedom Bridge over the Imjin River at noon precisely. Provided I did that, the officer had told me over the phone a few days before, everything should go like clockwork.

At eleven I was striding past yet another sprawling military base at the city of Munsan. A band was playing, its sousaphones and serpents gleaming in the steady sunshine. Two hundred soldiers in gleaming ceremonial helmets and white uniforms were wheeling and marching and countermarching on the parade ground. My feet moved involuntarily to the infantry pace, and I was out of town in moments and back in open country once more.

The railway line—the line that had been with me, on and off, ever since I left Mokpo more than a month before—passed across the road. But here it was rusty from disuse, and I saw that a few yards north of the road the rails had been taken up, and there was a pile of old sleepers and a small hill of sand, and the cutting that went under the old iron bridge was choked with grass and rosebay willow herb, and the bridge itself, still with its black stain of smoke, was thick with moss. This was the main line to Pyongyang—the line to Manchuria, to Mongolia, to Peking. It had been a busy line forty years ago, a trunk route, its timetables in *Baedeker* and the *Cook's Continental*. But now it stopped dead a couple of miles south of the Imjin and ran into a pile of old sand, and all because of the vagaries of politics, of ideology, and of war.

Suddenly from behind, a toot on a car horn, and a cheerful shout. "Hey! You're gonna make it, ol' son! Keep goin'! Don't stop!" It was Billy Fullerton, a large, ebullient Texan who has worked in the information office at the Yongsan U.S. Army Base for the last twenty years and who has befriended and helped everyone and anyone who has ever been interested in the country that he has adopted as his second home. It was Billy who had persuaded the UN bosses to allow me to walk to the Line—"Figured it'd be pointless you stopping at Seoul. You gotta go as far as you can git. They bought the argument in the end, but they weren't eager, I can tell you"—and it was Billy who had arranged the necessary escorts and the blue armband that the North Koreans insisted that I wear whenever in their line of sight. His driver slowed to my speed, and Billy took my order. "Gotta eat when you get to the bridge.

What'll you have—chocolate, peanuts, ice cream? All on me. Glad to help."
He was a blessing. I asked for a couple of cans of orange juice and a Hershey
bar, and then he zoomed off ahead of me, promising to have them ready.

Forty minutes later I came to the summit of a low rise and was looking down
into the valley of the Imjin-gang. Here on the hill it was sunny, with the
damp smell of balsam pines wafting from the thick woods beside me. Wildflowers grew in abundance. There were small houses with orange and bright
blue roofs, and farmers were tilling their fields for the late spring crops. It had
all been so different thirty years before: This small river valley, so savagely
fought over for so long, by so many forces going so many different ways as the
war ebbed and flowed, advanced and receded, had been utterly torn and bom-
barded to shreds. Twisted metal, huge artillery holes, discarded equipment,
stranded tanks, spent shell cases, ruined houses, and legions of dead and
maimed men—the valley had been littered with them all, whether they had
been covered by snow, half sunk in yellow mud, or baked in the summer sun.

❖   ❖   ❖

The Imjin! The name seems appropriately redolent of the Dakotas, of Custer,
of cavalry charges and stockades and embattlement a hundred years ago, when
the warriors were the Sioux and the Apache and the uniformed forces ordered
down from Washington. And just as the Dakotas have recovered physically
from those times but have never allowed them to be forgotten, so this countryside in Korea has sprung back too, as countryside always does, from the
immediate physical horrors of conflict. Except that here, as I walked down
toward the infamous stream, it was dismaying to see that man had planted
more than his customary share of memorials, since this war had only been
halted in its tracks and was still always on the verge of being fought again.
The peace that bathed the Imjin Valley today could be broken in an instant,
in a way that it never can be again ten thousand miles away on the high plains
of America.

I rounded a long bend, passing beneath another bridge barrier, its giant
building bricks looking as though they might topple and flatten me at any
instant. And then, just ahead, was a glitter of parked cars and a long, low
building festooned with flags and surrounded by monuments and, I could see
as I came closer, khaki-colored tanks and half-tracks and spiked guns. This
was the Imjingak Museum—the most northerly point on Route 1 that ordinary
South Koreans are permitted to visit. The place is dominated by a huge permanent exhibition of the follies of war, and each day—as on this Friday lunch-
time—it is crammed with bus-hauled visitors chattering with rapt fascination
as they are led from picture to picture, from tank to howitzer, from atrocity to
atrocity, to be reminded yet again of the war that has resulted in what seems
the permanent division of their peninsular country. From time to time a distinguished visitor passes through Imjingak and changes cars, and the crowds

have more to gawk at than usual: This morning a South Korean general was due to come on up to the Line for a meeting with an American colleague, and a caravan of long black cars swished into the bus parking lot, and heavily armed soldiers and aides with walkie-talkies conferred as jeeps maneuvered alongside them, and a small, fattish man in uniform, wearing dark glasses, was helped from the deep leather seats of the Lincoln onto the more austere vinyl of the Willys. A gold-braided South Korean national flag, with its colorful *taeguk* emblem, was raised on the jeep's wing, the outriders' visors were snapped down, powerful motors were gunned, and the new convoy sped away, and Army drivers parked the empty limousines under a shade tree and waited for orders, while curious children examined the paintwork and grinned at themselves in the gleaming chrome.

Billy Fullerton was waiting with my rations, which I fell upon with glee—I hadn't eaten breakfast back at Kumchon, and had been walking fast for the last three hours. And then here was a new man, a tall, kindly looking American lieutenant wearing the shoulder patches of an elite corps of foot soldiers. "Hi, sir," he said, stepping forward briskly and giving a half-salute. "I'm Lieutenant John Wiegand, first of the five-oh-sixth. Glad to meet you, sir. Well done. I'm your military escort for the last miles. Shall we get going? We've a fair way to march." He had an automatic pistol in a holster, and canvas walking boots, and he looked very fit. I collected my pack and my shepherd's stick and marched smartly past the parked limousines and the coaches filling up or disgorging their charges, and came to the sentry box at the left bank of the Imjin and the southern end of the Freedom Bridge.

❖　❖　❖

"Stand Alone—Suh!" screamed two voices in near unison, and the two American sentries shouldered their automatic rifles and slapped their hands across the magazines, making as much clatter and noise as they could. John returned the salute with equal vigor. "Rock Steady, Men!" he shouted, and we stepped beneath the steady gaze of the soldiers and onto the wooden planking of the rickety structure. "Sorry about the display," John said once we were out of earshot. "But that's the way we do things up here. It keeps the morale up, they say. These cute little exchanges between officers and men remind everyone why we're here. We used to have a little routine going where the soldiers would say 'One Man, Sir!' and we'd return the salute by shouting 'One Bullet, Men!' and everyone would get the message about economy with ammunition, and of effectiveness of fire. Nowadays we stress the simple importance of being up here, close to the Communists. We say 'Keep up the Fire, Men!' or 'In Front of Them All, Men!' They like it. It makes them feel good. And up here there's little enough opportunity for feeling good—especially in the winter."

Freedom Bridge is the one surviving link across the lower Imjin, the shattered stumps of the other (both were railway bridges, with the rail lines meeting at Munsan Junction) lying a hundred yards upstream, the brown waters of the flood swirling around them. The railway has gone from the surviving bridge, too, and now only a single line of road traffic—military vehicles or official cars granted permission by the UN authorities—bumps across the old planks, with American sentries at each end ordering southbound traffic to halt until the northbound convoys have cleared, and then vice versa. The bridge is in terrible condition, with dozens of holes gouged by armor-piercing gunfire, which remain unrepaired; when heavy trucks grind past the entire structure wheezes and groans.

But its symbolism alone is important enough to ensure its survival, just as it is. This, after all, is the bridge across which, once the armistice had been signed in 1953, thousands of prisoners were repatriated from Communist hands. They came streaming down from Panmunjom and from the tiny circle of no-man's-land where they had been checked and examined by the neutral inspectors; they had marched or been carried on litters down Liberty Lane, and they had arrived at Freedom Bridge and crossed the Imjin to the tent city known as Freedom Village. After all they had gone through, one can almost forgive the sentimentality.

The lieutenant and I marched steadily northward, up the other side of the valley. Billy Fullerton, who would be the first to admit that he is not a slender man, puffed and panted along behind us. His driver brought up the rear in the car. It was very hot, and we all had rivulets of sweat coursing down our faces. With the soldier as my pacemaker I was going a great deal faster than normal, and the miles slipped away easily. The countryside rose and fell, fire bases and battalion headquarters and ready rooms and forward-fire directorates appeared on the horizon, then came abeam, and fell away behind us. Finally, after about two hours of steady progress, we came to the brow of another long slope, at the bottom of which was a massive fence, sentry post, and a collection of heavily armed soldiers. This was the southern edge of the Demilitarized Zone—the DMZ.

The Korean Armistice Agreement—signed on July 27, 1953, in Kaesong by Marshal Kim Il Sung, supreme commander of the Korean People's Army and by Peng Teh Huai, commander of the Chinese People's Volunteers, and in Munsan by General Mark Clark, the American commander of the UN Forces—is the document that effectively created the division of the Korean Peninsula into two violently opposed countries. No treaty, no concordat, no instrument of state recognized by the real world created a country called North Korea or fashioned this miracle state called South Korea. Article One of the armistice says it all:

1. "A Military Demarcation Line shall be fixed, and both sides shall withdraw two (2) kilometers from this line so as to establish a Demilitarized Zone between the opposing forces. A Demilitarized Zone

213

shall be established as a buffer zone to prevent the occurrence of incidents which might lead to resumption of hostilities.

2. The Military Demarcation Line is located as indicated on the attached map. . . .

And so it was—the line the two groups of forces were deemed by their respective commanders to have reached when fighting was brought to a close. To a great extent it matched the line drawn at the Cairo Conference of 1945, which drew an arbitrary line across a map of Korea—north of the line the Russians would accept the surrender of the Japanese, and south of the line the Americans would. The conferees stood in their hot Cairene hotel suite poring over a map of the Korean Peninsula. Rear Admiral Matthias Gardner, probably keen to get away for a glass of beer, pointed to the thirty-eighth degree of north latitude—the famous 38th Parallel—and said simply: "Why not put it there?" And thus was the world's most heavily defended borderline created, for when the fighting was ended and the armistice signed, the armies were found to have reached a new line that more or less matched Admiral Gardner's parallel; it was a little to the south of it on the western side of the peninsula, a little to the north of it near the Sea of Japan. But essentially—and it remains one of the crueler ironies of a war that killed so many and maimed so many more, on both sides—the armies did not, in the end, either gain or lose any territory for their respective political masters. They ruined cities, they destroyed heritages, they ended and they broke hundreds of thousands of lives, but after three years of pounding and pillaging, the generals found themselves almost exactly where the admiral suggested they should be. They might as well have not fought at all.

The southern border of the DMZ, then, is an impressive frontier indeed, though it is not, in law, a frontier at all. There is an immense fence topped with coils of razor wire. There are trip lines. There is more barbed wire, bundled into rusting piles. Small notices with death's heads signal minefields two hundred yards deep. There are searchlights and ground sensors, sentry towers and constant patrols, and, ready to be rushed into action at a moment's notice, massive pieces of artillery, guns of awesome power and accuracy.

The soldiers checked our identities, and I was ordered to wear the sky blue armband identifying me as a noncombatant. I had to read and sign a piece of paper absolving the United Nations from any responsibility should I be subjected to hostile fire. And I had to promise that if I saw any Chinese or North Korean soldiers, I would make no gesture, no expression, no provocative act that might reasonably lead to a complaint or, worse still, to a retaliatory act. I read and signed and put on my armband. Soldiers saluted—"Keep Up the Fire, Sah!"—and a white car with a UN flag fluttering from its roof moved into the lead. Three large American soldiers—two of them black—joined as escorts. We were now eight—two cars, one ahead, one behind; four soldiers; Billy Fullerton, still game but pursuing; and me. And on we marched, deeper and deeper into neutral territory.

❖   ❖   ❖

The DMZ is 151 miles long, stretching across the country like a scar. Almost no humans go there—there are no farmers (other than a few I shall mention in a moment), no towns, few soldiers (since the vast majority operate *outside* the DMZ). The consequence of this is a profusion of wildlife within the zone—wildlife that is untroubled by the threat of the artillery that points menacingly in its direction, since it is wise enough not to understand the threat. So all manner of birds and beasts that have vanished from the more developed parts of Korea still live within the frontier fences. The Manchurian crane, *Grus japonensis*, a red-capped, black-wing-tipped bird of wonderful magnificence, still struts its stuff among the sedges of the DMZ; the Korean wildcat prowls beneath the arc lights; the little Korean bears—*Ursus thibetanus ussurious heuda*—that have a white stripe down their black furry backs can also be seen grubbing for food at the edge of the minefields. It is an ironic counterpoint to the awfulness of war that so much that is beautiful and rare flourishes where the human anger is greatest, and yet in those places where peace has translated into commerce, so much loveliness has vanished clear away.

A bus hurtled down the road toward us, swerving to avoid our scout car, and there was some good-natured fist-waving. "The damn Czechs," said the lieutenant, with a grin. "Off to go shopping in Seoul." There are representatives from four neutral nations up by the borderline—the Swiss and the Swedes on the southern side, the Poles and the Czechs to the north—and while for some unaccountable reason very few Swedes appear to want to go trawling through the bazaars of Pyongyang for bargains, the Poles and the Czechs make weekend expeditions to the South (as they are permitted to do under the terms of the armistice) to savor some of the delights of capitalism. "But see how they're all in civvies," said Wiegand. "The North Koreans take a very dim view of their neutral nations people going down in uniform. Great loss of face all round, it seems."

❖   ❖   ❖

And then, around another corner, we came to a dirt road that led to a village half a mile away on a hilltop. It was a place called Taesong-dong, or "Attaining Success Village"; some Americans like to call it "Democracy Village." The men and women who live and work there are paid by the government to do so. They all wear yellow hats to identify them to soldiers. Their town is dominated by a gigantic flagpole, which looks like the Eiffel Tower and on top of which, hundreds of feet above us, cracked and whipped a mighty edition of the *taeguk-ki*, the national flag. It is a show village, designed principally to display to the North Koreans that a full and productive life can be lived under the eccentric ways of near-beer democracy.

The North Koreans pay no heed. They have an identical village on the other side of the line—the Americans like to call it "Propaganda Village," and they make much of the fact that at night it seems empty, as though workers only toil there during the day. It too has a flagpole, and it is the first real glimpse of North Korea I had, even though I had been aware for some miles that the distant blue hills were in another world, a world as unattainable just now as were the stars. But here, not more than a mile in front of me, was the reality of North Korea—a mirror of the reality of the South—a flagpole.

"See the flag on top of that?" said one of my soldier-escorts and pointed to the blue and red-starred monster swinging heavily in the stiff breeze. "They say it weighs nearly half a ton. Know what? You get that son of a bitch down and down to the Blue House and over to President Chun, and you'll get a million dollars just like that. That's what they tell us. No one's been crazy enough to try. But just give it some time."

The breeze was still coming from the north, and wafting on it, distinct at most times, were martial tunes and the harsh, doglike barking of a North Korean propagandist in full spate. "It goes on all day and often all night," said the lieutenant. "That's the price those suckers pay for living in Taesong-dong. They have to listen to that garbage all the time. It gets real loud at times, when the wind's in the right quarter." And just as he said that, there came a gust of wind, and the sound blasted loudly, like a trumpet. But the yellow-capped workers in the rice fields didn't react at all. They had heard it all too many times before.

And now the end was but a few hundred yards away. We were nearly a mile inside the DMZ and were reaching the tiny island of neutrality that has long gone by the name of the village that—before the tank fire destroyed it utterly—once used to stand there. It was called Panmunjom, and by all accounts it was a miserably unspectacular hamlet, all thatch and *kimchi* jars and rice paddies, much the same in aspect and in the daily lives of its fifty or so inhabitants as any other farm village in the province of Kyonggi-do. But all had changed since the war, and where the *haetaes* might once have stood there was instead another guard post, and a UN soldier, and although the shorthand word Panmunjom is indeed used for this strange place, its official title is now the JSA— the Joint Security Area.

It is a rough circle, half a mile across, and it straddles the Demarcation Line. It is very heavily guarded—and on the Southern side there are barracks from where American troops, kept ever ready, their guns loaded and cocked, can pour into the neutral circle in a matter of seconds in case of trouble. The soldiers designated for duty in the JSA are all mighty specimens—none shorter than five feet ten, most of them well over six feet four—so that they tower above their North Korean colleagues (if "colleague" is the most appropriate way to describe the participants in this most curious of charades). Six of them detached themselves from various duties and walked beside me, with a large black sergeant in command. He greeted me expansively: He had been based in England once and knew the English liked walking. "Wish I could have done it all with you, sir," he said.

On the southern side of the line, inside the Panmunjom circle, are barracks and support buildings and a tall and vulgarly ornate viewing stand, modeled on those from which contemplative Buddhists might watch the rising moon or the stars. I clambered up the marble stairs and looked down on the strange assemblage of buildings below—and for my first view of a real, live North Korean.

There were in fact half a dozen of them, all on their side of a white-painted line that ran along the ground and then passed transversely through the long, warehouselike shed in which the truce talks stagger on, week after week after week. Each man wore a green drab uniform and one of those red-trimmed hats with unnaturally wide brims that seem to be favored by those who go soldiering for the Communist bloc. Each man wore a bright yellow armband, and a couple carried field glasses. They all looked profoundly uninterested in whatever their function was, except that as I watched one lazily raised a camera and pointed it at me and shot a couple of frames, for the record. He looked bored and not at all impressed by what he had seen.

I came down from the platform and ventured closer to the line, peering in through the windows at the infamous baize-topped table where the talks have stuttered on and off and where, it must be said, some measure of peace has been preserved across this most fragile of frontiers. The American soldiers began to shuffle uneasily at my wanderings, and a couple of them started to walk briskly toward me. There was a North Korean just a few feet away now—a man who looked no different at all, aside from his ill-tailored uniform coat, from all the soldiers I had seen in the three hundred miles behind me. Suddenly he smiled at me. I nearly jumped. I grinned back and said *"Annyong-haseyo,"* and he tipped his head toward me.

It was fleeting contact, but it was enough for my minders. There was a polite cough from behind. "I think we'd better be going, sir," a soldier said. "We've told the detail you'll be at the bridge in two minutes." And as if to reinforce his suggestion he spoke into a walkie-talkie and snapped it off, and we began to walk briskly off to the west.

We were still, notionally, on Route 1—the road that led all the way to Pyongyang and up into the wilds of Manchuria. But ahead of me, I had been told, was a narrow, weed-clogged stream that ran just behind the Demarcation Line. In front—and I was walking past it now, I realized—was the infamous elm tree where Americans encountered a posse of hysterically furious North Koreans one summer's day in 1976. The Americans had claimed that the tree prevented them from looking at the bridge with

217

their binoculars—the foliage obscured the view. So they tried to trim the branches back. There was a terrible fight, an hour of hand-to-hand combat that involved knives and axes and ended with two American soldiers being hacked to pieces by North Koreans. It was the worst border incident for many years, and the green baize table resounded with pounding fists, and the warehouse walls echoed with exchanges of abuse for months to come. But no shooting war broke out, and for that the Panmunjom process, clumsy and childish though its procedures may on occasion seem to be, deserves some credit.

❖   ❖   ❖

Now I was but a hundred feet from the end. The road drove on ahead, and in the distance I could see that it turned lazily off to the right and disappeared behind a low hill. But immediately in front, on the left, was a small blockhouse with a UN flag. Beside it stood the beginning of the small, otherwise insignificant bridge. A row of yellow steel poles, hip high, barred the way to any car that might want to cross. Beside the line of poles was an old rusty sign, with some of its old yellow paint still sticking. Military Demarcation Line, it read in English.

The bridge ran for perhaps a hundred feet beyond the line of poles, beyond the Demarcation Line. Thirty-odd years ago this line marked the end of a war. Today, it marked the effective end of a country, of an ideology, of an economic system that has helped make South Korea one of the world's great miracle states. It also marked the literal end of my progress along the length of Korea— and yet I was in no mood to stop. I wanted to press on, to see the rest of a country for which I had a new and abiding fascination.

There was a blockhouse on the northern side of the bridge, and within it I could see two heads bobbing in conversation. Two North Koreans, no doubt, sentries, making certain no mischief was being performed so close to their territory. As I approached they stood up, and one came out of the hut and watched my final steps. There was a North Korean car, black and rather dirty, waiting beside him, facing away from me with its engine running. It was all very quiet, except for the thud of our marching feet.

Idly—for I had no real intention of trying anything—I asked one of my escorts what would happen if I chose to walk on, between the steel poles and into North Korea. "We'd have to let you, sir," he said, gritting his teeth and not smiling. "We have no power to stop you. But they call this the Bridge of No Return. You do know that, don't you, sir?" He looked menacing. For the first time since I started walking I felt a wave of uneasiness pass over me, like a cold wind.

We walked on for the final feet. Someone said something quiet to my escorts, and three of them began to walk much more quickly than I and arrived at the steel poles a few seconds before. They turned around to face me and stood at ease, their feet placed squarely apart, their arms clasped behind their backs. There were only three, but they effectively commanded the approach to the bridge, and they had a resolved look about them.

I arrived at the line. It was 2:35 P.M. The stream, someone said, was called the Konshan-gang. "Please do not touch the MDL sign," said the black sergeant. "It's part of the armistice agreement." The American soldiers stood foursquare before me, looking sternly into the middle distance, unsmiling. Behind them, no more than a stone's throw away, the two North Koreans were now both out of their hut, looking with keen interest at this curious delegation. Someone mentioned—it may have been a joke—that the propaganda loudspeakers had just begun referring to this impoverished visitor who had been forced to walk all the way to the frontier, since he hadn't enough money to buy a car. Someone else reported that the North Koreans had invited me to cross over to their side. Was the black car, then, waiting for me? Did I fancy that the North Koreans were beckoning to me?

"A couple of quick pictures, sir, before we go?" said the sergeant, and the snaps were duly taken, and the American jeep was duly summoned, and it was suggested I might like to be driven away. I craned my neck to see across the border once again, but the black car had gone, and the drab-suited soldiers were back inside the hut. One seemed to be talking on the telephone. I got into the jeep. "It's all over," said Billy Fullerton. "You did it. Well done."

❖   ❖   ❖

On the way back I asked the sergeant—who by now was in a much brighter mood—whether I could in fact have walked across the bridge? "Well, of course you could. This is a free country. My men would have tried to persuade you not to, of course. They were big guys, weren't they? They could have been pretty persuasive if they tried. I don't think you would have wanted to go. Not really. Besides, this is a much better place. Don't you think?"

Behind me now the bridge faded into the distance, and we left sentry post by sentry post, to salutes and bugle calls and shouts of "Keep Up the Fire!" and "Rock Steady, Men!" The hills of North Korea, blue and misty in the late afternoon light, dimmed in the distance; the hills of South Korea, looking just the same, loomed ahead. And then there was the strong brown stream of the Imjin, and there the rickety old Freedom Bridge, and a few bumping moments later I was back on the smooth asphalt among the tour buses and caught in a routine traffic jam of those who had come up that day, as every day, to view the memorabilia of the war.

They had come—ordinary Koreans all—to see the ruin of war and also for a more powerful symbolism: For if it is here at the Imjin that the country's political geography ends, then equally it was here, three-odd decades ago, and with the armistice signed just a few miles away, that the country and its miracle rebirth really started. The Imjin, Panmunjom, the DMZ, and the Demarcation Line—the place, vitally important now to the new Korean mind, where the long war ended, and where the new state has had its birth.

"At Sunrising the Wind fell, which oblig'd us to lower our Sails and Row, to get further off, and prevent being discover'd. At about Noon the Weather began to freshen, and at Night we spread our Sail, directing our course by guess South-East. The Wind growing fresh at Night, we clear'd the point of Corea, and were no longer apprehensive of being pursu'd. . . ."

— HENDRICK HAMEL,
1668

EPILOGUE

❖ ❖ ❖

I STAYED AROUND THE FRONTIER ZONE FOR A WHILE
that Friday afternoon. While I had been in Seoul earlier in the week, an
invitation had come to me, in a roundabout way, from a man who, for the
previous three years, had lived and worked in and around the borderline: He
wanted to give me tea and to ask me how I had found the Korea through
which I had traveled. He was a man who rarely moved beyond his own immediate circle of specialist colleagues, and I jumped at the opportunity of
seeing him and of hearing his impressions of a country he was able to know
better than almost all other outsiders.

His ability to know Korea so very well stemmed from his uniquely privileged
position. He, unlike almost all foreigners who visit the peninsula, was permitted—and permitted by no less an authority than the terms of the 1953 armistice agreement—to travel more or less at will on both sides of the frontier
fences. Should he so choose he can take his breakfast in the present Southern
capital, Seoul; his lunch in a former all-Korean capital that is now sited in
the North, Kaesong; and his dinner in the present Northern capital, Pyongyang. Should he so demand he can wander by the Kum River one week, and—
after obtaining a permit, a document that is rarely denied to a figure of his
standing—by the Yalu River the next. He is able to commune with those who
aid and advise Kim Dae Jung on a Wednesday and with those who aid and
advise Kim Il Sung on the Friday following.

To identify this man by name or title or rank or even to describe his unusual duties is strictly forbidden—such were the terms of his invitation to tea. But it should be said at once that what he does is legitimate, is fully recognized and appreciated by all the governments concerned, and is—in his view, and in the view of his many supporters, admirers, and fans—one of the very few politically constructive tasks being undertaken by anyone on the Korean Peninsula.

The afternoon we met he had already had breakfast with a Chinese general up in Kaesong. He had taken his lunch with an American commander near the Imjin River, and he was planning to attend a small cocktail party that evening given by the North Korean Foreign Ministry in Pyongyang. His only complaint was that he didn't relish the prospect of driving along North Korean Route 1 after dark, for while Route 1 in the South was properly lit and metaled and cambered, in the North it was not much more than a cart track, lumbering with unilluminated military vehicles and the rough transports of the peasantry; the journey, even in a swift official Mercedes, was purgatory indeed.

He had been assigned by his European sponsors to his job in Korea for the last three years, and he knew most of the protagonists well. He loved Korea, quite passionately. And he was deeply saddened, he said, by what he thought had been the progressive deterioration of the situation across the frontier line during the last time he had had the opportunity to observe it.

"The suspicion, of one side by the other, is profound, we all know that. The buildup of military forces goes on, the tension increases, we all know that. But what has surprised and truly depressed me is that the obstinacy, the obduracy, the shortsightedness—the real bar to any progress—is nearly all to be found on the Southern side.

"I am not saying the Northerners are angels, far from it. They live in an astonishingly controlled state, as everyone knows. But so do the Southerners. And they, the ones we think might show some tendency to compromise, to reasonableness, show none at all. Every idea that comes down the pipeline and looks reasonable ultimately gets rejected by Seoul. The generals in Seoul are utterly intransigent, and that is with the knowledge, connivance, and probable support of the Americans. So long as the Americans call the shots in South Korea, there'll be no political movement. Things will simply get worse and worse."

He said all this in the early spring, a few days after President Chun had made his dismaying announcement that he was rejecting the apparently popular demands for political change in Korea. The country was in the grip of a very deep anger and exasperation, and this man's sadness mirrored, diplomatically, his own frustration over what, at the time, seemed to be an impossible situation.

But then, after a few heads had been broken and a few thousand rounds of Korea's particularly unpleasant brand of tear gas had been fired, President

Chun—to the liberal world's astonishment and delight—gave in. The political reforms that so many had seemed to want were promised (though whether they would actually be granted, and without limit, remained to be seen). Political prisoners were freed. There was heady talk of democracy and of a free press and of civil rights and of humanitarian reform—words and phrases that had not, for more than twenty years, been accommodated in Korea's political lexicon. The gloom began to lift. I then heard that my host at the frontier had left for another task on the far side of the Pacific Ocean, and that before he had embarked on the plane he had told friends that he had been considerably heartened by the news, though he continued to be skeptical and wondered how long the peace and harmony would last.

But he had made other remarks that teatime too, and one I remembered as seeming particularly poignant and strange. "I shall be very sorry to leave Korea," he said, "for I have made very many friends. I know many families, mainly senior people, on both sides of the Demarcation Line. I will try and keep in touch over the years.

"But I have a suspicion. From what I have seen, and from the conversations I have had, I actually believe that the people who will think of me as a friend, and who will write to me more constantly, will be the friends I made in North Korea. It has nothing to do with politics—I am no fan of Kim Il Sung, don't worry. But the people in the North seem, in a strange way, to be purer in their Koreanness. They are still gracious and kindly. There is something old-fashioned about them. There is a degree of sincerity and gentility that somehow seems to be evaporating, just a little, in the South. Many people I know in the South are too concerned with their own prosperity, with the rush of their lives, to remember their Koreanness. Perhaps it is my imagination, but I felt the Koreans north of the line were more—how shall I say it?—more unspoiled. I feel they will remain my friends for longer."

It was, indeed, a poignant moment. The hills beyond his living room, where we sat with our tea, were those of North Korea—for now as inaccessible to me as the mountains of the moon. The people who lived and worked in and beyond those hills, in farms and factories, in all the *ri* and *dong* and *shi* and *myun*, were very little different in an inner sense from the people who lived in the South. The people of the Yalu-gang were much the same as the people of the Kum-gang; the climbers on the Diamond Mountain of the North were every bit as Korean as the walkers in Sorak-san National Park; the people of Pusan were much the same as the people of Wonsan—all united by their race, their language, their script, their ancient history, their fear of invasion, their dislike of the Japanese and the Mongols and the Chinese, and quite probably of the Americans, the British, and the Russians too. For now the people to the south of where we sat were free, and the people to the north were not. All very sad, all very wrong—and all, no doubt, to be changed before too long. Whence all that has happened since the agreement that made this fence will

225

seem so pointless, such a waste of time and energy, a misuse of the intelligence of man.

And then, as we sat and mused in the fast-fading spring sunshine, a bird, perched on a branch of a tree that stood in North Korea, began to sing. It sang well and lustily for many minutes, and we both stopped talking and listened with pleasure. And then it stopped, and my host put down his teacup and stood up, suggesting silently that he must ready himself for his journey north.

"That bird," he said, pointing to the tree outside his window. "It was such sweet singing, don't you think? But you know in Korea the people don't say—they never have said—that the birds are *singing*. They say instead that the birds are *crying*, weeping for some tragic reason that is only known to them. Korean birds never sing. They always weep. What a very sad, sad country this always has been. Such a mournful place, and yet so very lovely. It is not a country that will be easy to forget."

And then my escort from the army reappeared and saluted, and I climbed into a jeep and in an hour was back across the Imjin and back among the skyscrapers in the capital, and the neon lights were on, and Korea didn't seem a sad place at all—not for this night, anyway.

GLOSSARY

❖ ❖ ❖

-do: Province.
-dong: Suburb.
-gun: County.
-jip: Literally, house, used as "restaurant."
-mun: Gateway, as in *Namdae-mun,* the great south gate in Seoul.
-myun: Borough.
-pan: Parish.
-ri: Village.
-saram: Person, e.g., *Meeguk saram,* American.
-shi: City-region.
-up: District.
A-joshe!: Hey, you! (said to a man).
Angibu: The Korean secret police.
Anio: No.
Anju: Snacks and salty appetizers served with beer.
Annyong-haseyo: Literally, Are you in peace? Used as "hello."
Annyong-hee kaesayeo: Good-bye (said by the one who is leaving to the one who isn't).
Anyonghee kashipshiyo: Good-bye (said by the one who isn't leaving to the one who is).
Arirang: A Korean mountain, and the title of a famous song.
Buk: North.
Bulgoki: Marinated and barbecued meat.
Cha-da: Sleep.
Chaebol: The major Korean industrial corporations, e.g., Hyundai, Samsung.
Cheju-do: Literally, the land over there.

Chige: Wooden A-frame-shaped carrier used by porters or *chige* men.

Chima: Long, floor-length skirt, traditional dress for women.

Chindo-kae: A tough little dog found on Chindo Island in southwest Korea.

Chogori: Jacket or blouse, traditional Korean dress.

Chokbo: Family-tree book kept by almost all Korean families.

Chonbok chuk: Rice and abalone gruel, popular in the south.

Chong mal?: Really?

Choson: Literally, Land of Morning Calm; old name for Korea.

Choson Minchu-chui Inmin Konghwa-guk: Democratic People's Republic of Korea (North Korea).

Cho-un: Good.

Chung wa dae: The Blue House—the Korean presidential palace.

Daegook: Literally, big country; also used to refer to China.

Daehan Minguk: Republic of Korea (South Korea).

Dong: East.

Gang: River.

Gwen chan sumnida: No thank you.

Haenyo: Diving women of Cheju Island, gatherers of abalone and sea cucumbers.

Hae-sam: Sea cucumber, a much favored seafood.

Haetae: Guardian beasts of a town, mythological mixtures of lion and dog.

Hanafuda: Japanese word for the Korean game *hwatu.*

Hangbok: Korean national dress.

Hangul: Korea's unique phonetic alphabet, designed by King Sejong.

Hanyak: Korean folk medicine.

Harubang: Standing "grandfather" stones, often found on Cheju-do.

Hodori: Baby tiger, symbol of the 1988 Seoul Olympics.

Hong cha: Red tea.

Hongsam: Red (steamed) ginseng root.

Hopak-dan chu: Ornamental amber buttons, used for fastening Korean clothing.

Hun min chong um: Early designation of hangul script.

Hwadu: Profound question set as a basis for Korean Buddhist meditation.

Hwan-gap: Sixty-first birthday celebrations.

Hwatu: A traditional Korean picture card game, played like gin.

Hyodo kwan guang: Literally, parental respect tour—holidays for the elderly paid for by their children.

Ibalso: Korean barbershop.

Ibul: Coverlet placed over *yo.*

Insam: Ginseng.

Ip chang: Face, as in the Oriental concept of pride and self-esteem.

I shipaloma: Grave insult; literally, a whore.

Jip-sin: Traditional Korean straw slippers.

Kalbi: Barbecued spare ribs.

Kinyombi: Monument.

Kimchi: Peppered, garlicked, and brine-pickled vegetables—a national staple.

Kkot saem chu wi: Literally, flower-jealousy weather—a snap of cold in early spring.

Koan: Riddle posed for Japanese Buddhist meditation.

Kobuk-son: The armored "turtle ships" of Admiral Yi Sun-shin.

Koguryo: Ancient northern Korean kingdom.

Kokoro: Japanese word for "heart."

Komusin: Korean slippers.

Koran-cho: Medicinal herb.

Koryo: Post-Shilla kingdom from which Korea took her name.

Kukbo: The National Treasures, the most valuable classification.

Kut: Shamanist devil-driving ceremony.

Mabu: A horseman.

Maekju: Beer.

Makkoli: Milky rice wine, the working man's principal drink.

Makkoli-jip: Working-class bar where *makkoli* is the favored, though not the only, drink.

Man: Ten thousand, as in *man won,* ten thousand *won.*

Man won gyon: Telescope.

Maum sang hada: Anguish over the loss of face (see *Ip chang*).

Meeguk: America.

Mian hamnida!: I am sorry!

Mogyok: Bath.

Mogyoktang: Public bath.

Moktak: Wooden clapper used in Buddhist ritual.

Mudang: Shamanist sorceress.

Mukkop-ta: Heavy.

Nakhwa-am: Rock of Falling Flowers in Puyo.

Naksonjae: Mansion of Joy and Goodness at Changdok Palace, Seoul.

Nam: South.

Nay: Yes.

Nunchi: An extraordinary Korean ability to discern someone's mood.

Odi isumnikka?: Where is?

Ojingoa: Dried squid, a favorite snack.

Oksusucha: Toasted-corn tea.

Ondol: Lacquered-paper floor, heated from beneath, common in Korean houses.

Onnyi: Literally, older sister; used by women, e.g., to summon bar hostesses.

Paduk: Korean version of the Japanese board game *go.*

Paekche: Ancient southern Korean kingdom.

Paekhwa jom: Department stores.

Paeksam: White ginseng root.

Paem sul: Snake wine.

Paem tang: Snake soup.

Paji: Trousers for men, traditionally worn baggy, ankle-length.

Pegae: Small pillow, filled with corn husks.

Pindae-ttuk: Bean-flour pancake; Korean pizza.

Pi pim pap: Rice and vegetables, staple food.

Pomul: Literally, treasured things—a secondary classification (see *Kukbo*).

Pori-cha: Toasted-barley tea.

Poshin-tang: Dog-meat soup; literally, soup for strength.

Putokkhamnida: Please.

Pyong: Unit of area measurement.

Sa: Temple.

Saemaul Undong: New Community Movement, a rural organization created by President Park.

Sajok: National Historic Sites.

San: Mountain.

Sangnom: "Unperson," outcast, untouchable.

Saunatang: Public bath with sauna and other luxuries.

Seoul: The word means "capital"; it cannot be written in Chinese.

Shilla: Ancient eastern Korean kingdom; later, the term represented the unified whole country.

Sijo: Form of Korean poetry.

Soh: West.

Soju: A strong sweet potato liquor, the Korean approximation of sake.

Sunim: Buddhist monk.

Sushi: Japanese-style raw fish and rice.

Taeguk: Yin and yang emblem used in the Korean flag.

Taeguk-ki: The Korean national flag, with *taeguk* and four trigrams.

Taehagkyo: University.

Taejungtang: No-frills public bath for the poorer people.

Taekwon-do: Korean martial art.

Tae-namu: The bamboo.

Tangun: The mythological founder of Korea.

Tojang: Name seal, equivalent to Chinese *chop*.

Ttok: Rice cakes.

Won: The unit of Korean currency.

Yangban: The Korean aristocracy, now officially defunct.

Yangnom: A Westerner—a term of mild abuse, similar to the Cantonese *gweilo*.

Yo: Thin mattress, placed on *ondol* floor at night.

Yogwan: An inexpensive roadside inn.

Yoinsuk: A very cheap Korean hotel for working men.

Yongduam: The Dragon Head Rock of Cheju-do.

Yong guk: England.

Yontan: Drum-shaped powdered-coal briquettes used for heating and cooking.

Yukgap: The five twelve-year cycles of life—the sixtieth year.

SELECTED BIBLIOGRAPHY

❖ ❖ ❖

Adams, Edward B. *Korea Guide.* Seoul: Seoul International Tourist Publishing Co., 1976.

———. *Korea's Kyongju.* Seoul: Seoul International Publishing House, 1979.

Amnesty International. *South Korea—Violations of Human Rights.* London: Amnesty International, 1986.

Asia Watch Committee. *Human Rights in Korea.* Washington, D.C.: Asia Watch, 1985.

Bartz, Patricia. *South Korea.* Oxford: Oxford University Press, 1972.

Bird, Isabella. *Korea and Her Neighbours.* Reprint. London: Routledge and Kegan Paul, 1985.

Buck, Pearl S. *The Living Reed.* New York: John Day Co., 1963.

Chung, Chong-Wha, and Boyd McCleary. *Korea and Britain Today—A Developing Relationship.* Seoul: Korea-British Society, 1986.

Clark, Allen D. *History of the Church in Korea.* Seoul: Christian Literature Society of Korea, 1971.

Cole, Lani, ed. *Peace Corps Guide to Korea.* Seoul: U.S. Peace Corps (undated).

Crane, Paul. *Korean Patterns.* Seoul: Royal Asiatic Society, 1967.

Crowther, Geoff: *Korea & Taiwan—A Travel Survival Guide*. Sydney: Lonely Planet, 1985.

Fodor's Korea. New York: Fodor, 1987.

Gore, M. E. J. *The Birds of Korea*. Seoul: Royal Asiatic Society, 1971.

Griffiths, William Elliot. *Corea, The Hermit Nation*. New York: Charles Scribner's Sons, 1904.

Hall, Basil. *Account of a Voyage of Discovery to the West Coast of Corea*. London: John Murray, 1818.

Hamel, Hendrick. *An Account of the Shipwreck of a Dutch Vessel on the Isle of Quelpaert, together with a Description of the Kingdom of Corea*. 1668. Reprint. Amsterdam: B. Hoetink, 1920.

Hastings, Max. *The Korean War*. New York: Simon and Schuster, Inc., 1987.

Henthorn, William. *A History of Korea*. New York: The Free Press, 1971.

Hong Kong and Shanghai Bank. *Korea*. Hong Kong: Hong Kong and Shanghai Bank (business profile series), 1986.

Hyun, Peter. *Koreana*. Seoul: Korea Britannica, 1984.

Insight Guide: Korea. Singapore: Apa Productions, 1981.

Kelly, Jeremiah F. *The Splendid Cause*. Seoul: Columban Fathers, 1983.

Kim, Dae Jung. *Mass Participatory Economy*. Cambridge, Mass.: Center for International Affairs, Harvard University, 1985.

Kim, Edward H. *Korea—Beyond the Hills*. Tokyo: Kodansha International, 1980.

Kusan, Sunim. *The Way of Korean Zen*. New York: Weatherhill, Inc., 1985.

Landor, Henry Savage. *Corea—The Land of Morning Calm*. London: Heineman, 1895.

Leckie, Robert. *The Korean War*. London: Pall Mall Press, 1963.

Ledyard, Gari. *The Dutch Come to Korea*. Seoul: Royal Asiatic Society, Korea Branch, 1971.

Lee, Ki-baik. *A New History of Korea*. Seoul: Ilchokuk, 1984.

Lee, Peter H. *Poems of Korea*. Honolulu: University of Hawaii Press, 1974.

MacMahon, Hugh. *The Scrutable Oriental*. Seoul: Sejong Company, 1975.

McCann, David, ed. *Studies on Korea in Transition*. Honolulu: University of Hawaii, 1979.

Michener, James A. *The Bridges at Toko-ri*. New York: Fawcett-Crest, 1953.

Middleton, Dorothy H., and William D. Middleton. *Some Korean Journeys*. Seoul: Royal Asiatic Society, 1975.

Office of Monopoly. *Korean Ginseng*. Seoul: Office of Monopoly, 1986.

Rees, David. *The Korean War*. London: Orbis, 1984.

Ridgway, Matthew B. *The Korean War*. Garden City, N.Y.: Doubleday, 1967.

Sands, William Franklin. *Undiplomatic Memories*. Reprint. Seoul: Royal Asiatic Society, 1975.

Suh, Kuk-Sung, et al., eds. *The Identity of the Korean People*. Seoul: National Unification Board, 1983.

INDEX

❖   ❖   ❖